Student Cookb...
For Dummie...

FOR DUMMIES
BESTSELLING
BOOK SERIES

D0841632

Quick Pasta and Tomato Sauce Recipe

If you're skint, have nothing in your cupboard but the Essential Ingredients List I talk about in Chapter 1 and are feeling peckish, don't worry, you can still rustle up something to eat. Here's a quick recipe using just those ingredients:

Pinch of salt

Enough pasta for 1

Olive oil

¼ onion, peeled and chopped

1 clove of garlic

½ tin chopped tomatoes

Pinch of mixed herbs

1 Fill a saucepan half full of water and put over a high heat to bring to the boil. When boiling, add a pinch of salt, pour in the pasta and stir.

2 Heat a glug of olive oil in a frying pan over a medium to high heat and add the chopped onion. Stir and cook for about 5 minutes.

3 Add the chopped garlic and fry for another minute or so.

4 Pour in the chopped tomatoes, add a pinch of the mixed herbs and stir with the onions and garlic.

5 Test to see if the pasta is cooked (after about 10 minutes, but check the packet), then drain the pasta and serve with the sauce on top.

If I Eat This, Will I Die?

Yoghurt looking a bit yucky? Tomatoes no longer tasty? This handy table tells you how long to store uncooked items in the fridge and whether you'll survive to make tomorrow's lecture.

Item	Will Keep in the Fridge for . . .	Item	Will Keep in the Fridge for . . .
Chicken breast	Up to 2 days	Tomatoes	Up to 10 days
Minced beef	Up to 2 days	Carrots	Up to 2 weeks
Fresh fish	Up to 2 days	Lettuce	Up to 1 week
Bacon	Up to 7 days	Mushrooms	Up to 4 days
Pizza	Up to 4 days	Opened yoghurt pot	Up to 4 days
Eggs	Up to 5 weeks	Milk	Up to 7 days

For Dummies: Bestselling Book Series for Beginners

Student Cookbook For Dummies©

Cheat Sheet

Volume Conversions

Imperial Fluid Ounces (fl oz)	Metric Millilitres (ml)	Imperial Fluid Ounces (fl oz)	Metric Millilitres (ml)
1	30	1 pint	570
2	55	1 ¼ pints	725
3	75	1 ¾ pints	1 litre
5 (¼ pint)	150	2 pints	1.2
10 (½ pint)	275	2 ½ pints	1.5
15 (¾ pint)	425	4 pints	2.25

Weight Conversions

Imperial Ounces (oz)	Metric Grams (g)	Imperial Ounces (oz)	Metric Grams (g)
½	10	7	200
¾	20	8	225
1	25	9	250
1 ½	40	10	275
2	50	12	350
2 ½	60	1 pound (16 ounces)	450
3	75	1 ½ pounds	700
4	110	2 pounds	900
4 ½	125	2 ¼ pounds	1 kilogram
5	150	3 pounds	1.35 kilograms
6	175		

Copyright © 2009 John Wiley & Sons, Ltd. All rights reserved. Item 4711-7.
For more information about John Wiley & Sons, call (+44) 1243 779777.

For Dummies: Bestselling Book Series for Beginners

Student Cookbook
FOR
DUMMIES®

by Oliver Harrison

A John Wiley and Sons, Ltd, Publication

Student Cookbook For Dummies®

Published by
John Wiley & Sons, Ltd
The Atrium
Southern Gate
Chichester
West Sussex
PO19 8SQ
England

Email (for orders and customer service enquires): cs-books@wiley.co.uk

Visit our Home Page on www.wiley.com

Copyright © 2009 John Wiley & Sons, Ltd, Chichester, West Sussex, England

Published by John Wiley & Sons, Ltd, Chichester, West Sussex

For general information on our other products and services, please contact our Customer Care Department within the U.S. at 877-762-2974, outside the U.S. at 317-572-3993, or fax 317-572-4002.

For technical support, please visit www.wiley.com/techsupport.

Wiley also publishes its books in a variety of electronic formats. Some content that appears in print may not be available in electronic books.

British Library Cataloguing in Publication Data: A catalogue record for this book is available from the British Library

ISBN: 978-0-470-74711-7

Printed and bound in Great Britain by TJ International Ltd

With thanks to Foodtest Laboratories Ltd for nutritional analysis

10 9 8 7 6 5 4 3 2 1

WILEY

About the Author

Oliver Harrison is one of the presenters and part of the team that create studentcooking.tv, the award winning website and podcast series dedicated to cooking at uni. With a long interest in food and cooking, Oliver set up the show as an answer to the lack of practical cooking advice on offer to students while at uni. With its irreverent humour and less than serious approach to cooking, the show was an instant success and is now run at several universities across the U.K. Watch it now at www.studentcooking.tv.

Author's Acknowledgments

First of all, many thanks to Mark Price at Loughborough University, for his invaluable help and advice on the recipes in this book and the show. Thanks to Simon, Tom and Jess for words of encouragement along the way; Nicole, Rachael and Sarah at Wiley for making it a smooth ride; and above all, my wonderful family – Mum, Dad and Laura, who got me into cooking and without whom I wouldn't be where I am now.

Publisher's Acknowledgements

We're proud of this book; please send us your comments through our Dummies online registration form located at www.dummies.com/register/.

Some of the people who helped bring this book to market include the following:

Acquisitions, Editorial, and Media Development

Commissioning Editor: Wejdan Ismail

Executive Project Editor: Daniel Mersey

Project Editor: Rachael Chilvers

Content Editor: Jo Theedom

Proofreader: Kelly Cattermole

Recipe Tester: Emily Nolan

Cover Photo: © D.Hurst / Almay (front); © topdog images/ Almay (back)

Cartoons: Ed McLachlan

Composition Services

Project Coordinator: Lynsey Stanford

Layout and Graphics: Samantha K. Cherolis, Melissa K. Jester

Proofreader: Amanda Graham

Indexer: Cheryl Duksta

Contents at a Glance

Table of Contents

Introduction

● ●

*C*hances are, before coming to uni and facing up to three years or more of independent living, you won't have spent too many hours in the kitchen at home, training and honing your culinary skills to a fine art.

Cooking's the kind of thing that you often leave to your parents, the meal that magically appears when you get called down to dinner. Maybe you feel that you don't really need to know how to cook, because you'll manage throughout uni on bland pasta and pizzas like everyone else. And yet uni is the perfect time to start learning how to cook, and it's utterly brilliant. Having a night in and cooking for your friends is amazing – the banter between mates, the laughs around the table and that warm feeling as you see everyone tuck in and enjoy something that *you* made . . .

Learning to cook isn't hard at all. In the words of my Mum (yep, she's the one who got me into cooking), 'If you can read, you can cook.' You read the recipe, you do what it says. Cooking certainly isn't economics, combined maths, medieval English or whatever degree you're studying; it's a simple way to create meals that taste great, and all on a student budget.

So whether you're a bit of a culinary connoisseur or you've yet to grill your first sausage, this book is for you. By the time you've tried some of these recipes, you'll be well on your way to effortlessly creating fantastic food, knowing what ingredients go well together and how you can eke out £10 to feed yourself for a week. Think you can't cook? Think again.

About This Book

So here it is, your Bible of food, your guide to student grub, everything you need to make some fantastic meals for you and your mates. Unlike other student cookbooks, this one doesn't patronise you and give you 50 different recipes for beans on toast. Just because you're on a budget doesn't mean you should be eating budget-style food. I know what you're likely to have in your kitchen, so don't suggest you use any fancy equipment or ingredients that you use once and then watch as they slowly fester and disintegrate in your sink or fridge.

Instead, this book gives you over 160 fantastic recipes that taste great and are simple to create. I go through how to feed yourself, your friends and even your entire hall (partay!) without having to extend your overdraft, as well as look at what ingredients to buy and where to buy them. Even if you're only armed with a microwave and a kettle, I still have recipes for you; so wherever you are and whatever kind of kitchen you have, prepare to get stuck in and get making some fantastic food.

Conventions Used in This Book

To make this book easy to read, you'll see that I use certain conventions:

- ✔ All web addresses appear in monofont.

- ✔ Occasionally, I use specific measurements for ingredients, but most of the time, they're pretty rough – such as a mug or a handful.

- ✔ If you come across a cooking term you've never heard before, take a look at the glossary at the back of the book to understand what I'm going on about.

- ✔ All the recipes are followed by a list that gives you a complete nutritional breakdown.

- ✔ A little tomato symbol next to a recipe means that the meal is suitable for vegetarians.

- ✔ When eggs or chicken appear in a recipe, please make sure that you buy free-range. Okay, so they cost a little more than battery chickens and their eggs, but an animal that's spent its life stressed out in a cage can't produce good eggs or meat.

✔ All oven temperatures are based on fan ovens – ovens with a fan that moves the heat around. If your oven isn't a fan oven, allow a little more cooking time for each recipe.

✔ When I mention a 'spoonful' of something in the recipes, I mean a dessert-spoon size. I explain when anything bigger or smaller is needed.

Foolish Assumptions

Every *For Dummies* book is written with a particular reader in mind, and this one is no different. I'm guessing you're:

✔ At, or will soon be going to uni and need a bit of a helping hand in the kitchen.

✔ Not stupid. It's not your fault if you don't know how to cook, and don't let anyone ever tell you differently.

✔ Wanting a bit of a laugh and aren't afraid to get your hands dirty making something that your friends will enjoy.

✔ A bit strapped for cash at the moment and don't want to spend too much money on food.

✔ Wanting to experience different flavours and tastes, and fancy going on a bit of a culinary journey without it sounding poncy.

How This Book Is Organised

This book is designed so that you can dive in anywhere and still get the most out of things. You don't have to read it from cover to cover, taking notes on every page. Here's what's waiting for you.

Part 1: Getting Started

Things kick off in Chapter 1 with a quick look at why cooking at uni is so great and some of the benefits that come with becoming the hall chef. I go through what you need (both ingredients and utensils), and look at what you *don't* need. Things get a bit yucky as I look at the lost art of kitchen hygiene and work out how long things last in the fridge and freezer before they become biohazards. Then it's off to the shops in Chapter 2 to look at how you can spend less and get more. Finally, in Chapter 3, I look at how what you eat affects how you feel and the nutrition in your nosh.

Part II: Breakfast, Lunch and Snacks

Part II gets you cooking, beginning in Chapter 4 as you whip up some healthy starts to the day and hangover-beating breakfasts. Lunch arrives before you know it, so in Chapter 5 you can slurp simple soups, packed full of vegetables and other healthy goodies as well as making quick and easy salads. I also give you some great little lunch recipes for two, covering everything for meat eaters to veggie visitors. Still feeling hungry? In Chapter 6 you can serve up snacks and dips to quieten that rowdy stomach, as well as making the best snacks to get you through a long night's revision.

Part III: Bringing On the Main Course

Chapter 7 is where you get stuck into making some great meals for when you're on your lonesome. No more ready-made meals for one as you'll soon be creating your own delicious dishes, whether they're meaty, fishy, vegetarian or vegan. In Chapter 8, you step up a gear and eat food to get you going; whether you need energy, brain food or meals to fight off fresher flu.

Discover how to make a chilli con carne in an electromagnetic box in Chapter 9 as you master microwave cooking and create meals you'd never thought possible. In Chapter 10, I look at how to make the most of time and money, making meals in under 10 minutes flat and getting the most out of any leftovers. I round things off in Chapter 11 with some decadent desserts and treats, spoiling the chocoholics among you and satisfying those who are hungry for more.

Part IV: Entertaining

Whether you're having a lads' or a girls' night in, Chapter 12 has the best recipes to entertain with, while in Chapter 13, you discover the surprisingly simple task of pulling together a Sunday roast, whether chicken, turkey, beef, lamb or pork. Someone special coming round? Turn to Chapter 14 as I show you the easy way to impress a date with your cooking. It's party time in Chapter 15, as I run through cooking for the ultimate uni party.

Part V: The Part of Tens

The final chapters read like the dream team of culinary top ten lists, all stuffed onto the few remaining pages of the book. Turn here for some quick and easy tips and money-saving suggestions about cooking at uni. And head to the Glossary if you need to know the difference between blanching and braising.

Icons Used in This Book

If you spot these icons in your book, don't worry, someone hasn't read through it before you and defaced the pages with witty little pictures; they're supposed to be there. They handily explain certain concepts and pointers:

Spot this sign and you know you'll have money leftover for a beer.

These are useful little pointers you won't want to forget in a hurry.

The target highlights little tips and tricks that help make cooking an easy and enjoyable experience.

Cooking can sometimes be dangerous, so make sure that you read these little pointers carefully.

Where to Go from Here

Get stuck in! Don't worry about starting at the beginning;
choose a recipe that tickles your tastebuds and give it a go!
Fancy a home-made chicken kebab? Turn to Chapter 5. Want
to treat yourself to a chocolate brownie? Chapter 11 will
satisfy your craving. Recipes for vegetarians and vegans
are in each chapter, so no one misses out.

Of course, if you do prefer to start at the beginning, you
have the added advantage of knowing what you need to start
cooking, as well as a few pointers about where to buy all
the ingredients that you require. Or if you're in a real hurry,
check out the Cheat Sheet or Part of Tens at the front and
back of the book.

Either way, get ready to get your hands dirty and you and
your friends laughing and enjoying something that too many
students are missing out on – proper home-cooked food,
made with a little bit of money, a big bit of passion and
probably fuelled by a lot of beer. Enjoy.

Part I
Getting Started

'To go with our nuts and fruit, we need a
<u>natural</u> sweetener – Quentin's just
gone to get that now.'

In this part . . .

Tighten your apron, arm yourself with spatula and frying pan and brace yourself as you begin to embark on a culinary quest against hunger! Feeding yourself at uni may feel like a quest as epic as finding a certain stolen ring, but trust me, with the help of this book, you'll find it a lot easier, cheaper and more enjoyable than you thought. Part I is where it all begins and where you get kitted out with everything you need for cooking at uni.

Chapter 1

Saying Hello to Your Kitchen

● ●

In This Chapter

▶ Cooking at uni – fun or fiendish?

▶ Kitting out your kitchen

▶ Storing and reheating food safely

● ●

*T*here's no better time to start cooking than when you're at uni, surrounded by friends who are constantly up for having a laugh and grateful for anything edible you can rustle up for them.

This book has everything you need to make that happen. Don't worry if the extent of your culinary expertise is making a cheese sandwich or if you struggle peeling a banana; throw away any ideas you have of cooking and get ready to start looking forward to every mealtime.

Before you get stuck in to making fantastic food, you're going to need something to make it with. This chapter goes over everything you need to kit out your kitchen, from essential utensils to store-cupboard favourites.

Student kitchens aren't renowned for their cleanliness, so I also go over some basic kitchen hygiene. You want your food to be safe to eat and to avoid anything nasty developing in the fridge . . .

But enough with the scary talk. Read on for why you'll soon be consulting this book with a spatula in one hand and a saucepan in the other.

Checking out the Benefits of Cooking at Uni

The benefits of cooking for yourself when you're at uni are seriously massive. Not enough students realise how a bit of time in the kitchen can do wonders for their health, bank accounts, relationships and, of course, appetites. Cooking at uni:

- ✔ **Saves you money.** A lot of money. Cashing out on ready meals or takeaways five nights a week soon adds up and rapidly depletes your student loan. With a bit of essential reading (that is, this book), you can eat very well and very cheaply while you're at uni. Instead of paying £4 or £5 for food each night (which could soon add up to £25 a week just on your evening meal), you can spend around the same amount of money but feed yourself three good meals a day, seven days a week. So while everyone else is squandering their money on fast food, you can be quietly saving for that new Playstation game, new dress or, of course, textbook on your reading list . . .

- ✔ **Keeps you healthy.** By cooking for yourself, you can see exactly what you're putting into your body. You know how much salt a meal has, or what vegetables are in there, plus you can choose what you eat. Getting into shape for the summer holidays is easy when you're cooking for yourself because you can decide what to eat and really feel and see the benefits of it.

  Having the ability to cook healthy grub not only keeps your skin glowing and your body in shape, but it also means you're less likely to catch any germs and bugs that are going round campus. Which means you spend less time in bed feeling sorry for yourself and more time out at parties.

- ✔ **Increases your attractiveness.** Seriously! Okay, so a floral apron and Marigolds don't do it for everyone, but there's something about a girl or guy who can cook. Mmm. No, I mean you'll have no problems making friends when you're at uni if you're handy in the kitchen. The ability to effortlessly cook a delicious meal is something that a lot of students will admire you for. The warm smell of a home-made lasagne cooking in the oven turns a hall of residence into a home, and you'll soon become a living legend and the centre of most social activities.

One of the best memories I have of uni is staying in on a night and cooking for my mates in the flat. Everyone would chip in some money and I'd go off and buy the ingredients and cook the meal, while they sorted out the beer and wine. In the evening, we'd all get together round the kitchen table, drink, listen to music and enjoy a fantastic home-cooked meal. These are just some of the great memories uni life can give you!

Check out the chapters in Part IV for loads of recipes perfect for a raucous night in.

✔ **Makes you part of the community.** Students come and go in towns and cities and put a lot of money into the local economy. But not many really become a part of the community. Cooking for yourself connects you a bit more to the shops and businesses around you. A trip to the local market or independent shop means you quickly get to know your butcher, fishmonger and grocer who can give you loads of culinary tips and advice. Your money can support the local farmers and food suppliers in the area. It's nice to feel a bit more rooted and know that you're doing your bit for the community.

✔ **Develops a great skill.** Now, I don't want to get all doom-mongering on you, but one thing you find when you finish uni is that life suddenly becomes a lot harder. All of a sudden you're in the real world with bills to pay, a job to get to every morning and less and less time to watch *Loose Women*.

You also find that your personal time becomes very precious. After spending all day at work, you have little time to learn how to cook – it either becomes something you look forward to, or something you dread. Cooking is like tying your shoelaces: it's something that everyone has to learn at some point in their lives (after all, you have to eat to live), so why not make the most of it and spend the time you have at uni creating food that makes every mealtime that bit more enjoyable. Okay, lecture over!

Looking at What You Need

The good news is that you don't need to buy much to cook at uni, and you certainly don't need any expensive or fancy kitchen utensils. You can kit out your kitchen in one swift shop at a supermarket or hardware shop and still have change from a tenner.

Whatever you're cooking, having a selection of store cupboard ingredients is really handy. Always try to have a few basic ingredients in stock because you'll use them for a lot of your cooking. Again, it's all cheap stuff; nothing too fancy or expensive.

Grabbing some essential utensils

You can get your hands on all sorts of kitchen utensils from your local hardware store or supermarket (the big, out-of-town, 24-hour places are the best ones to visit for non-food items). Don't bother buying any named brands or all-singing, all-dancing gadgets – the simple budget range is fine.

If you're not at uni yet, check what your future hall of residence provides in its kitchens. You may find that it already supplies most of these items.

Here's my top ten essential utensils list. Get these and you're sorted for cooking at uni:

- ✔ **Measuring jug.** The cheapest measuring jugs cost less than 50p, so don't worry about getting a silver-plated one signed by Ainsley Harriot; a cheap plastic jug is fine. You use this for measuring liquids (surprise, surprise) and for adding any stock or sauces to risottos, curries and soups.

- ✔ **Colander.** At number two in my culinary countdown is a colander, like a sturdy sieve for those not in the know. Again, a cheap plastic one is fine. You need a colander for draining potatoes, spaghetti and rice. Buy one with smaller, rather than larger draining holes (make sure strands of spaghetti won't fit through it) so you can use it for everything.

✔ **Potato masher.** A potato masher, with its flat grid-shaped end, is very satisfying to use after a frustrating day in the library. Take it out on boiled potatoes, swede, carrots – anything that you want mushed to a pulp.

✔ **Spatula.** You use a spatula to stir and break up food in the frying pan, and they cost about 20p. A simple wooden one will suit your purposes just fine.

✔ **Tin opener.** Nothing's more infuriating than getting half-way through a recipe and realising you have nothing to open your tin of baked beans. Tin openers are one of life's great inventions. Don't splash out on an electric one – go for a sturdy hand-operated tin opener (preferably with one of those little hooks for opening beer bottles too).

✔ **Frying pan.** You're starting to get into the important utensils now and the frying pan is in at number six. Great for frying, playing tennis and air guitar, get a fairly decent frying pan because this is one utensil you'll use all the time. Non-stick pans are good, but not essential.

✔ **Saucepan(s).** That little bracketed 's' means you're wise to get more than one saucepan because you quite often need to use more than one at a time. You can often buy saucepans in sets of two or three, in increasing sizes. The small ones are good for making sauces and cooking rice, while the bigger ones are good for soups and boiling potatoes. Buy at least two sizes.

You don't need to spend a lot on saucepans; a cheap set does the job. As long as they conduct heat well, they're suitable.

✔ **Ovenproof dish.** You need an ovenproof dish for lasagnes and cottage pies, two staple meals of student life. It's also a good dish to cook fish in, especially in the microwave (see Chapter 7 for the recipes).

A little rectangular Pyrex dish only costs a couple of quid and is sturdy enough to last you your time at uni, if not longer.

✔ **Chopping board(s).** Here's that plural 's' again. Get a decent wooden chopping board for all your bread and vegetables and a cheap plastic one for meat preparation. Having two chopping boards (one for raw meat and fish and one for vegetables and cooked meat) helps to keep your kitchen safe and hygienic and stops the chance of raw meat coming into contact with ready-to-eat food, leading to salmonella (food poisoning).

You'll use the wooden chopping board all the time, so try to get something nice and chunky. A good one will last you for years, so think of it as an investment. If you want to get something a little smaller and lighter, that's fine, but it won't last as long.

You won't use the plastic board as much as the wooden one so save your pennies and buy a cheap one. If you buy a really cheap thin board, place a tea towel underneath to stop it slipping on the work surface.

✔ **A good knife.** A smooth-bladed and sharp knife is *the* most important tool in your kitchen because you use it every time you cook. *Fork* out money on a knife (groan) and a good sturdy sharp one will not only last longer and perform better, but also be safer for you to use because a blunt knife may slip off food and cut you.

Hardware shops and supermarkets are good places to buy knives, although independent cook shops have a wider selection. Look to spend between £15 and £30 on a knife; it's a lot of money, but trust me, it's an essential buy. Scare your parents and ask them for a good knife as a leaving-home gift.

If you can bear to part with any more money, get a decent serrated knife too for slicing bread and carving roasts. 'When will I ever need to carve a Sunday roast?' I hear you ask. Well, read Chapter 13, and you'll be dying to try one.

Getting your hands on extra gadgets

The previous ten items can see you through your years of cooking at university and are a great start to kitting out your kitchen. However, if you've found yourself with a few quid left over and fancy pimpin' out your kitchen a little more, here are a few extra items that aren't essential, but are very useful and will impress your flatmates:

✔ **Blender.** I never had a jug-style blender while I was at uni, thinking that I'd never really use one. But now I have a blender, I use it every day, making fruit smoothies in the summer and toe-warming soups in the winter. A blender isn't essential, but is absolutely brilliant to have.

A hand blender (also called an immersion blender) is a cheaper alternative to an upright blender, but doesn't give you the same power and flexibility.

✔ **Scales.** Weighing scales are only really vital for baking when measurements need to be exact, but a cheap set of scales is still a useful item to have in your kitchen.

✔ **Cheese grater.** Another cheap utensil to buy, but one that's *grate* to have . . . I'll get my coat.

✔ **Casserole dish.** If you're a fan of casseroles (and let's face it, who isn't?), then casserole dishes are pretty important items in your life. A casserole dish is a large ovenproof dish with deep sides (and usually a lid) that allows you to make not only casseroles, but big fish pies, ratatouilles and anything that you cook in liquid. Some of the roasts in Chapter 13 benefit from being cooked in a casserole dish.

Casserole dishes aren't expensive. You can get a suitable one for around a fiver from a hardware store or large supermarket.

✔ **Large bowl.** You need a large bowl to be able to mix ingredients together, whether you're making a cake or an omelette. You can get a large bowl for less than a pound.

Compiling a Store Cupboard Hit List

You have your utensils sorted; now you need some food to start cooking. Coming up is a list of the ingredients to keep handy in your cupboard. Not only are they the foundations for a lot of the meals in this book, but also even if you're at the end of your overdraft and your cupboards are pretty much empty, as long as you have these ingredients, you can make a meal – see the Cheat Sheet for the Quick Pasta and Tomato Sauce recipe.

✔ **Onions.** Used all the time in Italian cooking, so perfect for your spag bols, lasagnes and many other meals, try to keep a few onions in your cupboard at all times.

White onions are used more often than red in most cooking, and are more readily available and cheaper.

Red onions are slightly sweeter than white onions and are nice when cooked slowly, or finely chopped and eaten raw in salads or with tuna mayo.

✔ **Garlic.** Useful for general cooking and fending off sudden vampire attacks, garlic is cheap to buy and another good store cupboard essential.

✔ **Pasta.** Pasta is perfect fast food. Bung the pasta in boiling water for ten minutes and you're halfway to making a meal. You can find loads of different types of pasta from the tubular style penne to the action man bow tie-esque farfalle. I advise buying a packet of spaghetti and something simple like penne or conchigli. Great for filling you up when your pockets are empty, keep a bag of pasta in your cupboard at all times.

✔ **Rice.** Rice is a staple ingredient for many Eastern dishes and fills you up on the cheap. If you have nothing else in your cupboards, a bowl of rice keeps you from feeling hungry. Like pasta, you can find many different types of rice. Basmati is good for Thai food and curries, while long grain rice is perfect for a good chilli con carne. Keep a packet of long grain rice in the cupboard, whether you choose the healthier (but longer to cook) brown rice or white rice.

✔ **Tinned chopped tomatoes.** Mix with a bit of pasta and you have a very cheap meal. You use chopped tomatoes in many Italian dishes, and a tin in your store cupboard always comes in handy, even if it's just for something to put on toast.

For a cheaper alternative, buy plum tomatoes and chop them up yourself.

✔ **Mixed dried herbs.** Herbs are great to work with and add a massive amount of flavour to your dishes. If in doubt, buy a jar of mixed dried herbs. A quick sprinkle of these before the end of cooking adds more flavour to your dish.

✔ **Stock cubes.** Sprinkled into the frying pan or dissolved in boiling water, stock cubes are another important store cupboard essential. Like herbs, they really enhance the flavour of your cooking. Vegetable stock cubes are good for soups, and beef stock cubes are good for meaty gravies. You can buy chicken, lamb and pork stock cubes too, although the last two are harder to find.

✔ **Olive oil.** You'll use olive oil all the time in savoury dishes. You don't need to buy expensive olive oil; the supermarket own-brand is fine. Olive oil is healthier for you than vegetable oil.

Naughtily named extra virgin olive oil is a lot lighter than normal olive oil and doesn't hold up well in high temperatures, so use it for drizzling over salads. Get normal olive oil for cooking or light frying.

✔ **Salt and pepper.** The recipes in this book call for salt and pepper (or *seasoning* to be all culinary about it) all the time. After buying salt and pepper mills, buy bags of salt (the free-flowing pre-ground stuff is fine) that you can fill up the mills with. The salt will last you years; probably the length of your degree! You can buy peppercorns, ready to grind in your mill, in the herbs and spices aisle in the supermarket.

Spicing things up

After you've been cooking for a while, you'll realise that herbs and particularly spices can make a real difference to the flavours in your cooking. In this section, I explain how you can use herbs and spices to their full effect.

Although fresh herbs aren't expensive, you may need to use a lot of them to get your money's worth. Dried herbs are a cost-effective alternative, but don't have the same flavour as fresh herbs. If you get serious about enjoying some herb action, you could always grow your own in a little pot by the windowsill. This is a very efficient and cheap way to use herbs in your cooking.

Spices tend to be dried or ground and are best bought from international food shops where shopkeepers can give you advice on what each spice is used for and the flavours they produce.

Tables 1-1 and 1-2 give a rough guide to the most popular herbs and spices and the flavours that they produce. Follow the recipes in this book to get used to using different herbs and spices.

Table 1-1	Guide to Herbs	
Herb	*Flavour*	*Uses*
Basil	Light and fresh	Italian dishes like spaghetti bolognaise and lasagne
Oregano	Woody	Pizzas and pasta sauces
Parsley	Very light and refreshing	Fish
Coriander	Light and peppery	Indian and Thai curries and Middle Eastern dishes
Rosemary	Woody and clean	Lamb and pork
Thyme	Warm and pungent	Chicken and lamb

Table 1-2	Guide to Spices	
Spice	*Flavour*	*Uses*
Cinnamon	Sweet and aromatic	Middle Eastern dishes
Turmeric	Strong and musty	Curries and other Indian dishes
Cumin	Sweet and aniseed	Curries, Middle Eastern dishes and some fish
Garam masala	A mixture of sweet smells and flavours, a bit like curry powder	Curries and some fish dishes
Saffron	Slightly bitter (smells like hay in a good way!)	Paellas and Middle Eastern dishes

Brushing up on Kitchen Hygiene

Student kitchens are never the cleanest of places, with most items more at home under a microscope than in a fridge. So it's extra important to get to grips with kitchen hygiene to avoid any nasty tummy bugs spreading along with the smell of rancid yogurt.

Stocking your fridge

Your fridge is where you keep roughly a third of all the food you buy, and as it's where you store fresh produce, it's ultra important to know where things should go.

If you need to store the contents from an open tin, empty the contents into a bowl and cover with cling film before refrigerating. Don't keep tins in the fridge because the food may start to taste like metal. Not good.

Meat

Store raw meat at the *bottom* of your fridge, on the lowest shelf. If you have a meat tray, keep raw meat in that, or keep it wrapped in a bag on a plate. This stops any blood or juices from dripping onto the bottom of the fridge and contaminating any cooked meat.

Keep cooked meat away from raw meat, on the shelf above.

Salmonella (the most common kind of food poisoning and nothing to do with salmon!) can occur if raw meat, eggs or shellfish come into contact with cooked meat or ready-to-eat food. You become ill if you ingest raw meat, eggs or shellfish that carry salmonella. The bug is destroyed through cooking, which is why you need to keep raw foods away from cooked, and to wash your hands after you handle raw meat.

Fish

Similar to raw meat, keep raw fish at the bottom of the fridge, wrapped up and on a plate to stop any juices dripping onto the bottom of the fridge.

Pongy fridge?

As a rule, cover with cling film any-thing in your fridge that's cooked or opened to stop any smells from escaping.

If you do find your fridge is becoming a bit smelly, put a couple of slices of lemon in a cup of boiling water and place in the fridge overnight. The cit-rusy smell fills the fridge and gets rid of any nasty pongs.

You can keep any cooked fish, like tuna or smoked salmon, on the middle or upper shelves, but make sure that you cover them.

Vegetables

Keep vegetables that need refrigerating in the vegetable drawer, if you have one. If not, keep them on the top two shelves of the fridge, ideally in a Ziploc bag or covered with cling film.

Table 1-3 gives you the low-down on storing vegetables.

Table 1-3	Storing Vegetables	
Vegetable	*Fridge*	*Cupboard*
Potatoes and sweet potatoes		√
Tomatoes	√	
Peppers	√	
Ginger	√	
Mushrooms	√	
Broccoli and cauliflower	√	
Onions		√
Chopped onions	√	
Parsnips	√	
Carrots	√	
Garlic		√

Chilling Out: Freezing Food

You can freeze most foods, and generally speaking they freeze better if they're raw. However, certain foods don't freeze well at all:

✔ Any greasy or fried food (they just get greasier)

✔ Mayonnaise

✔ Sour cream

✔ Gravy

✔ Yogurts

✔ Cheese

✔ Bananas, kiwi fruit, tomatoes, cucumbers, lettuce and other fruit and veg with a lot of water in them

✔ Eggs

Table 1-4 shows you how long you can keep things in the freezer and fridge.

Table 1-4	Guide to Fridge and Freezer Storage	
Food	*Can Stay in the Freezer For . . .*	*Can Stay in the Fridge For . . .*
Raw fish	6–8 months	1–2 days
Cooked fish	2–3 months	3–4 days
Raw minced beef/lamb/pork	3–4 months	1–2 days
Cooked minced beef/lamb/pork	2–3 months	3–4 days
Raw steak	6–12 months	3–5 days
Cooked steak	2–3 months	3–4 days
Raw chicken breast	9 months	1–2 days
Cooked chicken breast	2–3 months	3–4 days

Most foods are okay spending a few weeks in a cold climate. To freeze them properly, follow these tips:

✔ Always label any foods that you put in the freezer. Minced beef and minced lamb look very similar when they're frozen!

✔ Put food in a freezer bag (or wrap it in a carrier bag) before putting in the freezer. If the food touches the inside of the freezer this can cause *freezer burn*, where the food loses moisture. You can spot grey or white patches on the food, and it affects the taste and texture.

✔ When you freeze liquid, make sure you leave a gap at the top of the container because the liquid expands by 10 per cent when frozen.

✔ Don't just whack a plate of food in the freezer – the cold will cause the crockery to crack!

Knowing What You Can and Can't Reheat

Reheating food is another chance for potential bugs and germs to work their evil ways, so this section explains what foods you can and can't reheat.

Reheating foods safely

Imagine you've just cooked a delicious chilli con carne (and by the time you've finished this book, this will happen) and have some leftovers. In order to reheat the food and eat it the next day, follow these few simple steps:

1. **Allow the food to cool to room temperature.** This may take a few hours, so leave the leftover food in the pan, off the heat, and cover it with a lid to stop any flies or students nibbling at it.

2. **When at room temperature, refrigerate or freeze the food.** If you're going to eat it the next day or the day after, put it in a bowl, cover with cling film and whack it in the fridge. If you plan to finish it off any longer

than a couple of days, you need to freeze it. Spoon the food into a freezer bag or Tupperware container, seal it and write what's inside and the date. This helps you remember when you cooked it and if it's still safe to eat. Wave goodbye as you put it in the freezer.

3. **If refrigerated, reheat until hot throughout.** The best way to reheat food is in the microwave because it heats from the centre outwards.

   - Pierce the cling film with a fork then place the bowl in the microwave and heat on full power for 2 minutes.

   - Peel back the cling film, give everything a good stir, cover again and heat for another 2 minutes.

   - Check that the food is piping hot all the way through before eating.

4. **If frozen, remove from the freezer and allow to defrost overnight in the fridge.** Make sure that you put the frozen bag or box on a plate to stop any juices leaking into the fridge as it defrosts. When the food is completely defrosted, follow Step 3. If your microwave has a defrost function, you can use this, but letting the food defrost naturally is better.

You can keep defrosted meat and fish for about two days in the fridge before cooking it. If, after a day, you decide not to cook it you can freeze it again, but *only* if you defrosted it in the fridge.

Make sure that your food is hot all the way through when you reheat it. The food needs to be *hot*, not warm. Most bacteria grow between 4°C and 60°C, so the temperature of the food must be above 60°C to destroy the bacteria.

What can't I reheat?

The number one rule is that you can only reheat food once. Any bacteria that's survived the initial cooking process also survives the less intense reheating process, meaning it increases the chances of bacteria multiplying.

Only cook rice once and never reheat it. Uncooked rice can sometimes contain spores called Bacillus cereus. When the rice is cooked, the spores can still survive. If you leave the rice at room temperature, the spores grow into bacteria and multiply, and won't be destroyed during reheating.

For more advice on storing and freezing food, check out this great website: www.stilltasty.com/questions or the excellent government website www.eatwell.gov.uk/asksam.

Throwing stuff away

An overflowing bin in a student kitchen, stuffed with glass bottles, cardboard and paper is a shamefully regular sight. It doesn't take much to get into the habit of recycling, with many campuses now having their own recycling facilities or some close by.

Just remember that whatever you throw into a bin is thrown into a landfill. So get into the habit of sorting out your rubbish into recyclable and non-recyclable materials.

It's not just packaging that ends up in the bin. Instead of instantly chucking away any leftover meat from a meal or less than perfect fruit, think about how you can use them again in another meal – a vegetable soup for example, or a chicken curry. Check out Chapter 10 for more ideas for leftovers.

Chapter 2

Going Food Shopping

··

··

*W*hen you're trying to feed yourself on a budget, knowing how to shop for food is the first step in saving yourself a lot of moolah. Buying food on a budget isn't just looking out for the best supermarket deals and seeing if Asda is cheaper than Tesco. Planning meals, making a list and buying in bulk all help to keep food costs down.

Also in this chapter, I show you the advantages and disadvantages of shopping at both the supermarket and the market. While the supermarket is great for some things, you'll often find much fresher and cheaper ingredients at your humble market. And while the market has its fair share of deals, you just can't beat some supermarket offers. I explain which to use when.

Spending Less and Buying More

Although it sounds a bit like a zen-esque mantra, learning how to spend less and buy more is an art that can save you a lot of money at uni. In this section, I share a few handy tips to make your student loan stretch a little bit further.

Food is one thing you have to spend your money on every week, if not every day, while you're at uni. When you're coming to the end of term and your wallet is getting thinner and thinner, you can cut back on buying music and alcohol, but you still have to shell out on food. So working out how to get the most for your money and how to waste as little of it as possible really makes sense.

Planning ahead

Planning your meals is probably the best way to save an absolute fortune on food.

Although it sounds a little geeky (but hey, no one needs to know you're doing it), try planning your week's meals. Look through recipe books, magazines or on the Internet for ideas and meals you can make throughout the week.

Plan what you're going to cook on each day and try to choose recipes that share ingredients. For example, if you planned a spinach and sweet potato curry on one night, look for another recipe later on that week that uses sweet potato or spinach again. This stops you from using ingredients once, and then spending the rest of their lives sitting in your cupboards or fridge, slowly going mouldy.

Try to make meals that use up leftovers from the meal the day before. For example, if you do a roast chicken for your flat-mates on Sunday night, do a chicken curry on Monday night to use up any leftover chicken or veg. Using leftovers is a fantastic way of getting two meals for the price of one!

Here's an example of a good meal plan for the week:

- ✔ **Sunday:** Roast chicken

- ✔ **Monday:** Chicken curry with coriander *(using up roast chicken leftovers from Sunday night)*

- ✔ **Tuesday:** Salmon with new potatoes, carrots and peas *(most fresh fish comes into the fishmonger's on a Tuesday, so this is a great day to buy and eat fish – buy some fish for Friday too, freeze it when you get back and defrost it on Thursday night)*

- ✔ **Wednesday:** Carrot and coriander soup and a baguette *(using up your carrots and coriander)*

✔ **Thursday:** Vegetable lasagne with new potatoes and salad *(Finishing off any new potatoes from Tuesday's salmon)*

✔ **Friday:** Fish pie (an easy way to make sure you're getting two portions of fish a week)

✔ **Saturday:** Well, everyone has a night off some time!

By planning meals ahead, straight away you know exactly what you need to buy for that week.

Meal planning also ensures you enjoy a healthy and varied diet, with a balance of meat, fish and plenty of vegetables to keep you fit, healthy and less likely to catch that cold that's going round campus.

Making a list, checking it twice

After planning your meals, it's time to draw up that all-important shopping list, the blueprint to saving your cash. Break apart your recipes and work out the ingredients that you need to buy, making sure that you check your cupboards to see what you have already – no point buying another tub of gravy granules when you already have one tucked behind the baked beans . . .

By making a shopping list, you can make a rough guess at how much your food will cost. If you seem to have a lot of ingredients on the list, it's obviously going to be an expensive week, so it might be worth rethinking and swapping some recipes for cheaper ones.

Along with planning your meals, making a shopping list stops you wandering around the supermarket aimlessly, buying food and ingredients that you *think* you'll use, but actually will waste. Sticking to a list ensures you only buy what you need.

Buying in bulk

You can make some great savings when you buy in bulk. I'm not suggesting you take a trip down to the local wholesalers and buy 4 kilos of rice, but buying a 1-kilo packet rather than the 500-gram one usually works out much cheaper.

See how much money you can save when you buy in bulk:

> 2 x 500g pasta shells: £1.56
>
> 1 x 1kg pasta shells: £1.24
>
> **Saving: £0.32**
>
> 2 x 250g cornflakes: £2.58
>
> 1 x 500g cornflakes: £1.69
>
> **Saving: £0.89**
>
> 2 x 200g baked beans: £0.96
>
> 1 x 415g baked beans: £0.64
>
> **Saving: £0.32**
>
> 2 x 250ml olive oil: £2.56
>
> 1 x 500ml olive oil: £1.98
>
> **Saving: £0.58**
>
> **Total Saving: £2.11**

Saving 32p on a can of baked beans doesn't sound like much, but these savings soon add up. By buying items in this way, you're buying as much as you normally would over a couple of weeks, but saving money at the same time.

As well as dry ingredients, buying meat or fish in bulk also saves a few pennies, although works in a slightly different way. For a start, buying meat in bulk at an independent butcher's or market is more likely to save you some money than buying meat at the supermarket, because these traders are more likely to give you better deals when you buy a lot of produce from them. Independent butchers often round down the final price of the meat and throw in a few extra pieces for free if you ask nicely.

Splitting and freezing

If you buy meat and fish in bulk, you can split it up into freezer bags and save it for later. Divide all the cuts into single portions; so about a handful of minced beef, or single pork chops. Pop each portion into a bag and write the contents and your name on the bag. Telling the difference between minced beef and minced lamb is tricky when it's frozen, and writing your name on the bags may stop people pinching them from the freezer.

Dividing the meat into portions this way makes it very easy when cooking for different numbers of people. Cooking spaghetti for four? Get four bags of mince from the freezer. Cooking for one? Take one bag out. You minimise wasted food and money by not defrosting more than you need.

 To thaw out frozen food quickly, place the frozen item in a watertight and sealed bag (over the bag it's already in) and place in a bowl of cold water. Change the water every half an hour until the food is completely thawed (usually about two hours for one portion). Check by pushing a knife into the meat. It should be able to go all the way through.

Supermarket Sweep

Supermarkets are convenient; they have everything you need under one roof, are easy to get to and often have good offers on.

They do have their downsides though. Supermarkets are far less flexible when it comes to individual pricing. While you can easily haggle and sweet talk for a lower price at the market, the price you see at the supermarket is the price you pay (although they do give refunds – very rare at a market). Also, butchers and fishmongers in supermarkets aren't usually as knowledgeable about their products as independent butchers and fishmongers.

Supermarkets are great for buying all your dried and tinned foods, such as rice, pasta, chopped tomatoes and cereal.

 Supermarkets often sell cooking utensils. You can pick up items like wooden spoons and baking trays for a really good price as they're designed to be cheap and cheerful and not made to an amazingly high quality.

Choosing between brands

The two deciding factors when considering whether to buy the supermarket's own brand or a named brand are quality and price, with the supermarket brand supposedly being lower in both.

The truth is, telling the difference in taste between the two is usually difficult. Whether you use a named brand or a supermarket brand tin of chopped tomatoes in a lasagne, it'll be very difficult to tell any difference in taste when you also have the flavour of the onions, garlic, beef and herbs going on in there. Products like chopped tomatoes, rice and pasta don't vary a tremendous amount in quality. It's only when you start paying for specialist brands of say, olives, that you get a noticeable difference in taste and quality.

The difference in price between a branded product and the supermarket's own can be pretty big:

Branded basmati rice 1kg: £3.49

Supermarket basmati rice 1kg: £1.95

Saving: £1.54

Branded fusilli pasta 1kg: £2.19

Supermarket fusilli pasta 1kg: £1.24

Saving: £0.95

Branded olive oil 500ml: £2.78

Supermarket olive oil 500ml: £1.98

Saving: £0.80

Total saving: £3.30

Don't be fooled by the plain packaging of supermarket budget ranges; what's inside is perfect for the cooking you'll be doing at uni.

Taking advantage of special offers

BOGOFs (*buy one get one free* – which should win an award for being the world's only offensively-named special offer) are one of the many pitfalls of supermarket shopping. Know how to use them, and you're laughing. Get them wrong and you end up with a trolley full of two of everything you don't need – the special offer becomes more attractive than the actual product.

The solution is simple: write the all-important shopping list that I mention earlier and stick to it. When you're on a budget, sticking to it stops you getting sucked into buying things that you don't need. And there's nothing worse than buying one thing you don't need and getting another one for free.

The only time when BOGOFs are useful is when they apply to things that you'd normally buy anyway or items that will keep or freeze. So if you don't usually use fancy marmalade, there's no point getting two jars of the stuff, even if you only had to pay for one. But if you're a bit of a porridge junkie, and the local supermarket has a BOGOF on your favourite bowl of breakfast goodness, then get stuck in!

Getting to Know Your Local Markets

The market is the student's friend when it comes to food shopping. Markets have much more flexible pricing than supermarkets and can offer discounts and round down prices where supermarkets can't. Supermarkets are ruled by a nationwide company policy, but independent shops and stalls are their own bosses. They can decide what to sell and what price to sell it at.

Ask a market stall or independent shop if they do student discounts. A lot of traders knock a few pounds off the amount at the end; something you can't do at the supermarket checkout.

Independent butchers and fishmongers are also likely to be better trained than most staff in supermarkets. So, when you want to have fish for dinner, but have no idea how to cook it, your independent fishmonger can pass on his or her expert advice.

Independent retailers can advise you on cheaper cuts of meat or species of fish. For example, if you wanted something like cod, but can't really afford it, they can suggest alternatives like pollock or coley.

Knowing when to go

Unlike supermarkets, you get different deals from the market depending on the day of the week and the time of the day you go. Late afternoon is the best time to go. (See why markets are a student's friend?) By late afternoon, traders are starting to pack their stands away and want to get rid of as much produce as possible. Traders are more likely to do better deals and throw a few extra bits and pieces into your bag. The last thing a greengrocer wants is to carry boxes full of apples back to the van.

While meat and veg come into the market all week long, fish is a little different. Most fresh fish doesn't come into the market on a Monday because fewer fishermen work at the weekend, so anything you buy on a Monday has been stored all through the weekend. This isn't a problem and won't really affect the quality, but you may have to cook and eat the fish that night. Ask the fishmonger for advice.

Some markets have a half-day closing during the week, and most are closed on Sundays. Check the Internet for the opening times of your local market.

Buying seasonally

Different fruit and vegetables are harvested at different months of the year in Britain. If a particular vegetable isn't in season, it's often imported into Britain from another country. Buying seasonally means ensuring that most, if not all, the food you buy is grown in season in Britain.

Shunning foreign exports in favour of local produce from Blighty has both advantages and disadvantages.

For a start, food that's travelled the least is fresher than food that has had a long journey to get here. (How would you feel after a 5,000-mile plane journey across the Atlantic?) The more fresh produce has to travel, the more it deteriorates. So buying in season means you're buying locally (from Britain), eating the freshest produce, reducing CO_2 emissions from transport and supporting local producers.

The problem is that if followed completely, eating seasonally can really restrict what you eat and narrow down choice in your diet. It also has an adverse effect on the communities around the world that supply food.

A happy medium, especially when you're on a budget, is to try to buy as much food as you can seasonally and locally, but don't bust a gut trying to restrict everything in your diet.

Visit www.eattheseasons.co.uk and www.bbcgoodfood.com/content/local/ for free advice on what's in season and recipes.

Chapter 3

Bring On the Balanced Diet

● ●

In This Chapter

▶ Eating your five-a-day

▶ Enjoying a balanced diet

▶ Mining information on vitamins and minerals

● ●

*T*he idea of students living off tins of baked beans and
beer while at uni is a pretty old-fashioned one. Today,
it's much more likely to be vodka and kebabs. Seriously
though, students today are much more aware of the risks
and problems a bad diet can cause. Night after night of mass
alcohol consumption topped off with cheesy chips starts to
take its toll on your body, leaving you feeling run-down and
exhausted, and dying for that long Sunday lie-in so your body
can have a chance to recover.

The old saying 'you are what you eat' is true. Everything that
you eat and drink has a direct relationship to how you think,
feel and act. The obvious example is coffee – one cup and
you're in the zone, five cups and you're in shakey-shake headache land. Your diet has a long-lasting effect. A good diet not
only makes you feel better and healthier on the inside (and
helps you avoid all the yucky colds and fresher flus), but it
also makes you look better on the outside, improving your
hair and skin and increasing your pulling power!

The good news is that it's easy (and best of all cheap) to
change your diet from a bargain bucket of caffeine and carbohydrates to one that's full of fresh fruit and vegetables and all
the goodness your body needs, leaving you looking and feeling simply spiffing.

Getting Your Five-a-Day

Even if you can't name five different portions of fruit and veg, chances are you know what the Five-a-Day initiative is all about. Way back in 1991, the World Health Organization started to recommend an intake of 400 grams of fruit and vegetables a day. One portion is 80 grams, so five portions adds up to 400 grams, swiftly turning into the more memorable five-a-day. Remember, this is the amount your body needs to function at its best; any more is a bonus. And although you can go on loads of crazy diets and get different nutritional advice from experts, one piece of advice is always the same: eat more fruit and veg. Why? Well, fruit and veg:

- ✔ Are low in fat and calories, helping you to feel full but not put on loads of weight.

- ✔ Are full of the vitamins and minerals your body needs to function.

- ✔ Reduce the risk of heart disease and cancer and keep your body running like the well-oiled machine it is.

- ✔ Aren't expensive to buy, making your money go further.

- ✔ Are pretty damn tasty and make great snacks instead of crisps and biscuits.

So what counts towards your five-a-day? Thankfully, Mother Nature has made it simple, because nearly all fruit and vegetables count. Even frozen vegetables and fruit, such as peas or berries count, as well as dried fruit like bananas and raisins. Tinned fruit, like pineapple rings, count as well, as do smoothies and fruit juices.

When fruit and vegetables are frozen, their goodness gets locked in. So, unlike fresh fruit, their quality and nutrients don't deteriorate.

Cooked fruit and vegetables all count towards your five-a-day. Soups, stews, salads, stir-fries and curries with vegetables in all count towards the five-a-day mark. Even ready meals containing vegetables count, but be careful because along with the vegetables usually comes a high level of salt.

Potatoes and similar vegetables such as sweet potatoes and yams *don't* count. This is because they're starchy and lack the level of nutrients that other fruit and vegetables have.

And although vitamin and mineral tablets may have the same vitamins as fresh fruit and vegetables, they lack the other nutritional benefits that fruit and vegetables provide, so don't count towards the five-a-day.

Eating a rainbow

Get colourful when you choose your fruit and veg and aim for a rainbow diet (hang on in there; it's not as hippy as it sounds). Here's the science: different-coloured fruit and vegetables contain different chemicals. For example, dark green leafy vegetables such as spinach and pak choi are packed with omega-3 essential fatty acids that help to build good quality cells in the body; while orange fruit and vegetables such as carrots and pumpkins contain carotenes, which are important antioxidants. So by getting a colourful mix in your diet, you're giving your body the mix of all the important chemicals and nutrients it needs.

Table 3-1 shows the benefits of eating a food rainbow.

Table 3-1	The Benefits of Different-Coloured Fruit and Veg	
Colour	*Nutrient*	*Benefits*
Red *(tomatoes, cherries, red grapefruit, red apples)*	Lycopene	Lowering blood pressure and reducing the risk of prostate cancer
Orange and yellow *(oranges, carrots, pineapples)*	Beta-carotene	Fighting harmful free radicals in your body
Green *(asparagus, broccoli, spinach)*	Fibre	Helping with digestion

(continued)

Table 3-1 *(continued)*

Colour	Nutrient	Benefits
Blue and purple *(blueberries, aubergines, grapes, raisins)*	Lutein	Maintaining your eyesight
White *(mushrooms, garlic, parsnips)*	Lignans	Strengthening your immune system

Doing the maths: Eating five-a-day in three meals a day

Getting your five portions of fruit and veg a day is surprisingly easy. If you have a fairly average diet, you don't need to change much to keep hitting your five-a-day goal. Here are a few ideas for getting some extra fruit and veg goodness into each of your meals without looking like a new-age fitness instructor:

✓ **Breakfast**

- Start your day with a smoothie or fruit juice. That's one portion downed straight away!

- Sprinkle some chopped strawberries or a banana over your cereal, porridge or muesli. Remember, you can also use dried fruit, like raisins.

✓ **Lunch**

- Choose salad or fruit salad pots in your union (or make them up at home) for a nice healthy snack that knocks down a few more portions. Try the salads in Chapter 5.

- Finish off your sandwich with a banana, apple or pear rather than crisps.

✓ **Dinner**

- Try making vegetarian versions of meat dishes. A good vegetable lasagne is often as tasty as its meaty alternative, but far cheaper and healthier. Have a go at the Vegetable Lasagne in Chapter 7.

- Add a bit of veg variety to your plate. Carrots, peas, green beans; the choice is yours!

Got a load of fruit that's past its best and a bit soft? Chuck it in a blender and blitz it into a sexy smoothie, getting another portion of fruity goodness! (Turn to Chapter 4 for smoothie ideas.)

(Portion) size matters

Knowing what makes up a portion is probably the most confusing thing about getting your five-a-day because the portion sizes between fruit and vegetables can vary so much. While two kiwi fruit make up a portion, it only takes one tablespoon of raisins, and no matter how much fruit juice you drink, it still only counts as one portion!

The reason for this mixed-up set of rules is because every kind of fruit and vegetable, whether dried, fresh, juiced or tinned, has different nutritional values. For example, dried fruit loses a lot of water through the drying process, while all the other nutrients (and sugars) become more concentrated, hence the small amount needed to make up the portion size. Kiwi fruit, on the other hand, are 80 per cent water, so you need two to get the appropriate nutrients to make up a portion.

But don't let this put you off your quest for a healthier, fruitier lifestyle. Table 3-2 is a really quick and easy method to work out portion sizes:

Table 3-2	Portion Size Guide
1 Portion of:	*Is Roughly:*
Fresh or tinned fruit *(bananas, apples, strawberries, peaches and so on)*	1 full handful
Dried fruit *(raisins, dried bananas, prunes and so on)*	What you can hold in one lightly closed fist
Juice *(fruit or vegetable juice or smoothies)*	One glass

(continued)

Table 3-2 *(continued)*

1 Portion of:	Is Roughly:
Cooked, tinned or frozen vegetables	1 small handful
(carrots, peas, broccoli, cauliflower and so on)	
Pulses and beans	
(kidney beans, chickpeas and so on)	
Raw vegetables	
(celery, tomatoes, cucumber and so on)	

You can find more in-depth portion information on the NHS's official five-a-day website at www.5aday.nhs.uk.

Stocking Up on Carbs and Protein

Variety plays a really important role in a good diet. Not only is eating a wide range of fruit and vegetables essential for maintaining that healthy radiant glow, but also eating a well-proportioned mix of carbohydrates and protein completes a well-balanced, healthy diet.

What foods apart from fruit and veg can you eat to get that all round health-tastic diet?

You don't need food like meat and cheese as much as you need fresh fruit and vegetables. Figure 3-1 shows the balance of food groups to aim for.

Looking at Figure 3-1, you may be surprised to find that you need to eat the same amount of bread, rice and other starchy carbohydrate foods as fruit and veg. These kinds of foods aren't fattening; it depends what you serve with them. A slice of bread is fine, but not so great when you slather it in butter . . .

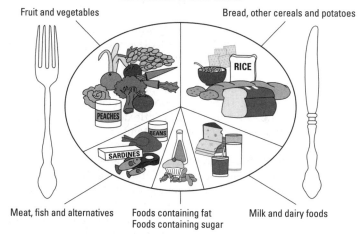

The Balance of Good Health

Fruit and vegetables   Bread, other cereals and potatoes

RICE

PEACHES

BEANS

SARDINES

Meat, fish and alternatives   Foods containing fat   Milk and dairy foods
                                Foods containing sugar

Adapted from model from the Food Standards Agency

Figure 3-1: The balance of food groups to aim for.

Bread, rice and potatoes are good sources of energy and also contain fibre, calcium, iron and lots of vitamin B. Like fruit, these foods also do a good job of filling you up (and stopping you snacking later on) without piling on the pounds.

 Choose brown rice, wholemeal bread and pasta, and low-fat dairy products for a healthier option with these two food groups.

Discovering Vitamins and Minerals

When it comes to finding out about vitamins and minerals in food, things can get pretty in-depth and a little microscopic. After all, aren't minerals in rocks?

In this section, I give you an idea of what vitamins and minerals are, how they work and what effect they have on your body. And don't worry, I keep things simple!

From A to K: Vitamins

Vitamins help your body work in different ways. If you have a cold, you need plenty of vitamin C; if your skin is a bit spotty, get some vitamin A down you.

Vitamins can be water or fat soluble, and they regulate bodily functions. They build bones, skin cells and nerves, as well as acting as hormones and antioxidants. The human body only requires tiny amounts of vitamins in order to function properly.

People have known about the benefits of certain foods for years. In the 18th century, the Royal Navy started to use citrus fruits to fight scurvy (a wasting disease resulting from vitamin C deficiency), giving Brits the nickname *limeys*. Want another cool fact? A Polish scientist called Casimir Funk (I'm not kidding) first 'discovered' vitamins in 1912. But it's only fairly recently that specific vitamins have been linked to specific effects in the body. Here's a quick rundown:

- ✔ **Vitamin A** is your beauty vitamin. It gives you healthy skin and hair, is essential for good growth and is fat soluble, meaning it dissolves in the fat in your body. You can find vitamin A in oily fish like mackerel, trout and herring; dairy products like milk, cheese and eggs; and in chicken, kidneys and liver. Another source of vitamin A is in a substance called beta-carotene, found in fruit and vegetables like carrots, mangoes and watercress. When inside you, your body converts beta-carotene to vitamin A.

- ✔ **Vitamin B** is water soluble and doesn't get stored in your body like fat-soluble vitamins. Vitamin B exists in several forms: B1, B2, B3, B6, B12 and folic acid. The body doesn't need much B1, 2 or 3, while vitamins B6 and B12 work at repairing cells, digesting food and helping your immune system keep fighting fit. Vitamin B12 is typically found in animal and dairy products, making it a problem for vegans. However, soya milk and breakfast cereal are good B12 providers.

- ✔ **Vitamin C** is everyone's favourite vitamin when they have a runny nose. Vitamin C is the fighter in your immune system and speeds up wound repair. It's also water soluble. The main sources of vitamin C are citrus fruits and smoothies.

✔ **Vitamin D** is vital for healthy bones and teeth as it helps the body to absorb calcium. Part of vitamin D (which is fat soluble) is created inside you when sunlight hits your skin. Even us lot in rainy Britain usually get enough vitamin D every day.

✔ **Vitamin E** looks after your heart, nerves, muscles and reproductive system. It's also involved in protecting your body from unstable compounds called free radicals, which cause damage to healthy cells. Vitamin E is fat soluble and is in oily fish like mackerel and salmon, olive oil, nuts and wholegrains.

✔ **Vitamin K** comes to the rescue when you cut yourself shaving and helps your blood clot on the wound. Vitamin K is in dark green leafy vegetables like spinach and broccoli, but most of it is produced in your large intestine by healthy bacteria, and is fat soluble. Sugary and fatty foods can change the balance of this good bacteria, so that's one more reason to leave the biscuits alone.

Uncovering minerals

Minerals come from non-living things like water, rocks and soil. You get minerals in your diet through a chain: plants get minerals from the soil, animals eat the plants, and then you eat the plants or the animals.

Minerals are classified according to the amount your body needs:

✔ **Major minerals** are those humans need more than 100 milligrams of a day.

✔ **Minor minerals** (or *trace elements*) are those humans need less than 100 milligrams of a day.

Here's a rundown of the benefits of minerals:

✔ **Calcium** is essential for strong bones and teeth. Dairy products provide a high amount of calcium. Broccoli, almonds, sesame seeds and dried apricots also contain lots of calcium.

✔ **Iron** is important for healthy blood and muscles; too little can cause symptoms such as tiredness and irritability. Women lose iron when they menstruate and one in four don't get enough. Apricots, blackcurrants, baked beans, broccoli (again!), eggs, wholegrain cereals and nuts are all really good sources of iron.

✔ **Magnesium** is involved in controlling your blood pressure and regulates energy release and your body temperature. It also helps the body absorb and break down other vitamins and minerals like calcium and vitamin C. Magnesium is in lots of foods like milk, meat, courgettes, brown rice, nuts and raisins.

✔ **Zinc** is vital for growth, wound healing and in producing testosterone. A lack of zinc often results in skin problems and a low sexual libido – not good. Red meat and meat products are good sources of zinc, as are milk, eggs and fish.

✔ **Potassium** helps in the transmission of nerve impulses, heart rhythm and relaxes muscles. It also helps in secreting insulin to control blood sugar and provide constant energy. Most fruit and vegetables contain potassium, and bananas, strawberries and orange juice are the best sources.

Here are the benefits and sources of trace elements:

✔ **Selenium** is found in the soil, so the amount you get depends on the farming methods used in the fruit and veg you eat. Over-cultivation of the land (a problem in the UK) results in a drop in the selenium level of crops. The best sources of selenium are cashew nuts, onions, green vegetables and chicken (because of the animal's diet).

✔ **Manganese** is sadly no relation to the Japanese comics, but part of an enzyme that metabolises carbohydrates. It's also pretty important for a healthy reproductive system. You can find manganese lurking around in nuts, fruits, vegetables and even tea.

✔ **Copper** is an antioxidant that helps fight free radicals that may have formed inside you. Copper also helps bones and blood vessels grow. You can get a small amount of copper in most things you eat: bread, meat and vegetables all contain trace elements of copper.

> ✔ **Iodine** is involved in tissue and bone growth and in maintaining a healthy nervous system. The best sources of iodine are in milk, seafood and in vegetables grown in coastal regions.

A well-balanced and varied diet full of vitamins and minerals is amazingly beneficial. So swap crisps for carrots, and bacon butties for healthy cereals, and very quickly you'll see an improvement in how you feel and look. Give it a go, and set your foundations for a long, healthy and fun life.

Part II
Breakfast, Lunch and Snacks

In this part . . .

1 cover everything you need to eat from the moment you get up to just before your evening meal (main meals are in Part III). I also give you some tips on what you can eat to boost your brainpower when you're revising. Top score!

Chapter 4

Bigging Up Breakfast

In This Chapter

▶ Making quick and healthy breakfasts

▶ Juicing super smoothies

▶ Gorging on all-day breakfasts

▶ Beating hangover blues

*W*here better place to start your cooking adventures than with the most important meal of the day: breakfast. If you're missing out on some early morning (or possibly late afternoon) eating action, hang your head in shame! Eating a good breakfast means that you get a fantastic start to the day and have less chance of wanting to gorge on snacks before lunch, which means saving those precious pennies for more important things. And if you happen to have spent those pennies on too much alcohol, this chapter includes breakfasts for dealing with the after-effects. Forget crazy hair-of-the-dog remedies and tedious daytime TV, I give you hangover-busting breakfast recipes that'll get you back on your feet and ready for that morning lecture.

Making Healthy Breakfasts in a Hurry

Let me guess; you've overslept and have a date with Marxist Sociology in less than an hour. So you need a quick fix. But don't underestimate the benefits of getting a healthy start to the day. Not only will you feel more alert and be giving your body all the energy it needs to get out of bed, but also you'll be getting a few portions of your recommended five-a-day of fruit and veg. So knock up one of these quick and healthy breakfasts and keep hunger locked up till lunchtime!

⌒Pimp'd Up Porridge

Porridge doesn't have to be boring and look like wallpaper paste. Try adding some of these great toppings to pimp up your bowl of oaty goodness. Plain oats or instant packets of porridge are fine for this recipe. Plain oats are cheaper and more versatile (you can use plain oats in muesli as well as cooked up as porridge), but the instant sachets are very quick and easy if you have a microwave. Most instant packets also show you how to measure the right amount of milk into the mix, which can be handy if you don't have a measuring jug.

Although this recipe is cooked in a microwave, porridge is just as easy cooked on the hob – check the back of the packet for instructions.

Preparation time: *5 minutes*

Cooking time: *2 minutes*

Serves: *1*

6 tablespoons of porridge oats

200 millilitres of cold milk (about a mugful)

Selection of toppings – choose what you want to use from:

Handful of raisins

1 chopped banana

Drizzle of honey or maple syrup

Pinch of cinnamon

Handful of blueberries

Handful of chopped strawberries

Sprinkle of pumpkin seeds

1 Spoon the porridge oats into a bowl.

2 Pour in the cold milk and stir well.

3 Place the bowl in the microwave and cover with a bit of kitchen roll.

4 Microwave on full power for one minute.

5 After a minute, stir the mixture and then cover and microwave again for one minute.

6 Using a tea towel or oven gloves (the bowl will be hot), take the porridge out of the microwave and stir in your choice of toppings. If you want thicker porridge, let it sit for a minute or two before tucking in.

Variation: *Try experimenting! Have a look in your cupboards and scour your local market to see how you could pimp up yo' porridge!*

Per serving: *Calories 404 (From Fat 104); Fat 11.6g (Saturated 5.7g); Cholesterol Trace; Sodium 114mg; Carbohydrate 63.1g (Dietary Fibre 3.6g); Protein 11.9g.*

⏺Banana and Strawberry Smoothie

Smoothies – whizzed up fruit drinks – make great breakfasts. They're packed full of fruity goodness, giving you the completely natural boost your body needs at the start of the day, and are super quick to prepare – what other breakfast comes in a glass?

This recipe is actually a great starting point for creating your own tasty smoothie. You can swap the strawberries for other fruit, particularly if strawberries aren't in season and are a bit expensive. Have a look round your local market and on the Internet to find out what's in season and what you could use instead.

Preparation time: 5 minutes

Cooking time: 30 seconds

Serves: 1

2 bananas, peeled and chopped into small chunks

1 handful of strawberries, washed and cut in half, with the green bits removed from the top

1 cup of orange juice

1 cup of ice cubes

1 spoonful of honey

Pinch of cinnamon (optional)

Pinch of brown sugar (optional)

1 Place all the prepared ingredients in a blender.

2 Blend until smooth – all of 30 seconds!

Variation: Try using blueberries or raspberries rather than strawberries.

Per serving: Calories 376 (From Fat 9); Fat 1g (Saturated 0.2g); Cholesterol Trace; Sodium 27mg; Carbohydrate 87.4g (Dietary Fibre 3.4g); Protein 4.3g.

Tip: If you don't have time to clean your blender afterwards, soak it in some warm soapy water and come back to it later. The warm water stops any smoothie drying hard onto the inside, making it a lot easier to clean later on.

⌒Superfood Smoothie

Superfoods are foods that are high in certain vitamins and minerals and are particularly healthy for you. So, for an instant feel-good vitamin boost, try this fantastic superfood smoothie.

 Frozen fruit is just as good as fresh fruit, particularly if you're just using it for making smoothies (as it can sometimes be a bit mushy when it defrosts). Frozen fruit can also be a lot cheaper than buying fresh and is still as good for you. Fresh fruit loses nutrients as it ages, whereas the nutrients in frozen fruit are locked in; kind of frozen in time.

Preparation time: *5 minutes*

Cooking time: *1 minute*

Serves: *1*

4 chopped strawberries

1 chopped kiwi fruit (remember to peel off the tough outer skin first)

Handful of blueberries

1 peeled and chopped banana

1 glass of orange juice

2 spoonfuls of natural yogurt

Place all the ingredients into a blender and whizz until smooth.

Variation: *Pop in a few raspberries and a drizzle of honey if you have a sweet tooth.*

Per serving: *Calories 366 (From Fat 23); Fat 2.5g (Saturated 0.7g); Cholesterol Trace; Sodium 52mg; Carbohydrate 79.8g (Dietary Fibre 5.9g); Protein 6.1g.*

ᘛDried Fruit Salad

You can make up this fruit salad in advance and store it in your cupboard for ages, then grab a bowlful when you're on the run (just remember to add the yogurt before you eat it). A plastic food-storage box keeps it nice and fresh. You can pick up a lot of these ingredients at your local market or health food shop.

Preparation time: *5 minutes*

Cooking time: *Nil*

Serves: *6*

100 grams dried apricots (a small handful)

100 grams prunes or dates (a small handful)

100 grams mixed dried fruit (a small handful of sultanas, currants and raisins)

100 grams dried banana slices (a small handful)

50 grams hazelnuts

Pinch of ground cinnamon (optional)

300 grams natural yogurt (about 7 spoonfuls)

1 Combine all the dry ingredients together in a container and mix well.

2 Fill up your breakfast bowl with the fruit and spoon the yogurt over the top.

Variation: *For an extra dash of goodness, sprinkle some seeds over the yogurt, or add the dried fruit salad to muesli or breakfast cereal to liven up standard breakfast fare.*

Per serving: *Calories 257 (From Fat 66); Fat 7.3g (Saturated 1.6g); Cholesterol Trace; Sodium 33mg; Carbohydrate 42.7g (Dietary Fibre 7.8g); Protein 5.2g.*

⑤Fresh Fruit Salad

You can make fresh fruit salad in advance and keep it in the fridge for up to three days for when you need brekky in a hurry; just make sure you leave out the banana for now (because it will go brown) and add it just before eating.

 If you don't fancy some of the fruit in the ingredients list below, choose your own!

Preparation time: *10 minutes*

Cooking time: *Nil*

Serves: *6*

2 peeled grapefruit, cut into bite-sized chunks

2 peeled oranges, cut into bite-sized chunks

2 apples, cored and cut into bite-sized slices

100 grams tinned pineapple (about a small handful)

100 millilitres of orange juice

50 grams seedless grapes, washed and halved

1 banana, peeled and sliced into chunks

300 grams natural yogurt (about 7 spoonfuls)

1 Place the grapefruit, orange, apple and pineapple pieces in a bowl.

2 Pour in just enough orange juice to cover the fruit.

3 Add the halved grapes to the bowl.

4 Chuck in the banana slices (if you're eating the fruit salad straight away). Carefully mix the fruit together.

5 Place into serving bowls and add the yogurt.

Variation: *Other fruit, like kiwi fruit, mangoes and pears, are delicious additions.*

Tip: *Mix whatever you have in your fruit bowl into your fruit salad – it's the perfect way to use up fruit that's slightly past its best because you'll be chopping it all up anyway!*

Per serving: *Calories 151 (From Fat 18); Fat 2g (Saturated 1.1g); Cholesterol Trace; Sodium 32mg; Carbohydrate 29.6g (Dietary Fibre 3.8g); Protein 3.7g.*

Enjoying All-Day Breakfasts

Let's face it, getting up before midday might be a rare thing while you're a student, especially at the weekend. So here's a rundown of the best breakfasts to have whatever time you get up, whether that's a late afternoon lie-in, or a post-clubbing nosh-up for the times when you're still up at 4 a.m.

Some of the following recipes use eggs. Always try to buy free-range eggs.

Healthy Full English

Who said a full English breakfast has to be a barrage of cholesterol and grease? This recipe's indulgent yet healthy, so ditch the guilt and grab an apron.

Add a few sausages if you want to create the full Monty. Supermarket sausages have cooking instructions on the packet (most sausages take about 15 to 20 minutes to grill). Cooking the sausages takes longer than the rest of this meal, so start them off 5 minutes before the rest of the recipe.

Preparation time: *10 minutes*

Cooking time: *10 minutes*

Serves: *1*

1 tomato, halved	*Salt and pepper*
2 rashers of bacon, rind cut off	*1 egg*
1 small tin of baked beans	*2 slices of wholemeal bread*
Handful of mushrooms, chopped into quarters	*Low-fat spread*

1 Turn the grill on at a medium setting and have two pieces of kitchen paper laid out in readiness to drain the excess water from the poached egg.

2 Half-fill a saucepan with water, and place on a medium heat to bring to a simmer (when the water is lightly bubbling).

3 Place the tomato and bacon onto the grill pan and place under the grill.

4 Pour the beans into a bowl, cover with a square of kitchen roll and heat on full power in the microwave for two minutes. If you don't have a microwave, pour the beans into a saucepan and place on a medium heat on the hob. Keep stirring occasionally.

5 Heat some oil in a frying pan and when hot, add the chopped mushrooms. Sprinkle a little salt and pepper over them while they're cooking.

6 By now, the water for the egg should be simmering (very lightly bubbling). Carefully crack the egg into the just simmering water and allow to *poach* (gently cook in the water). Just leave the egg to do its thing – avoid the temptation to mess with it.

7 Turn the bacon over and remove the tomato if it's starting to turn golden or burn.

8 Give the beans a stir, cover again and reheat in the microwave for another minute.

9 Place the bread in the toaster and spread with low-fat spread when toasted. Place on a plate.

10 Add the beans, bacon and tomato to the plate.

11 When the mushrooms look golden brown, carefully spoon them onto the plate, leaving most of the oil in the pan.

12 Carefully lift the poached egg out of the pan with a spoon (preferably a slotted spoon if you have one) and drain on the kitchen paper, before placing onto the plate.

Variation: For a vegetarian option, swap the bacon with some veggie sausages. You cook them the same way as normal sausages, by grilling or frying. If you're grilling them (the healthy option), place the sausages underneath a hot grill for about 20 minutes, turning them 10 minutes in. If you're frying them, add a drop of oil to a frying pan over a medium heat, add the sausages when the oil is hot and fry for about 15 minutes.

Per serving: Calories 395 (From Fat 113); Fat 12.5g (Saturated 3.7g); Cholesterol Trace; Sodium 1827mg; Carbohydrate 47.2g (Dietary Fibre 10.1g); Protein 23.4g.

○Grilled Tomatoes on Toast

Everyone knows beans on toast, but what about a colourful alternative? Tomatoes are fantastic things, full of vitamin C and *lycopene,* a natural antioxidant that gives them their red look. So when choosing tomatoes, look out for really bright red ones, because these contain the most lycopene.

 Cooking tomatoes releases even more of their nutrients and is as good, if not better, for you than eating them raw.

Preparation time: *3 minutes*

Cooking time: *5 minutes*

Serves: *1*

3 small tomatoes, sliced in half	Low-fat spread
2 slices of wholemeal bread (or white bread if you prefer)	Salt and pepper
	Brown sauce (optional)

1 Turn on the grill.

2 When the grill is hot, place the tomatoes under the grill. Grill for 5 to 7 minutes, until the tomatoes become soft and the tops turn a dark golden colour.

3 Toast the bread and spread with low-fat spread. Add the grilled tomatoes.

4 Add a shake of salt and pepper.

5 Add a dash of brown sauce for a little kick.

Variation: *Use cherry tomatoes for that extra sweetness, or if you have half a tin of chopped tomatoes that needs using up, fry them in a little olive oil and pour on the toast.*

Per serving: *Calories 225 (From Fat 52); Fat 5.8g (Saturated 1.4g); Cholesterol Trace; Sodium 704mg; Carbohydrate 35.8g (Dietary Fibre 4.6g); Protein 7.3g.*

⟲Wholemeal Bagels with Cottage Cheese and Grilled Tomatoes

Turn your kitchen into a New York deli with these delicious bagels. I've chosen health-conscious wholemeal bagels, but you can always use white bagels instead.

 Check the Reduced section of the supermarket for going-out-of-date bread and bagels at bargain prices. When you get home, split up the bread and freeze in freezer bags. Use slices or bagels as and when you need them, defrosting them the night before.

Preparation time: *5 minutes*

Cooking time: *5 minutes*

Serves: *4*

4 tomatoes, cut into quarters

Salt and pepper

4 wholemeal bagels

300 grams cottage cheese

1 Turn on the grill to a medium setting.

2 When hot, place the tomatoes onto the grill tray, sprinkle a little salt and pepper over them and place under the grill for about 5 minutes.

3 Cut the bagels in half and place in a toaster for about a minute (use your toaster's bagel setting if it has one, to toast the flat side more than the curvy side).

4 Spread the cottage cheese on each toasted bagel.

5 When the tomatoes turn soft and golden brown, remove from the grill and carefully place onto the bottom half of each bagel. Place the other half of the bagel on top.

Variation: *As an alternative to grilling the tomatoes, you can also cut them up smaller and fry them in a pan with a little olive oil.*

Per serving: *Calories 306 (From Fat 43); Fat 4.8g (Saturated 2.1g); Cholesterol Trace; Sodium 632mg; Carbohydrate 47.4g (Dietary Fibre 2.6g); Protein 18.4g.*

Scrambled Eggs and Smoked Haddock Student-Style

Pretend you have loads of money with this luxurious-tasting breakfast. Thankfully, it's actually pretty cheap to make. You can find smoked haddock at your local fishmonger's or supermarket. Buy it ready skinned and de-boned so you don't have to mess about with it.

 Smoked fish doesn't necessarily mean it's precooked. Fish can be *hot smoked* (cooked during the smoking process) or *cold smoked* (smoked over a low temperature and not cooked). Check on the packaging or with the fishmonger to see if your fish needs cooking.

Preparation time: 15 minutes

Cooking time: 15 minutes

Serves: 1

Chunk of butter	2 eggs
100 grams smoked haddock (skinned and de-boned)	2 slices of wholemeal bread
	Salt and pepper

1 Preheat the oven to 200°C.

2 Cut a square of tin foil large enough to wrap the haddock in and rub it with the chunk of butter.

3 Place the haddock in the middle of the buttery foil and bring the edges together to make a sealed parcel. Place on a baking tray in the middle of the preheated oven and leave to cook for 10 minutes.

4 After 10 minutes, take the fish out of the oven and leave to stand, keeping the foil sealed.

5 Crack the eggs into a bowl and whisk for a minute until you have a light liquid (use a fork if you don't have a whisk).

6 Heat a saucepan over a medium heat and add a chunk of butter.

7 While the butter melts, open the fish parcel and check that the haddock is cooked by gently pulling a piece of the fish away with your fork. If it falls away easily, the fish is cooked. If it's still quite firm, wrap it back up and put back in the oven for another 5 minutes. When the haddock is cooked, break it up into small pieces using your fork.

8 By now, the butter should be melted, so add the egg mixture and cook the eggs until they become thick and creamy, continually turning and folding the mixture in on itself with a wooden spoon or spatula. Add the flaked haddock and keep stirring and folding the mixture for about 3 to 5 minutes. When the eggs are just about to go firm but are still runny, remove from the heat.

9 Toast and butter the bread.

10 Add a bit of salt and pepper to the fish and eggs and spoon over the toast.

Variation: Use kippers rather than the haddock. Cut off the heads and tails with some scissors or a knife and put the fish under a medium grill skin side up. After about a minute, flip them over and spoon or brush melted butter over the flesh side and put them back under the grill for another minute.

Per serving: *Calories 656 (From Fat 365); Fat 40.6g (Saturated 20.0g); Cholesterol Trace; Sodium 1740mg; Carbohydrate 27.9g (Dietary Fibre 3.3g); Protein 44.7g.*

Hangover-Beating Breakfasts

Oh dear. I guess you're reading this with double-vision, a throbbing headache and a promise to yourself that you'll never drink again. Put on some sunglasses and stagger to the kitchen as I'm going to bring you back to life with these hangover-beating breakfasts.

Just why does drinking too much alcohol make you feel so bad? A hangover is when your body is dehydrated, has low blood sugar levels and is trying desperately to get rid of the toxins from last night's alcohol intake. The bad news is that the only real way to beat a hangover is to limit your alcohol intake and drink plenty of water throughout the night out and the morning after.

However, if it's too late for the good advice, here are some good hangover-helping foods:

✔ Bananas are especially good hangover fighters because they contain the potassium and sugars your body is desperately crying out for.

✔ Try drinking fizzy drinks (or flat if you can't handle fizzy). The sugar helps to break down the alcohol in your body. Energy drinks such as Lucozade and Irn-Bru can be helpful hangover remedies.

✔ Green tea or lemon juice in hot water are also good comfort drinks and help to top up your fluid levels.

Your liver needs approximately one hour to break down one unit of alcohol. When one pint contains nearly two and a half units, it's no wonder you feel bad the next day!

Banana and Honey Smoothie

Here's a quick and easy hangover cure. Bananas replace the potassium you're missing, honey raises the blood sugar levels and the orange juice and ice cubes replace lost liquid. Just brace yourself for the noise when it blends together!

 This is also a great smoothie to have after a workout at the gym because it contains all the nutrients your body has lost during exercise.

Preparation time: 5 minutes

Cooking time: 1 minute

Serves: 1

2 peeled and chopped bananas

Spoonful of honey

Glass of orange juice

Glass of ice cubes

Pinch of cinnamon (optional)

Place all the ingredients in a blender and whizz for a couple of minutes until smooth.

Variation: Add some strawberries or blueberries for a change in colour and increase your five-a-day.

Per serving: Calories 402 (From Fat 10); Fat 1.1g (Saturated 0.2g); Cholesterol Trace; Sodium 34mg; Carbohydrate 93.5g (Dietary Fibre 2.9g); Protein 4.5g.

⏱Hangover-Beating Beans on Toast

I doubt you need much help with making this one, but it's a great hangover cure! Beans are full of protein and help break down the alcohol while releasing a slow stream of sugar into your body.

Preparation time: *1 minute*

Cooking time: *5 minutes*

Serves: *1*

Small tin of baked beans   2 slices of toast (brown if possible)

1 Pour the beans into a pan and heat over a low heat on the hob for a few minutes (making sure that they don't boil and damage the flavour). If you have a microwave, stick the beans in a bowl, cover and microwave at full power for two minutes. After two minutes, stir the beans, cover and microwave again for another minute.

2 Place the bread in the toaster and toast.

3 Butter the toast and pour the cooked beans over the toast.

Variation: *Try mixing in a dash of Worcestershire sauce to the beans before you microwave them (buy vegetarian Worcestershire sauce if you're veggie). Adding grated cheese on top of your beans on toast also adds to the protein kick.*

Per serving: *Calories 334 (From Fat 26); Fat 2.9g (Saturated 0.6g); Cholesterol Trace; Sodium 1434mg; Carbohydrate 59.8g (Dietary Fibre 11.1g); Protein 17.1g.*

ℭMasala Omelette

This omelette is a bit of a kick start to your day! The ginger and spices open your airways and get you feeling alive again in no time. Plus, the protein in the eggs is just what you need to fight the remaining alcohol in your bloodstream.

 Always wash your hands thoroughly after preparing chillies. Getting chillies in your eyes or on other areas of your face can seriously hurt!

Preparation time: *3 minutes*

Cooking time: *5 minutes*

Serves: *1*

2 eggs

Half a red pepper, chopped into small cubes

A small piece of ginger, peeled and chopped into little bits (you can use ground ginger)

Half an onion, peeled and chopped into pieces

1 green chilli, chopped into small pieces (remove the seeds if you want to reduce the heat!)

1 garlic clove, peeled and chopped

Pinch of chopped coriander (optional)

Olive oil

1 Crack the eggs into a bowl and whisk until smooth (use a fork if you don't have a whisk).

2 Pour the remaining ingredients into the egg mixture and mix well.

3 Add a glug of oil to a large frying pan (preferably nonstick), swirling round to coat all the pan, and heat up on a hob.

4 When the oil is very hot, pour in the omelette mixture and swirl round so it coats the entire pan.

5 Fry the mixture until it becomes a semi-solid omelette. You should be able to move the pan and the omelette stays together.

6 To cook the other side, place a plate over the frying pan and twist them both over, so that the plate is underneath and the frying pan on top. Lift the frying pan off, put back on the heat and slide the omelette back in, so the other side is facing up.

7 Continue cooking the omelette for about another minute, then slide it onto a plate and eat.

Variation: If this is too spicy, leave out the green chilli, or if you haven't got any chillies, add a generous pinch of chilli powder.

Per serving: Calories 451 (From Fat 308); Fat 34.2g (Saturated 6.8g); Cholesterol Trace; Sodium 204mg; Carbohydrate 18g (Dietary Fibre 3.5g); Protein 17.7g.

Chapter 5

Making Great Lunches

In This Chapter

▶ Enjoying tasty soups, hot and cold

▶ Creating fresh and healthy salads

▶ Making lunch for two

*T*he average student spends nearly £500 each year on sandwiches, crisps and lunchtime snacks at uni! Making a great lunch at home not only works out cheaper than buying a bland sandwich from the union shop, but also is healthier and a bit of a laugh. Too many students skip lunch, brunch or whatever you want to call that important meal at midday, but now it's time for a change. The recipes in this chapter are guaranteed to tingle your tastebuds and get you hankering for a bit of lunchtime eating action!

In this chapter, I look at souping up soups, and for the health conscious, I give you some fantastic salads that are great even in winter months. I also reveal how to wow that special person with a delicious lunch for two. Get stuck in!

Serving Simple Soup

Soups are one of those hearty, feel-good comfort foods that are just brilliant. They're a great way of using up any vegetables you have lurking in the bottom of your fridge, and you can make enough to last you through the week – pour it into a flask and take it into uni for a warm top-up on a winter's day. Soups don't have to be warm – I'm going to show you some fantastic cold soups to cool down the hottest of summer days.

ᕕClassic Tomato Soup

Tomato soup is everyone's favourite. Far better than anything from a tin, this classic soup is a winner every time.

If you want to, make a big batch of this soup and eat over several lunchtimes during the week. Simply leave it to cool, then pour into bowls, cover with cling film or kitchen foil and put it in the fridge. When you're hungry for more tomato soup, re-heat it in the microwave for one minute, stir, then reheat again for another minute. This soup freezes well; just defrost it, and then re-heat it thoroughly.

Preparation time: *5 minutes*

Cooking time: *40 minutes*

Serves: *4*

Olive oil

1 onion, peeled and chopped

2 cloves of garlic, peeled and crushed or finely chopped

2 sticks of celery, washed and chopped into pieces

2 carrots, peeled and chopped

500 grams ripe tomatoes, chopped into chunks

1 teaspoon of sugar

Squeeze of tomato purée

1 litre of vegetable stock

Big pinch of mixed herbs

Salt and pepper

1 Heat a glug of olive oil in a large saucepan over a medium heat.

2 When the oil is hot, add the chopped onion, garlic, celery and carrots and gently fry until soft.

3 After 10 minutes, add the chopped tomatoes and sugar. Squeeze in a big splodge of tomato purée and mix thoroughly.

4 Add the vegetable stock, mixed herbs and some salt and pepper, and then give your soup a good stir and bring to a simmer (so it's lightly bubbling).

5 Simmer for 20 to 30 minutes or until the vegetables are nice and tender. Remove from the heat and leave to cool slightly.

6 Blend with a hand blender (one you can immerse in the pan) or pour the soup into a food processor or blender.

Variation: *If you don't have any fresh tomatoes, use two tins of chopped tomatoes or plum tomatoes.*

Per serving: Calories 129 (From Fat 53); Fat 5.9g (Saturated 0.8g); Cholesterol Trace; Sodium 1302mg; Carbohydrate 15.8g (Dietary Fibre 3.2g); Protein 3.2g.

⟳Leek and Potato Soup

Here's another classic soup that's really easy to make and is great comfort food. Leeks are in season from November through to April and are packed with nutrients and antioxidants to fight off those winter blues.

You need to thoroughly clean leeks before cooking. Chop off the white root end of the leek and cut off and bin most of the tough leafy end. Cut a line into the remaining leafy section, parallel to the direction of the leek. Then fan out the leaves and rinse under a cold tap to wash away the mud and dirt that gets trapped under the leaves.

Preparation time: *5 minutes*

Cooking time: *30 minutes*

Serves: *2*

Chunk of butter

1 leek, washed and sliced

1 clove of garlic, crushed or finely sliced

1 onion, peeled and sliced

1 potato, peeled and chopped into chunks

500 millilitres vegetable stock

1 Melt the butter in a large saucepan over a medium to high heat.

2 Add the leek, garlic and onion and fry until soft (about 10 minutes).

3 Add the chopped potato and the vegetable stock, and then season with some salt and pepper.

4 Simmer for about 10 to 15 minutes or until the potato has gone soft (check by pushing a knife into a piece).

5 Remove the pan from the heat and leave to cool for a minute.

6 Pour into a blender (or use a hand blender) and blend until smooth. If the soup starts to look a bit thick, add half a mug of hot water to it and blend a bit more.

Tip: *If you don't have a blender, cut all the vegetables a bit smaller at the beginning and serve the soup chunky.*

Variation: *Add some chopped mint or watercress before you blend it at the end to give the soup a bit of a kick.*

Per serving: Calories 299 (From Fat 122); Fat 13.6g (Saturated 8g); Cholesterol Trace; Sodium 1330mg; Carbohydrate 37.1g (Dietary Fibre 5.9g); Protein 7.0g.

ℭCarrot, Apple and Celery Soup

This soup is nice and chunky but comes with a delicate flavour. It's great for using up any apples in your fruit bowl that are going a bit soft.

Preparation time: *5 minutes*

Cooking time: *20 minutes*

Serves: *2*

Chunk of butter

1 onion, sliced

2 carrots, peeled and chopped

2 cloves of garlic, peeled and chopped

1 apple, skin removed and chopped into pieces

2 sticks of celery, chopped

350 millilitres vegetable stock (use two stock cubes for a fuller flavour)

Big pinch of dried tarragon (optional)

Couple of bay leaves (optional)

Salt and pepper

1 Melt the butter in a saucepan over a high heat.

2 Add the onion and stir well, coating it in the butter.

3 After a few minutes, add the carrots, garlic, apple and celery. Stir well and leave to cook for 5 minutes.

4 Add the vegetable stock and the dried tarragon and bay leaves if you're using them. Season with some salt and pepper.

5 Turn down the heat to medium and put the lid on the saucepan. (If you can't find the lid, put some kitchen foil over the top). Simmer for about 10 minutes.

6 Chuck out the bay leaves if you put them in (they just give the soup some flavour). If you like your soup chunky, pour into a bowl and enjoy; if you like it a bit smoother, add some more stock and give it a quick blend in a blender.

Variation: *Add a chopped chilli if you like things spicy!*

Per serving: *Calories 249 (From Fat 121); Fat 13.4g (Saturated 7.9g); Cholesterol Trace; Sodium 1056mg; Carbohydrate 28.6g (Dietary Fibre 6.3g); Protein 3.6g.*

⌒Gazpacho

Gazpacho is a classic Spanish tomato soup that's served cold. As such, it's a great refreshing snack, ideal for cooling down during a hot day. This soup is also unbelievably quick to make.

Preparation time: *5 minutes*

Cooking time: *5 minutes (plus 2 hours' chilling)*

Serves: *1*

400-gram tin of plum tomatoes

1 garlic clove, crushed or sliced into small pieces

Splodge of tomato purée

¼ cucumber, diced (cut up into small cubes)

1 teaspoon of caster sugar

1 tablespoon of olive oil

Salt and pepper

1 Combine all the ingredients into a blender, season with salt and pepper and whiz until smooth.

2 Pour into a bowl and pop into the fridge until chilled and ready to serve (about 2 hours). Season again with some salt and pepper before tucking in.

Variation: *Shake in some Worcestershire sauce (vegetarian if necessary) before serving, to add a lightly spiced flavour.*

Per serving: *Calories 252 (From Fat 140); Fat 15.5g (Saturated 2.1g); Cholesterol Trace; Sodium 382mg; Carbohydrate 22.3g (Dietary Fibre 3.9g); Protein 5.7g.*

⌒Beetroot Soup with Greek Yogurt

Here's another cold soup for those chill-out hot days. This recipe is one of my favourites. I love beetroot, and the cream-iness of the Greek yogurt really cuts through the richness of the vegetable.

Beetroot stains very easily, so forget style and wear an apron, or at least don't wear a white top when you make this!

Preparation time: 5 minutes

Cooking time: 30 minutes

Serves: 2

Olive oil

1 onion, peeled and sliced

1 clove of garlic, peeled and finely chopped

1 to 1½ large beetroot, peeled and chopped into chunks

200-gram tin of chopped tomatoes

200 millilitres vegetable stock

Salt and pepper

Small pot of Greek yogurt

1 Fry the onion and garlic in a glug of olive oil in a saucepan over a medium heat until soft.

2 Add the beetroot and chopped tomatoes and mix together well. Fry for 5 minutes.

3 Add the stock and simmer for 15 minutes, or until the beetroot is tender. Season with salt and pepper.

4 After 15 minutes, take the soup off the heat and allow to cool for 5 minutes before blending until smooth.

5 Spoon into bowls and place in the fridge until chilled.

6 When you're ready to serve, drizzle a circle of Greek yogurt into the soup, grind over a bit more pepper and enjoy.

Variation: Rather than the Greek yogurt, add a spoonful of crème fraîche to the soup just before serving.

Per serving: *Calories 222 (From Fat 126); Fat 14g (Saturated 4g); Cholesterol Trace; Sodium 681mg; Carbohydrate 18g (Dietary Fibre 2.7g); Protein 6.1g.*

Whipping Up Light Bites

If you're looking for sandwiches, you've come to the wrong place. What you'll find here are far more exciting ideas for what you can do with a cupboard full of ingredients.

⟋Roast Vegetable Tortillas

Vegetarian friendly and very tasty, this Roast Vegetable Tortilla recipe may look like it takes a while to prepare, but in fact the oven does all the hard work. These tortillas are really nice with some hummus (see the nearby sidebar for a handy recipe).

Preparation time: *10 minutes*

Cooking time: *30 minutes*

Serves: *2*

1 red pepper, deseeded and sliced into strips	½ red onion, peeled and chopped into small chunks
½ courgette, sliced into circles	6 cherry tomatoes
½ aubergine, sliced into circles then chopped into small pieces	Olive oil
	4 tortilla wraps
	Hummus, if desired

1 Turn the oven on to 180°C.

2 Place the prepared vegetables on a baking tray and pour a generous amount of olive oil over them, shaking the tray to coat them well.

3 When the oven is hot, place the baking tray inside. Roast the vegetables for 30 minutes, giving them a stir halfway through.

4 Five minutes from the end, prepare the wraps according to the packet instructions (usually you pop a few on a plate, cover with cling film and microwave for around 30 seconds).

5 Using oven gloves or a tea towel, take the baking tray from the oven and dish the vegetables into the middle of the warm tortilla wraps. Spoon over some hummus if you're using any, and then wrap them up and eat.

Variation: Use as many or as few vegetables as you want for this. This recipe is a great way of using up vegetables that are going a little soft or are a bit past their best.

Per serving: Calories 550 (From Fat 209); Fat 23.2g (Saturated 3.2g); Cholesterol Trace; Sodium 595mg; Carbohydrate 71.9g (Dietary Fibre 5.2g); Protein 13.3g.

Hummus: The dip that makes you go 'mmm'

Hummus is a dish that can be found in both the Middle East and the dip section of your local supermarket. Hummus may sound fancy, but it's essentially mashed up chickpeas. Home-made hummus is very easy to prepare. Simply pour half a tin of drained chickpeas, a generous glug of olive oil, a chopped clove of garlic, some paprika and the juice from half a lemon into a blender, and blend until smooth. If the mixture is too thick, add a few tablespoons of water or more lemon juice to thin and blend well. Delicious.

Honey and Tarragon Chicken on Toasted Ciabatta

Imagine succulent chicken coated in a generously sweet marinade on crispy, warm ciabatta. Doesn't really sound like student food, but believe me, it is. This lunch is cheap, easy to make, and best of all, tastes fantastic.

 Use a separate chopping board when you prepare meat. And be sure to wash your hands and knife after handling meat.

Preparation time: *15 minutes*

Cooking time: *20 minutes*

Serves: *1*

2 big spoonfuls of honey	*Salt and pepper*
3 tablespoons of olive oil	*1 chicken breast, cut into bite-sized pieces*
Big pinch of dried tarragon	
Squeeze of half a lemon	*1 ciabatta, sliced in half*

1 Spoon the honey into a bowl and add the olive oil, tarragon and lemon juice, and then season with salt and pepper. Add the chicken pieces and mix well. Leave the chicken to marinate for 15 minutes. In the meantime, turn the grill on to full power.

2 When the grill is hot, remove the chicken pieces from the marinade and place onto a grill tray under the grill.

3 Turn the chicken regularly to make sure it goes golden brown on all sides and coat with any leftover marinade. This gives more flavour to the meat and helps keep it moist. When each side is brown, check a piece by cutting it open. It should be completely white inside.

 Always cook chicken until it's white inside. If the meat appears pink when the chicken is cut open, it's not fully cooked, so place it back under the grill.

4 Remove the chicken from the grill and replace with the sliced ciabatta. Place back under and grill until lightly browned (about 2 minutes).

5 Place the grilled ciabatta on a plate and top with the grilled chicken.

Variation: *For a vegetarian and vegan option, swap the chicken for tofu. You can also swap the ciabatta for some tortilla wraps or a crispy baguette.*

Per serving: Calories 1078 (From Fat 479); Fat 53.2g (Saturated 8.2g); Cholesterol Trace; Sodium 730mg; Carbohydrate 75.4g (Dietary Fibre 2.4g); Protein 74.5g.

ᐁNaan Bread Pizza Strips with Mint Yogurt Dip

Italy meets India in this fantastic snack. These slabs of home-made pizza have an Indian naan bread base. They go great with a mint yogurt dip.

Preparation time: 10 minutes

Cooking time: 10 minutes

Serves: 1

Small handful of fresh mint leaves, chopped

2 large spoonfuls of natural yogurt

1 naan bread

½ jar of sun-dried tomato pesto

½ packet of mozzarella, cut into slices

1 Turn on the oven to 200°C.

2 In a bowl, stir the chopped fresh mint into the natural yogurt.

3 Spread the sun-dried tomato pesto over the naan bread and top with the slices of mozzarella.

4 Place in the pre-heated oven and bake until the mozzarella has melted. Remove from the grill and slice into strips. Serve with the mint yogurt.

Per serving: Calories 1032 (From Fat 536); Fat 59.5g (Saturated 19.8g); Cholesterol Trace; Sodium 2367mg; Carbohydrate 87.6g (Dietary Fibre 7.1g); Protein 36.6g.

Quick 'n' Easy Salads

Salads have a bad reputation of being as satisfying as drinking a glass of water. However, a good salad can be a fantastic lunch, filling you up and keeping you studying hard (ahem) until dinnertime. Don't believe me? Well, try your hand at one of the recipes below and see if you still feel hungry during that mid-afternoon lecture.

ᑏ Sun-Dried Tomato Pasta Salad

Mmm, sounds good, doesn't it? I cheat a little bit here and use sun-dried tomato pesto rather than the real deal, but if you fancy treating yourself, go ahead and buy some delicious sun-dried tomatoes.

This salad keeps in the fridge for about three days, but make sure you cover it with some kitchen foil or cling film, or better still, keep it in a plastic storage container.

Preparation time: *10 minutes*

Cooking time: *15 minutes*

Serves: *3*

Pinch of salt

2 mugs of pasta (penne or whatever you have)

2 big spoonfuls of sun-dried tomato pesto

½ a lettuce (something leafy like curly leaf is best, but you can use whatever you have), sliced into pieces

½ a cucumber, diced

1 red pepper, deseeded and diced

½ tin of cannellini beans, drained and rinsed

Drizzle of olive oil

1 Fill a saucepan three-quarters full of water, put on the hob and bring to the boil.

2 When boiling, add a pinch of salt and then pour in the pasta.

3 Cook for about 12 minutes, or until tender (taste it to see – run a piece of pasta under cold water to cool it).

4 When cooked, drain in a colander, shake and leave to one side.

5 Get a big bowl and add the chopped lettuce, cucumber, pepper and beans. Mix well.

6 When the pasta has cooled to room temperature, pour back into the empty saucepan and plop 2 big spoonfuls of the sun-dried tomato pesto into the pasta. Mix well.

7 Transfer the pasta to the bowl of salad, drizzle with olive oil and mix again. Put on a plate and serve. You can cover the rest and put it into the fridge for a super-quick lunch tomorrow.

Variation: You can always use whatever vegetables you have to hand instead of the ones I list here. Radishes, celery and strips of carrot make good alternatives.

Per serving: *Calories 522 (From Fat 111); Fat 12.3g (Saturated 1.8g); Cholesterol Trace; Sodium 239mg; Carbohydrate 84.3g (Dietary Fibre 2.9g); Protein 18.5g.*

Squishy green goodness: Preparing avocados

Dark green or black on the outside, green on the inside, avocados are an underused fruit but are delicious in salads. They're also extremely good for you – they're packed full of fibre and naturally lower your cholesterol.

Many people don't buy avocados because they don't know how to prepare them. Here's how to get into and eat this super-nutritious fruit:

1 To prepare an avocado for a salad, cut it in half, running your knife around the stone in the centre of the fruit. Using your hands, twist the two halves apart. Prise your knife underneath the exposed stone and carefully remove it.

2 Spoon the avocado flesh out or cut each slice in half and peel the skin away from the flesh.

3 Chop up the avocado flesh into bite-sized pieces.

The green flesh of avocados can quickly turn brown when exposed to air. Try tightly wrapping the avocado in cling film or, better still, squeeze a few drops of lemon juice over it first. The acid from the lemon juice reacts with the flesh to slow down the browning process.

᭒Citrus Couscous Salad in Pitta Breads

My friends know how much I rave on about the joys of couscous. Apart from having a daft name, this quick, healthy and cheap snack should be a hit with students across the globe. Couscous is like a natural pot noodle. Just pour boiling water over the couscous, leave it for a bit and it's done. What could be easier than that?

Preparation time: *5 minutes*

Cooking time: *10 minutes*

Serves: *1*

1 vegetable stock cube	¼ red onion, peeled and diced
½ mug of couscous	Drizzle of olive oil
½ red pepper, deseeded and diced	2 pitta breads
¼ cucumber, diced	1 lime

1 Crumble the vegetable stock cube into a measuring jug and then flick the kettle on. Pour boiling water over the stock cube and fill the jug to about 200 millilitres. Get a fork and stir well.

2 Pour the couscous into a bowl and pour the vegetable stock over the couscous until it's just covered. Cover the bowl with a clean tea towel. Wait about 10 minutes, or until the couscous has absorbed all the water.

3 Get a fork and run it through the couscous, breaking it up. Add the red pepper, cucumber and red onion pieces and drizzle with olive oil. Mix well.

4 Put the pitta breads in the toaster.

5 Grate a little bit of the skin of the lime over the couscous (move over Gordon Ramsay, you're now adding some zest). Then cut the lime in half and squeeze the juice from both pieces over the bowl. Mix again.

6 By now the pitta breads should be done, so cut them in half to open them up and fill with couscous.

Variation: Try adding some freshly chopped coriander. I know it makes it a little bit more expensive, but you'll use coriander again in curry dishes (see the recipe for Creamy Chicken Curry in Chapter 12), and it makes people think you're an amazing cook when they see it in the fridge.

Per serving: Calories 778 (From Fat 132); Fat 14.7g (Saturated 1.7g); Cholesterol Trace; Sodium 2805mg; Carbohydrate 137.7g (Dietary Fibre 12.7g); Protein 23.8g.

Chicken and Avocado Salad

If there was such a thing as a salad hall of fame, this dish would certainly have a space somewhere on the wall. Yes, having a hall of fame for salads would be a bit bizarre, but anyway, this salad is a winner.

This is a good salad to have after you've cooked a roast chicken because it uses up any leftover meat.

Preparation time: *5 minutes*

Cooking time: *Nil*

Serves: *1*

½ avocado, peeled and chopped into pieces (see nearby sidebar)

200 grams cooked chicken, cut into pieces

100 grams radishes, sliced

6 cherry tomatoes

1 Granny Smith apple, peeled and chopped into pieces

2 spoonfuls Greek yogurt

½ lemon

½ lettuce

Drizzle of olive oil

1 Put all the ingredients including the chicken into a big bowl, except for the lettuce, yogurt and lemon.

2 Add the yogurt to the bowl and mix well.

3 Squeeze the lemon through your (washed) hands to make sure no pips fall in and then mix well again.

4 Put the lettuce into a different bowl and drizzle with some olive oil. Then spoon the chicken and avocado mix on top. Enjoy!

Per serving: Calories 779 (From Fat 392); Fat 43.6g (Saturated 12.1g); Cholesterol Trace; Sodium 280mg; Carbohydrate 34.6g (Dietary Fibre 10.9g); Protein 62.0g.

Niçoise Salad

This recipe is for one healthy salad. You get protein from the egg and tuna, mixed with vitamins and antioxidants from delicious fresh vegetables, which are bursting with goodness. This is a good all round salad to fight off hunger till evening.

Preparation time: *10 minutes*

Cooking time: *15 minutes*

Serves: *1*

1 egg	*Handful of black olives*
4 new potatoes	*4 cherry tomatoes*
Handful of green beans	*Squeeze of lemon juice*
½ tin of tuna, drained and flaked into bits with a fork	*Drizzle of olive oil*
	Salt and pepper

1 Hard-boil the egg (should take about 6 minutes), remove from the water and add in the new potatoes. Boil for 5 minutes, and then add in the green beans and boil both for a further 3 minutes. Drain when cooked.

2 While the egg, new potatoes and green beans are cooling, put the tuna, olives and tomatoes in a bowl.

3 When the other ingredients have cooled down, cut the potatoes and green beans in half and add to the other ingredients.

4 Cut the egg into quarters and add to the bowl.

5 Squeeze some lemon juice and drizzle some olive oil in there and mix well. Season with salt and pepper and then serve.

Variation: *Add a dollop of mayo for an indulgent alternative.*

Per serving: *Calories 511 (From Fat 212); Fat 23.5g (Saturated 4.4); Cholesterol Trace; Sodium 822mg; Carbohydrate 44.4g(Dietary Fibre 9.5g); Protein 30.4g.*

Let's Do Lunch: Midday Meals for Two

Don't have lunch on your lonesome – make it into a bit of an event by inviting a friend round. Share some gossip, get some help with an essay or plan tonight's escapades. And remember to make sure your mate returns the favour tomorrow lunchtime!

⌒Home-made Tomato and Feta Pasties

You won't be able to find this delicious pasty in your local bakers, as this is pure home-made magic. It takes a little bit of effort, but is a lot of fun to make.

Use fresh, not dried thyme for this recipe if possible.

Preparation time: *20 minutes*

Cooking time: *20 minutes*

Serves: *2 (makes 2 pasties)*

Olive oil	1 egg
Handful of cherry tomatoes	100 grams feta cheese, crumbled
Salt and pepper	Fresh thyme
Sprinkle of plain flour	Salad of your choice – whatever you want to put with lettuce
125 grams ready-made puff pastry	

1 Turn on the oven to 200°C, and lightly oil a baking tray to stop the pasties from sticking to the tray.

2 Heat a glug of olive oil in a frying pan over a medium heat on the hob. When hot, add the cherry tomatoes. Heat the cherry tomatoes until they go soft (about 4 minutes). Press down on them with a fork to squash them, making them into a tomato mixture. Season with some salt and pepper, and then take off the heat and leave to one side.

3 Sprinkle some flour onto a clean dry flat surface or a chopping board and roll out the puff pastry. The pastry should be big enough to cut out four saucers.

> If you don't have a rolling pin, use a bottle of olive oil or wine!

4 Using a sharp knife, cut out two circles in the pastry – about as big as saucers. Place them on the baking tray.

5 Break the egg into a bowl and whisk until it's smooth and yellow.

6 Add the feta cheese into the middle of each circle, leaving about a centimetre gap around the edges.

7 Spoon the tomato mixture over the cheese and sprinkle with some thyme. Cover with some more crumbled feta cheese. Brush some of the egg over the exposed edges of the pasty. You can use the back of a spoon to do this if you haven't got a pastry brush.

8 Cut out another two circles that are slightly bigger than the ones before to make the top of your pasties. You may have to scrunch up the puff pastry and roll it out again to make more room to cut the circles out.

9 Lay the bigger circles over the bottom layers and seal down with a fork. You may have to cut off the overlapping bit with a sharp knife. Score a cross in the top of the pasty and brush with the egg yolk. The egg mixture makes the pasties go golden brown in the oven.

10 Place the baking tray in the preheated oven for about 20 minutes or until the pasties have turned golden brown.

11 When done, take your pasty out of the oven and serve it with a salad.

Variation: *You could change this into a bigger meal for dinner by adding some roast root vegetables or some baked beans.*

Per serving: *Calories 625 (From Fat 428); Fat 47.5g (Saturated 15.3g); Cholesterol Trace; Sodium 961mg; Carbohydrate 32.6g (Dietary Fibre 1.4g); Protein 16.8g.*

Healthy Chicken Kebabs

Kebabs don't need to be the grease-fest that you get from a dodgy van on a night out. Try these delicious healthy chicken kebabs for a light and tasty midday snack and remind yourself of what kebabs are supposed to taste like.

You need two wooden skewers for this recipe – you can find kebab or barbecue skewers in most supermarkets. Before you start cooking, soak the skewers in a bowl or tray of water to stop them burning under the grill.

Preparation time: *10 minutes*

Cooking time: *15 minutes*

Serves: *2*

2 skinless chicken breasts, cut into bite-sized pieces

Drizzle of olive oil

Mixed spice

Ground coriander (not essential)

2 cloves of garlic, chopped

½ a lemon

1 Place the chicken pieces in a bowl and drizzle with olive oil. Then add a pinch of mixed spice, ground coriander (if you're using any) and the chopped garlic, followed by a big squeeze of lemon. Mix all the ingredients together and leave for around 20 minutes for the chicken to absorb the flavours of the lemon and spices.

2 Turn the grill on to full power.

3 Push the meat on the skewers, evenly spaced apart, and place under the preheated grill.

4 Rotate the skewers every so often so that all sides turn golden brown, and brush on the marinade while they cook.

5 After about 15 minutes, or when the meat looks golden brown, remove from the grill. Check that the meat is cooked by cutting open a piece and seeing if the inside is white (cooked). If it's still pink, put it back under the grill for another 5 minutes.

6 Serve with some couscous (see the Citrus Couscous recipe earlier in this chapter), salad or just enjoy them on their own as a quick snack.

Per serving: Calories 345 (From Fat 85); Fat 9.4g (Saturated 1.9g); Cholesterol Trace; Sodium 111mg; Carbohydrate 0.8g (Dietary Fibre 0.2g); Protein 64.3g.

Olive and Tomato Quesadillas

Quesadillas (pronounced *kay-sa-dee-yas*) are a Mexican dish and literally mean 'little cheesy thing' in Spanish. I remember one of my flatmates making this for me in my first year at uni and after eating them, I was hooked! Think of them as Mexican sandwiches; whatever you put between two pieces of bread usually works in a quesadilla. Well, maybe not peanut butter. Or marmite . . .

Check out Chapter 6 to see the different dips you can have with quesadillas.

Preparation time: 3 minutes

Cooking time: 10 minutes

Serves: 2

Olive oil	Handful of olives (stones removed)
2 flour tortillas	2 spring onions, sliced into pieces
100 grams grated Cheddar cheese	1 chilli (or 2 if you like it hot!)
4 tomatoes, chopped into small pieces	

1 Add a little oil to a frying pan and swirl it round until it coats the base of the pan.

2 Place the pan onto a work surface and place one of the tortillas in the pan.

3 Cover the tortilla with half of the grated cheese. Spread out all the other ingredients over the top and cover with the remaining cheese.

4 Cover this with the second tortilla and press down gently. Place the frying pan onto a medium heat and cook for about 5 minutes or until the bottom has turned golden.

5 Grab the quesadilla by sliding a fish slice or spatula underneath and holding the top with a fork. Turn the quesadilla over and cook the other side for a further 5 minutes.

6 When done, slide the quesadilla onto a chopping board and cut into quarters.

Variation: *For a meaty alternative, cover the first tortilla with ham and then half the cheese. Add a few fried sliced mushrooms, the rest of the cheese and seal with the second tortilla.*

Per serving: *Calories 494 (From Fat 270); Fat 30.0g (Saturated 12.6g); Cholesterol Trace; Sodium 1359mg; Carbohydrate 35.9g (Dietary Fibre 3.8g); Protein 20.2g.*

Chapter 6

Serving Up Snacks

In This Chapter

▶ Satisfying your snack attacks

▶ Making instant brain food

▶ Whipping up dips

Snacks are funny old things. They're those in-between-meal meals that aren't quite meals at all. Less than a lunch, but just a bit more than a packet of crisps or a piece of fruit, snacks are light bites to keep you working hard(ish) until the next meal time.

The snacks in this chapter are great little recipes to know. If you fancy something to eat but don't want a full-on meal, try Spicy Mushrooms on Toast or tuck into a Tomato and Mozzarella Toastie. Got a long night's cramming before an exam? Get some Home-Made Garlic Potato Wedges down you or try your hand at a Chicken, Spinach and Walnut wrap. Or if you have some friends round and fancy a nibble and a natter, find the tasty way to impress them by doing some delicious dips like home-made Guacamole or Mint and Yogurt Dip; and I'll also show you what you can dip in them!

Another great thing about these snacks is that you can have them any time of day (or night) and they don't take long to make. So no slaving over a hot stove, making a mountain of washing up; instead, these snacks are quick to prepare, using only a few ingredients and are dead simple to make.

So if you fancy working some culinary magic on something light and tasty, get stuck in and get snacking on some good home-made grub!

Making a Snack in 5 Minutes Flat

Considering you're a student, with around six hours of lectures per week, people would think you've got loads of free time on your hands. How wrong can they be? After waking up at 11 and catching your routine dose of Loose Women, there's the worrying check of what drunken text messages you sent last night, flatmates to chat to and a session on the Xbox to squeeze in. All before you get dressed.

On days like this, time in the kitchen needs to be kept to a minimum. A quick get in, get out is needed, making sure you come out with something lip-lickingly tasty and with minimum washing up. Everyone knows how to make cheese or beans on toast, so coming up are a few alternative ideas for what to put on a slice of toasted bread, followed by a series of different snacks you can cook in five minutes or less. Go!

Spinach, Mushrooms and Cheese on Toast

This recipe is a bit of a change from regular cheese on toast, and adds spinach and mushrooms for extra taste and vegetable goodness. Two of your five a day in one quick snack – now that's what I call healthy!

Spinach is amazingly good for you (when was the last time you saw Popeye ill?), and this is a great way of getting it into your diet almost without you realising it!

Spinach is packed full of vitamins and antioxidants, helping to keep you healthy and alert. (When Popeye was created, spinach was thought to have ten times the amount of iron it actually contains. The mistake was down to a German nutritionist putting the decimal point in the wrong place . . .)

Preparation time: *2 minutes*

Cooking time: *5 minutes*

Serves: *1*

A glug of olive oil

A few mushrooms, sliced

Big handful of spinach leaves (and I mean big. The spinach shrinks a lot when it's heated.)

Salt and pepper

2 slices of wholemeal bread

Butter or low-fat spread

Small handful of grated cheese (Cheddar works best)

Dash of Worcestershire sauce (vegetarian if necessary)

1 Heat the grill to a medium heat.

2 Heat the olive oil in a frying pan over a medium heat and when hot, add the sliced mushrooms.

3 When the mushrooms have been in the pan for a couple of minutes, add the spinach. Fry until the mushrooms are lightly browned and the spinach has shrunk and turned dark green. Add a sprinkle of salt and pepper, mix well and remove the pan from the heat.

4 Toast the bread (in a toaster or under the grill) and spread with the butter or low-fat spread.

5 Put the spinach and mushroom mix on top of the toast and top with the grated cheese.

6 Place under the grill and grill until the cheese has melted.

7 Add a dash of Worcestershire sauce to finish off.

Tip: *Have some spinach leftover? Check out Chapter 8's Spinach and Chickpea Curry or Spinach and Beetroot Salad.*

Variation: You can always swap the mushrooms for some sliced toma-toes or some tinned chopped tomatoes. If you're using sliced tomatoes, add them after the spinach has turned dark green, because they won't take as long to cook.

Per serving: *Calories 762 (From Fat 525); Fat 58.3g (Saturated 25.8g); Cholesterol Trace; Sodium 1231mg; Carbohydrate 30.4g, Dietary Fibre 4.8g; Protein 28.9g.*

Tuna Mayo Toastie

A cool and refreshing filling between two slices of hot, crunchy toast, this Tuna Mayo Toastie is good brain food and pretty tasty too.

Preparation time: *5 minutes*

Cooking time: *Nil*

Serves: *1*

2 slices of bread

½ tin tuna

2 spoonfuls of mayonnaise

2 spoonfuls of tinned sweetcorn

Salt and pepper

1 Place the bread in a toaster.

2 While that's toasting, mix the tuna, mayo and sweetcorn in a bowl and season with salt and pepper.

3 When the toast's ready, spread the tuna mayo mixture over one slice and put the other one on top. Cut in half to form a delicious tuna mayo toastie.

Per serving: *Calories 498 (From Fat 222); Fat 24.7g (Saturated 3.9g); Cholesterol Trace; Sodium 938mg; Carbohydrate 31.7g, Dietary Fibre 1.9g; Protein 37.3g.*

⌒Tomato and Mozzarella Toastie

Go continental and sandwich Italian cuisine between a very British snack. Tomatoes and mozzarella cheese are a simple but classic combination, so try whipping up this snack to impress your housemates.

Preparation time: 5 minutes

Cooking time: Nil

Serves: 2

4 slices of bread	Salt and pepper
4 tomatoes, thinly sliced	Drizzle of olive oil (optional)
150 grams of mozzarella, sliced	

1 Toast the bread.

2 Put a layer of tomatoes on two of the slices of toast and cover with a layer of mozzarella. Cover the layer of cheese with another layer of tomatoes and season with salt and pepper. Add a light drizzle of olive oil if you like. Put the remaining two slices of toast on top. Mwah!

Tip: If you have any fresh basil, add a couple of basil leaves on top of the mozzarella to make it a truly Italian feast.

Variation: Try using thick, floury ciabatta bread. Toast under the grill if you can't fit it in the toaster.

Per serving: Calories 370 (From Fat 150); Fat 16.7g (Saturated 10.7g); Cholesterol Trace; Sodium 653mg; Carbohydrate 34.8g, Dietary Fibre 2.7g; Protein 20.1g.

☙Spicy Mushrooms on Toast

This snack turns up the heat in the kitchen by adding a bit of spice to your everyday mushrooms on toast, but, best of all, it's just as simple to make.

Preparation time: *5 minutes*

Cooking time: *5 minutes*

Serves: *1*

Glug of olive oil

¼ onion, finely sliced

Handful of mushrooms, chopped into little pieces

Generous pinch of curry powder

50 millilitres (couple of large spoonfuls) of double cream

2 slices of bread

1 Heat the oil in a frying pan over a medium heat and fry the onions until they start to turn golden brown.

2 Mix the mushrooms with a pinch of curry powder. Add the mushrooms to the pan and fry until they too turn a light brown colour (about 5 minutes).

3 Toast the bread.

4 Add the cream to the mushrooms and gently fry until the cream thickens.

5 Spoon the creamy, spicy mushrooms over the toast.

Variation: *Add a dash of Tabasco at the end if you like your mushrooms really spicy!*

Per serving: *Calories 609 (From Fat 436); Fat 48.4g (Saturated 19.8g); Cholesterol Trace; Sodium 324mg; Carbohydrate 35.7g, Dietary Fibre 2.7g; Protein 7.6g.*

Toasted Bean and Bacon Sarnie

You can't beat a good bacon sarnie, can you? Well, actually, now you can, by adding some other goodies to the bacon and placing it all between two slices of toasted bread. Give it a whirl and taste the difference.

Preparation time: *5 minutes*

Cooking time: *5 minutes*

Serves: *1*

2 rashers of bacon (or, to save cooking and washing up, some ready-cooked strips of bacon from the supermarket)

1 small tin of BBQ baked beans

2 slices of bread

Dash of Worcestershire sauce

1 If you bought raw bacon, fry it in a frying pan until cooked and leave to cool. When cool, cut it into strips. If you bought pre-cooked bacon, move on to Step 2.

2 Empty the beans into a microwavable bowl, cover with a sheet of kitchen roll and place in the microwave. (See the tin for cooking times.)

3 Toast the bread in the toaster.

4 When the beans are heated through, add the bacon strips and a dash of Worcestershire sauce and spoon onto one slice of toast. Pop the other slice on top, press down, cut in half and enjoy.

Variation: *You can use different kinds of tinned beans, such as normal baked beans or beans and sausages. Or swap the beans for some chopped plum tomatoes.*

Per serving: Calories 471 (From Fat 106); Fat 11.8g (Saturated 4.2g); Cholesterol Trace; Sodium 1978mg; Carbohydrate 65.8g, Dietary Fibre 12.8g; Protein 25.3g.

Vegan (or Not) Rarebit

Rarebit isn't the meat from a rabbit, but the name of a sauce
served over toast. The sauce is usually made with cheese,
but this rarebit is suitable for vegans if you use vegan cheese.

 If you're not vegan, swap the vegan cheese for Cheddar and
the soy milk for ordinary milk.

Preparation time: *5 minutes*

Cooking time: *5 minutes*

Serves: *1*

Handful of grated vegan cheese or small tub of vegan cheese spread	*Small teaspoon of mustard*
30 millilitres soy milk	*2 slices of bread*
Dash of vegetarian Worcestershire sauce	*Salt and pepper*

1 Place a small saucepan over a medium heat and add the cheese or
cheese spread, milk, Worcestershire sauce and mustard. Stir over
the heat until smooth and bubbling.

2 Meanwhile, toast the bread. When the rarebit looks thick and
smooth, spread it over the toast and season.

Variation: *Add some spinach leaves or roast vegetables onto the toast*
before adding the rarebit.

Per serving: *Calories 565 (From Fat 303); Fat 33.7g (Saturated 21.0g); Cholesterol xTrace;*
Sodium 1310mg; Carbohydrate 33.5g, Dietary Fibre 1.5g; Protein 31.9g.

Scrambled Eggs with Chorizo on Toast

Scrambled eggs on toast are more usual at breakfast, but there's nothing stopping you from eating it any time of the day. Besides, eggs are full of protein, which helps you to concentrate and can help to get you through that long night of revision.

Chorizo is a cured Spanish sausage (easily found in the supermarket). You can also use smoked sausage rather than the chorizo.

Preparation time: *5 minutes*

Cooking time: *5 minutes*

Serves: *1*

2 eggs	Salt and pepper
2 tablespoons of milk (fill up the lid of the milk bottle four times as a rough equivalent)	Butter
	2 slices of bread
Generous dash of Worcestershire sauce	Small chunk of chorizo (about as big as your thumb) chopped up into very small pieces

1 Break the eggs into a large bowl and add the milk and Worcestershire sauce. Season with salt and pepper and whisk with a fork or hand whisk until the liquid turns smooth.

 The longer you whisk, the fluffier the scrambled eggs become because more air gets into the mixture.

2 Add a chunk of butter to a frying pan over a medium to high heat.

3 Put the bread in the toaster.

4 When the butter has melted, pour in the egg mixture. Leave the egg mixture for about 10 seconds until it starts to set.

5 Grab a spatula or a fork and fold the edges of the egg into the centre, breaking up the mixture. Doing so seems as if you're ruining a perfectly good omelette, which in a way is what you're doing. Keep breaking up the egg mixture into little chunks.

6 While the egg mixture is still slightly moist, add the chopped chorizo and take the pan off the heat. Keep mixing and mashing it until the eggs turn into a scrambled egg consistency.

7 Spoon the mixture over the toast and tuck in.

Variation: Try frying half an onion, chopped into small pieces, in the butter before adding the egg mixture.

Per serving: *Calories 492 (From Fat 313); Fat 34.8g (Saturated 14.2g); Cholesterol Trace; Sodium 963mg; Carbohydrate 18.7g, Dietary Fibre 0.6g; Protein 26.1g.*

Creating Cramming Snacks

A big exam looms tomorrow, which means you're in for a long night cramming in long overdue revision. For these kind of nights, along with the coffee, you need something to help you motor on through the wee small hours, keeping you full and focused.

Most of the snacks in this section are full of slow-releasing energy; finger food designed to help you work through the night, cram in as much as possible and give you a fighting chance for the exam in the morning. Good luck!

Jacket Potato with Tuna and Feta Cheese

Brain power on baked energy – that's what this recipe is. Tuna, like all fish, keeps you feeling sharp as a button thanks to its high protein and low fat levels, while the potato is stuffed full of slow-releasing energy to keep you truckin' through the night. And the feta cheese? Well, that just tastes nice.

This dish takes a while to bake, so put the potato in the oven at the start of your revision sesh, and then come back to it when it's cooked. Cooking time depends on the size of your spud. If the potato fits in your palm, cooking time is 40 minutes; if it's the size of your fist, 50 minutes will do; and if it's a big 'un, about a fist and half size, keep it cooking for around 70 minutes.

Preparation time: *5 minutes*

Cooking time: *Various (see tip above)*

Serves: *1*

1 potato	*½ tin of tuna*
Olive oil	*Handful of feta cheese, crumbled into*
Salt	*chunks.*

1 Preheat the oven to 200°C.

2 Prick the potato with a fork and rub with olive oil. Sprinkle some salt over it. The oil and salt make the skin turn nice and crispy. (If you don't like crispy potato skin, prick the potato, but don't use the oil or salt.)

3 Place the potato in the middle of the preheated oven and leave to bake for the appropriate amount of time. Carry on or start revising.

4 After your time is up, take the potato out of the oven.

 Check if the potato's cooked by pushing a knife into it. If the knife can go all the way through, then the potato's cooked. If not, put it back in the oven for a bit longer.

5 Cut a large *X* into the top of the potato and (using a towel or something to protect your hands) carefully open out the potato.

6 Add the flaked tuna and then top with the crumbled feta cheese. Drizzle some olive oil over the top and eat.

Per serving: *Calories 563 (From Fat 279); Fat 31.0g (Saturated 15.2g); Cholesterol Trace; Sodium 1741mg; Carbohydrate 35.9g, Dietary Fibre 2.6g; Protein 35.1g.*

Wicked Tortilla Wraps

Tortilla wraps are so versatile as a snack. Pretty much anything – meat, vegetables or grated cheese – works wrapped up in a tortilla. Usually you fry ingredients to put inside them, but for a late night option when you don't want to wake anyone up with a sizzling frying pan, this recipe doesn't need any cooking at all.

Preparation time: *10 minutes*

Cooking time: *Nil*

Serves: *1*

2 flour tortillas	Handful of cooked chicken
2 spoonfuls of mayonnaise	½ red pepper, cut into strips
¼ red onion, finely sliced	½ green pepper, cut into strips
½ carrot, grated or peeled into strips using a vegetable peeler	Handful of iceberg lettuce, cut into slices
2 tomatoes, sliced	

1 Place the tortillas in the microwave for around 30 seconds.

2 Take the tortillas out of the microwave and spread a circle of mayonnaise around the centre.

3 Place half the ingredients in the middle of one of the tortillas and roll it up.

4 Repeat with the other tortilla and scoff.

Per serving: *Calories 940 (From Fat 385); Fat 42.8g (Saturated 9.1g); Cholesterol Trace; Sodium 913mg; Carbohydrate 83.0g, Dietary Fibre 7.6g; Protein 55.6g.*

⌕*Cheese and Spring Onion Jacket Potato*

If you like cheese and onion crisps, you'll like this recipe. In fact, even if you don't like cheese and onion crisps, you'll probably like this recipe. The sharp taste of the spring onions mixed with the warm melted cheese tastes fantastic in this jacket potato. Try it and see for yourself!

Preparation time: *10 minutes*

Cooking time: *Varies depending on size (see Jacket Potato with Tuna and Feta Cheese)*

Serves: *1*

1 potato	*Handful of grated Cheddar cheese*
Olive oil	*2 spring onions, finely chopped*
Salt	*1 big spoonful of mayonnaise*

1 Preheat the oven to 200°C.

2 Prick the potato with a fork and rub with olive oil and salt if you like the skin crispy.

3 Place the potato in the middle of the oven and leave to bake.

4 After the appropriate time, take the potato out of the oven and while it's cooling down slightly, prepare the cheese and spring onions.

5 Cut the potato in half and scoop out the potato flesh into a bowl.

6 Add the grated cheese, spring onions and a big spoonful of mayo to the potato flesh and mix well.

7 Spoon the mixture back into the crispy potato shells, season with some salt and pepper and enjoy.

Per serving: *Calories 827 (From Fat 548); Fat 60.9g (Saturated 25.5g); Cholesterol Trace; Sodium 913mg; Carbohydrate 37.9g, Dietary Fibre 4.1g; Protein 31.8g.*

⚘Roast Vegetables and Cheese Toasted Sandwich

What's better than two slices of toast? Placing stuff in between them and turning them into a toasted sandwich, that's what. And this is one *good* toasted sandwich. Roast vegetables mixed with melted cheese. Mmmm.

Preparation time: *10 minutes*

Cooking time: *10 minutes*

Serves: *1*

½ an onion, sliced

Handful of sliced peppers (use mixed ones if possible to give the snack loads of different colours)

¼ courgette, sliced

Clove of garlic, peeled and chopped into bits

Glug of olive oil

2 slices of bread

Handful of grated cheese (use Cheddar, or slices of mozzarella if you have any)

Pinch of dried or fresh basil (optional)

1 Preheat the oven to 230°C.

2 Put the onion, peppers, courgette and garlic on a roasting tray and drizzle with some olive oil. Place it in the hot oven.

3 After five minutes, take the tray out (use a tea towel or oven gloves) and turn the vegetables over, coating them a bit more in the olive oil. Continue roasting for 10 minutes until the veggies turn soft and darken in colour.

4 Toast the bread in the toaster and turn the grill on to a medium heat.

5 When the veg is done, leave them to one side to cool down for five minutes. Then spoon onto one slice of toast, cover with the cheese and sprinkle with the basil (if using).

6 Place under the grill until the cheese has melted, remove and cover with the other slice of toast. Cut in half and eat.

Tip: Serve with salad or Home-Made Garlic Potato Wedges.

Variation: Try replacing the veggies with celery, aubergines or leeks.

Per serving: *Calories 830 (From Fat 510); Fat 56.7g (Saturated 24.9g); Cholesterol Trace; Sodium 1032mg; Carbohydrate 44.3g, Dietary Fibre 5.6g; Protein 35.6g.*

Tuna and Olive Melt

Yum, yum, this one's good. Think tuna pasta bake, but swap the pasta with olives and shove it in some soft ciabatta bread. Sounds good, doesn't it? Well, here's how to make it . . .

Preparation time: *10 minutes*

Cooking time: *10 minutes*

Serves: *2*

Dash of olive or groundnut oil

½ onion, sliced

½ tin of chopped tomatoes

1 tin of tuna, drained of brineHandful of black olives, chopped into pieces

2 ciabattas, cut in half

8 slices of mozzarella

1 Turn on the grill to a medium heat.

2 Heat a drop of olive oil in a frying pan over a medium heat.

3 When the oil's hot, add the sliced onions and fry until they start to turn golden.

4 Add the chopped tomatoes and tuna, breaking up the tuna when it's in the pan.

5 Gently fry until most of the liquid from the chopped tomatoes has evaporated (about 5 minutes) and then add the olives.

6 Meanwhile, lightly toast the ciabattas under the grill.

7 Spoon the tuna mixture onto the two bottom halves of the ciabattas and top with the sliced mozzarella.

8 Place under the grill until the mozzarella starts to melt and then cover with the top halves of the ciabatta bread.

Variation: *You can always use normal bread for this, although ciabatta tastes a lot nicer!*

Per serving: Calories 590 (From Fat 202); Fat 22.4g (Saturated 8.7g); Cholesterol Trace; Sodium 1202mg; Carbohydrate 60.5g, Dietary Fibre 4.5g; Protein 36.5g.

⟳*Home-made Garlic Potato Wedges*

These wedges are a fantastic finger food that goes great with some of the dips later on in this chapter. Potato is an energy-releasing food, and wedges are easy to nibble at while you're writing down notes!

Preparation time: *10 minutes*

Cooking time: *15 minutes*

Serves: *1 (makes 6 wedges)*

1 large pre-baked jacket potato (put in the oven at 200°C for around 40 to 50 minutes to bake it)

Olive oil

1 large clove of garlic, whole and peeled

Salt

1 Turn on the oven to 200°C.

2 Cut the jacket potato into wedges by slicing it in half lengthways and then slicing each half into three wedges.

3 Line a baking tray with kitchen foil and drizzle olive oil over it. Add the potato wedges and garlic clove, season with salt and then place in the oven for 5 to 7 minutes.

4 When they turn golden brown and slightly crispy, take the wedges out and toss, coating them in the oil a little more. Return the tray to the oven. Cook for another 5 to 7 minutes.

5 When cooked and nice and crispy, remove the garlic and gobble up the wedges.

Variation: This is a basic recipe that you can very easily adapt. Try sprinkling garam masala on the wedges halfway through cooking for an Indian taste, or chilli powder for something a bit Mexican-esque.

Per serving: Calories 292 (From Fat 95); Fat 10.5g (Saturated 1.4g); Cholesterol Traces; Sodium 96mg; Carbohydrate 43.7g, Dietary Fibre 3.4g; Protein 5.6g.

Chicken, Spinach and Walnut Wraps

I don't think you can get a healthier or more energy-packed wrap than this! Spinach and walnuts are known as *superfoods*, foods unusually high in certain properties, in this case, energy. This wrap is light, but filling and perfect for getting that boost of energy, whatever you need it for.

Preparation time: 5 minutes

Cooking time: Nil

Serves: 1

A large handful of sliced cooked chicken (you can usually find packets of cooked chicken in most supermarkets if you don't want to cook your own)

Handful of baby spinach leaves, roughly chopped

50 grams chopped walnuts (a sprinkle)

1 apple, cut into small chunks

2 spoonfuls of Greek yogurt

Squeeze of lemon juice

Salt and pepper

2 tortillas

1 Put all the prepared ingredients (minus the tortillas) into a large bowl. Season with salt and pepper and mix well.

2 Put the tortillas in the microwave, full power, for 10 seconds. When done, spoon the chicken, spinach and walnut mixture into the middle and roll up.

Per serving: Calories 1176 (From Fat 528); Fat 58.7g (Saturated 10.8g); Cholesterol Trace; Sodium 974mg; Carbohydrate 86.1g, Dietary Fibre 7.9g; Protein 75.8g.

Baked Sweet Potato with Cream Cheese and Bacon

Try swapping your normal spud for a sweet potato, for a slightly sweeter (surprise, surprise) baked potato. Sweet potatoes are slightly smaller and less dense than a normal potato, so take less time in the oven. You can find sweet potatoes next to the normal spuds in the market or supermarket.

Preparation time: 5 minutes

Cooking time: 50 minutes

Serves: 1

Olive oil

Salt and pepper

1 sweet potato

2 rashers of bacon (or, to save cooking and washing up, some ready-cooked strips of bacon from the supermarket)

Three spoonfuls of cream cheese

1 Preheat the oven to 200°C.

2 Cut a piece of kitchen foil large enough to wrap the sweet potato in. Make a well in the foil, drizzle a generous amount of olive oil in and sprinkle some salt over the foil.

3 Prick the sweet potato all over with a fork and put it in the middle of the kitchen foil. Wrap the foil around the sweet potato, forming a parcel.

4 Place the sweet potato in the oven for about 50 minutes.

5 After 40 minutes, fry the bacon (if you bought pre-cooked, skip to Step 6) and when cooked, leave to cool for a bit before cutting into matchstick-size strips.

6 Put the cream cheese into a bowl and add the bacon. Mix well and season with salt and pepper.

7 By now the sweet potato should be cooked, so carefully remove it from the oven, discard the foil and cut the potato in half. Put the bacon and cream cheese mixture in the middle of the potato and eat. Yum.

Per serving: Calories 693 (From Fat 423); Fat 47.0g (Saturated 19.5g); Cholesterol Trace; Sodium 1238mg; Carbohydrate 53.3g, Dietary Fibre 6.0g; Protein 14.3g.

Doing Delicious Dips

Hands up if you've ever made a dip from scratch. No? Well, shame on you! Dips are super-easy to whip up. If you're looking for something to nibble on – crisps, breadsticks or sliced vegetables – add a bit more flavour with a tasty dip. The dips in this chapter are also perfect for when your friends come round or if you're throwing a party. They're easy to make and even easier to eat!

So next time you're snacking and trying to get through a heavy essay on New Wave Cinema, don't forget about whipping up a quick, easy and delicious dip to go with it. Mmmm.

⟲Blue Cheese and Chive Dip

Cheesier than Timmy Mallet's Mega Mix playing at an 80s themed club night, this dip is a must for all cheese (and chive) fans. Very quick to make and great with a few crisps or Ryvitas. Get stuck in.

Preparation time: *5 minutes*

Cooking time: *Nil*

Serves: *2*

4 spoonfuls of mayonnaise

100 grams (about a fistful) of grated blue cheese (Roquefort, Stilton or St Agur)

Big pinch of chopped chives (fresh if possible, dried don't really work)

Grind of pepper

Squeeze of lemon juice

1 spoonful of double cream (optional)

Add all the ingredients into a large bowl and mix together. Serve.

Per serving: *Calories 453 (From Fat 399); Fat 44.3g (Saturated 17.4g); Cholesterol Trace; Sodium 531mg; Carbohydrate 1.0g, Dietary Fibre 0.1g; Protein 12.5g.*

ᛒMint and Yogurt Dip

I suppose for a kind of replacement Sunday lunch, you could dip lamb-flavoured crisps into this tasty mint and yogurt dip and pretend you're back home with the rents. Or you could just enjoy this mint and yogurt dip with a few breadsticks . . .

Preparation time: *5 minutes*

Cooking time: *Nil*

Serves: *2*

4 big spoonfuls of natural yogurt

2 teaspoonfuls of mint sauce

Big pinch of fresh mint or parsley (optional)

1 Mix the yogurt and mint sauce in a bowl.

2 Add the herbs (if you're using them) on top and serve.

Per serving: *Calories 23 (From Fat 9); Fat 1.0g (Saturated 0.6g); Cholesterol Trace; Sodium 32mg; Carbohydrate 2.2g, Dietary Fibre Trace; Protein 1.3g.*

ᛒGuacamole

Guacamole is a great Mexican dip made from avocados. It's goes dead nice with spicy nachos and you can add it in tortilla wraps too. This recipe takes a little bit of preparation, but no cooking's involved, and the home-made taste is fantastic. (Chapter 5 has some hints for preparing and storing avocado.)

Preparation time: *10 to 15 minutes*

Cooking time: *Nil*

Serves: *4*

2 tomatoes

1 chilli (red or green, doesn't matter) or some Tabasco sauce

3 large avocados

1 clove of garlic, peeled and crushed

½ medium onion, finely chopped (optional)

2 to 3 tablespoons of lemon juice

Salt and pepper

1 Cut the tomatoes in half and scoop out the seeds with a spoon. Finely chop the tomatoes.

2 Chop the top off the chilli, slice in half lengthways and remove the seeds. Now finely chop and add to the tomatoes.

 As a rough guide, the smaller the chilli, the hotter the taste. Be really careful when preparing chillies and wash your hands in hot soapy water after handling them. Getting any chilli or extract of chilli in your eyes or a cut *really* hurts.

3 Remove the avocado stone and, using a spoon, scoop out the flesh into a clean bowl and add the lemon juice. Mash the mixture to your preferred consistency – chunky or smooth.

4 Add the chilli (or Tabasco), tomato and onion (if using) and mix well.

5 Season with salt and pepper to taste. You may need to add a bit more lemon juice.

6 If not using it immediately, cover tightly with cling film and place in the fridge.

Per serving: Calories 243 (From Fat 200); Fat 22.2g (Saturated 4.7g); Cholesterol Trace; Sodium 38mg; Carbohydrate 7.6g, Dietary Fibre 5.0g; Protein 3.1g.

☺ *Hummus*

Hummus, made from puréed chickpeas, is a dish from the Middle East. It's a really easy dip to make, although for best results, use a blender. If you don't have a blender, use a potato masher, but your hummus will turn out a little more chunky.

Preparation time: *10 minutes*

Cooking time: *Nil*

Serves: *2*

1 200-gram tin of chickpeas, rinsed and drained

1 clove of garlic

1 tablespoon of lemon juice

2 tablespoons of olive oil

Small dash of Tabasco sauce

Salt and pepper

¼ mug of water

1 Combine all the ingredients in a food processor and blend together until smooth.

2 Check the consistency. If it's a little dry, add a drop more olive oil and blend again. Otherwise, spoon into a dish and enjoy.

Per serving: Calories 470 (From Fat 184); Fat 20.4g (Saturated 2.6g); Cholesterol Trace; Sodium 110mg; Carbohydrate 50.0g, Dietary Fibre 10.8g; Protein 21.5g.

ᏅNachos

Okay, so nachos aren't a dip, but after making that guacamole and hummus, you need a recipe for tortilla chips. This recipe provides enough to share between two, or just be dead greedy and finish it off by yourself.

You can use a jar of salsa or make it yourself – see the Tomato and Red Onion Salsa recipe a little later in this chapter.

Preparation time: *5 minutes*

Cooking time: *30 seconds*

Serves: *2*

Big bag of tortilla chips

8 big spoonfuls of salsa

Big handful of grated Cheddar cheese

Few sliced jalapeños (optional)

1 On a large microwavable plate, scatter a layer of tortilla chips and spoon over 4 spoonfuls of salsa. Cover with half of the grated cheese. Add some jalapeño peppers if you're using them.

2 Cover with another layer of tortilla chips, the rest of the salsa and the rest of the grated cheese.

3 Pop the plate in the microwave and cook until the cheese starts to melt (about 30 seconds). Eat on their own or dip into some home-made guacamole or hummus (or both if you fancy) and get messy.

Per serving: Calories 937 (From Fat 448); Fat 49.8g (Saturated 18.1g); Cholesterol Trace; Sodium 3010mg; Carbohydrate 93.3g, Dietary Fibre 12.1g; Protein 28.9g.

⟁Garlic and Chive Dip

This dip is garlicky enough to keep vampires, werewolves and any other horrors at bay, so make this an essential item, along with your crisps and cushion to hide behind, while watching a scary film.

Preparation time: *5 minutes*

Cooking time: *Nil*

Serves: *2*

4 spoonfuls of mayonnaise

1 to 2 cloves of garlic, peeled and crushed or finely chopped

Big pinch of fresh chives

Salt and pepper

1 Spoon the mayo into a bowl.

2 Add half the garlic and mix well. Taste a bit to check how strong the garlic is. (If you make it in advance, the garlic flavour will get stronger.) Add more garlic if you need to.

3 Add the salt, pepper and chives and mix well.

4 Serve with crisps or breadsticks.

Per serving: *Calories 211 (From Fat 204); Fat 22.7g (Saturated 3.4g); Cholesterol Trace; Sodium 175mg; Carbohydrate 1.0g, Dietary Fibre 0.2g; Protein 0.6g.*

⟁Tzatziki

Tzatziki is a dip from Greece, served cool, so it's perfect for chilling out on balmy summer evenings.

Tzatziki is a bit runnier than hummus or guacamole, so it's more for dipping in fresh vegetables like strips of carrot or cucumber; something that won't go soft.

Preparation time: *5 minutes*

Cooking time: *Nil*

Serves: *4*

1 medium cucumber

250 grams thick Greek or natural yogurt

Big pinch of chopped fresh dill or mint

1 clove of garlic, crushed

1 glug of olive oil

Dash of Tabasco sauce

Salt and pepper

1 Peel the skin off the cucumber with a vegetable peeler, chop the ends off and discard.

2 Slice the cucumber in half lengthways and carefully scrape out the seeds with a small spoon.

3 Finely chop or grate the cucumber into a bowl.

4 Add the yogurt, herbs, garlic and olive oil to the cucumber. Add a dash of Tabasco to taste.

5 Place the dish in the fridge to chill for an hour or two. Add the salt and pepper just before serving.

Per serving: *Calories 116 (From Fat 80); Fat 8.9g (Saturated 3.3g); Cholesterol trace; Sodium 133mg; Carbohydrate 5.0g, Dietary Fibre 0.7g; Protein 3.9g.*

⟲*Creamy Curry Dip*

This dip has a spicy flavour to wake up your tastebuds. It goes great with some grilled naan or pitta bread cut into strips.

This recipe calls for some freshly chopped coriander. I know it's a little bit pricey, but you'll use coriander again in curry dishes (see Creamy Chicken Curry in Chapter 12) and people will think you're an amazing cook when they see it in the fridge.

Preparation time: *5 minutes*

Cooking time: *Nil*

Serves: *4*

3 spoonfuls of mayonnaise

1 spoonful of korma sauce (from a jar)

1 spoonful of mango chutney

2 spoonfuls of natural yogurt (optional)

1 spoonful of fresh coriander or chives, chopped

1 Spoon the mayonnaise into a mixing bowl, add the korma sauce and mango chutney (and yogurt if you're using it) and mix together.

2 Sprinkle the herbs over the top and serve.

Per serving: *Calories 101 (From Fat 87); Fat 9.7g (Saturated 1.8g); Cholesterol Trace; Sodium 108mg; Carbohydrate 2.9g, Dietary Fibre 0.2g; Protein 0.6g.*

✎*Tomato and Red Onion Salsa*

Although some may disagree, I class salsa as a dip. After all, it tastes great and you can shovel the salsa into your mouth using a crisp. Elegant? No. Tasty? Oh yes.

Preparation time: *10 minutes*

Cooking time: *Nil*

Serves: *4*

5 or 6 tomatoes

1 small red onion

½ to 1 fresh chilli or a dash of Tabasco sauce

Big pinch of chopped fresh coriander

1 teaspoon vinegar (balsamic vinegar if you can afford it)

1 clove of crushed garlic (optional - if you want a bit more of a kick)

Salt and pepper

Pinch of sugar

1 Cut the tomatoes in half and remove the seeds with a spoon. When deseeded, chop the tomatoes into small pieces and place in a bowl.

2 Peel and dice the red onion and add to the diced tomato.

3 Slice the chilli in half lengthways and remove the seeds. Finely chop the chilli and add half to the tomato. Wash your hands with hot soapy water after handling the chilli!

4 Add the coriander, vinegar and garlic (if you're using it) and carefully combine.

5 Season with salt and pepper and add a pinch of sugar. Taste the salsa and add more chilli if you want.

6 Place into a serving dish, cover with cling film and chill in the fridge for a couple of hours. Chilling it really brings out the flavours.

Per serving: Calories 29 (From Fat 3); Fat 0.3g (Saturated 0.1g); Cholesterol Trace; Sodium 45mg; Carbohydrate 5.5g, Dietary Fibre 1.3g; Protein 1.0g.

Part III
Bringing On the Main Course

'That was a <u>fantastic</u> stew, Kevin – where did you get all that great meat from?'

In this part . . .

Time to get stuck into some serious nosh in this part as you bring on the main course. Whether you're going to knock up a delicious dish for yourself, let the microwave do all the hard work, or finish things off with a divine dessert, Part III has everything you need to do some serious (well, kind of serious) cooking.

Chapter 7

Cooking For One

*E*ven though at uni you're surrounded by friends and mates, you sometimes find yourself on your lonesome for an evening meal. Everyone slinks off back to their flats or halls to rummage around in their cupboards and attempt to make something edible. It's at this point, armed with this trusty book that you can show off your culinary genius and whip up a meal that's the envy of everyone in your hall.

Don't feel like a Billy No-Mates – cooking for one is brilliant. You get to experiment with recipes, do trial runs ready for that important date and if it all goes wrong, well, no one's around to find out. Plus you can make that curry as spicy as *you* like it and that toad in the hole as big as *you* want. You have free range over what you devour. And when you get that recipe bang on, when you make something that tastes fantastic, you can give yourself a big pat on the back. In this chapter, I share with you some marvellous meals with meat and fish as well as some great vegetarian and vegan dishes too.

A dish for one

Consider buying a small Pyrex dish so you can cook your meals for one. You can buy them in most supermarkets and hardware shops. If you only have a bigger dish to cook in, double the quantity for the recipe and share with a mate, or save the leftover half for another night. (Reheat in the microwave or in a hot oven until the middle of the dish is piping hot and reheat food only once.)

So rather than wallow in a haze of gloom over eating for one, crack open a beer and have a ruddy good time cooking some of these recipes.

Always make sure you have a chopping board for meat and fish and a separate chopping board for veg. Using two chopping boards stops raw meat getting mixed with cooked meat or vegetables, which can cause food poisoning. I suggest a plastic chopping board for the meat because it's easier to clean than a wooden one.

Making a Meal with Meat

In Britain, meat tends to be in most meals. While eating this quantity of meat may not be the best for your diet because of its high level of saturated fat (particularly in red meat), you do get some really great hearty meals. The first set of recipes in this meaty section are more traditional and are great for when you're on a tight budget; later on I show you some slightly more luxurious dishes, so you can sit down and treat yourself after a long day's work.

Sausage and Bean Stew

This recipe is dead quick to make and also pretty cheap. It goes really nicely with some mashed potatoes, which you can use to mop up the stew. (Put the water on to boil the potatoes after you put the grill on, so they'll be cooked by the time the stew is done.)

Preparation time: *10 minutes*

Cooking time: *15 minutes*

Serves: *1*

Olive oil

½ red onion, peeled and finely chopped

1 clove of garlic, chopped

Splodge of tomato purée

2 sausages

½ tin of chopped tomatoes

¼ tin of red kidney beans, drained and rinsed

½ tin of mixed vegetables, drained and rinsed

100 millilitres of vegetable stock

Big pinch of oregano (or mixed herbs)

Salt and pepper

1 Turn the grill on to a medium to hot setting.

2 Heat a drop of oil in a saucepan on the hob over a medium heat and add the chopped onions and garlic when the oil is hot. Fry for about 5 minutes, until the onion goes soft.

3 Add the splodge of tomato purée and mix well.

4 Chuck in the chopped tomatoes, kidney beans, mixed vegetables and vegetable stock and mix everything together.

5 Pop the sausages under the grill. (If you're doing mashed potatoes, put some cubed potatoes into some salted boiling water in a pan on the hob now).

6 Keep turning the sausages under the grill to make sure they're completely cooked, and keep stirring the stew. If the stew starts to look dry, add a little boiling water.

7 Check that the sausages are cooked by cutting into one. The inside should be light in colour and piping hot.

8 Add the oregano and salt and pepper to the stew and mix well. Spoon onto a plate, add the sausages on top and serve with mashed spuds.

Per serving: Calories 978 (From Fat 410); Fat 45.6g (Saturated 14.9g); Cholesterol Trace; Sodium 1983mg; Carbohydrate 92.8g, Dietary Fibre 26.8g; Protein 49.0g.

Drunk Toad in the Hole

What is it with British dishes and confusing names? Yorkshire pudding isn't a pudding, toad in the hole isn't made from amphibians and cottage pie doesn't provide ideal living conditions . . .

Toad in the hole is a fab budget recipe to know. The sausages are encased in a crispy, light batter that I've given a bit of a student makeover to – by adding beer.

Preparation time: *10 minutes*

Cooking time: *25 minutes*

Serves: *1*

Olive oil	*1 egg*
2 or 3 sausages	*70 millilitres (about half a mug) of milk*
50 grams (about a handful) of plain flour	*70 millilitres (about half a mug) of beer (use real ale, not lager)*
Salt and pepper	

1 Preheat the oven to 200°C.

2 Add a glug of oil to a heatproof dish and add the sausages, coating them in the oil. Place in the preheated oven and bake until the sausages are a light brown colour (about 10 minutes). They don't need to be fully cooked because they'll be going back in the oven later on.

3 While they're baking, add the flour and salt into a bowl and crack the egg in. Add a bit of milk and mix into the flour and egg. Keep adding in the milk a bit at a time and stir together.

4 Gradually add in the beer. Mix until you get the consistency of cream. If it's too thin, add a pinch more flour to thicken things up.

5 By now the sausages should be brown, so take the dish out of the oven and pour in the batter. You want the batter to be about a centimetre deep in the bottom of the dish, and don't worry if it splashes over the sausages. Place back in the oven and bake for 25 minutes, or until the batter has completely risen.

Don't open the oven door during this time because you knock the air out of the batter and it deflates.

6 Take out of the oven and serve with mashed potato, roasted root vegetables and greens. Oh, and a drizzle of gravy.

Per serving: Calories 1127 (From Fat 723); Fat 80.3g (Saturated 25.6g); Cholesterol Trace; Sodium 2057mg; Carbohydrate 66.1g, Dietary Fibre 3.8g; Protein 34.9g.

Lemon and Chilli Chicken Stir-Fry

How easy is a stir-fry to make? You fry it. You stir it. You fry it a bit more. Then it's pretty much done. Stir-fries are nice and cheap to make and are a great way of using up any vegetables you have knocking around that need eating up. This recipe adds a bit of a kick to an otherwise plain chicken breast.

Preparation time: 5 minutes

Cooking time: 15 minutes

Serves: 1

Groundnut or vegetable oil

1 chicken breast, chopped into strips

1 chilli, finely chopped

1 clove of garlic, finely chopped

Squeeze of lemon juice

Salt

Assortment of vegetables (broccoli, spring onions, mushrooms, baby sweetcorn)

1 block of noodles or 1 mug of rice

1 Half fill a saucepan with water and bring to the boil on the hob.

2 Add a drop of olive oil to a bowl and add the chicken, chilli and garlic. Add a squeeze of lemon, mix well and leave to one side for the flavours to seep into the chicken.

 Wash your hands after handling raw chicken or chillies. Spreading raw chicken on other items increases the risk of salmonella (food poisoning), while getting raw chilli into a cut or your eye really hurts!

3 Add a pinch of salt and your rice or noodles to the boiling water on the hob.

4 Heat a drop of oil in a frying pan over a high heat and when hot, add the chicken. Keep stirring and frying (hence the name stir fry).

5 When the chicken's lost its pinkness, add some of the other vegetables and keep stirring and frying.

6 Add the rest of the vegetables and stir. And fry.

7 If you have any lemon juice left, squeeze a bit over the chicken in the pan. Keep frying until the chicken turns a light brown colour. To check if the chicken is cooked, cut open the biggest piece and see if the inside of the chicken has turned white. If it has, it's cooked; if it's still pink or a little wet, keep cooking until it turns white and dry.

8 Check to see if the rice or noodles are cooked by tasting and then drain and spoon onto a plate. Add the stir fry on top and then bring out the chopsticks.

Per serving: *Calories 836 (From Fat 182); Fat 20.2g (Saturated 4.5g); Cholesterol Trace; Sodium 401mg; Carbohydrate 62.4g, Dietary Fibre 19.7g; Protein 101.1g.*

Skint Shepherd's Pie

Here's your starter for ten: what's the difference between shepherd's pie and cottage pie? Answer: cottage pie contains beef, shepherd's pie contains lamb. And Skint Shepherd's Pie? Well, that's my version and it contains mutton. Mutton is basically mature sheep, which means there's more flavour in the meat, but the texture is a little tougher than lamb. But when the mutton is minced, as in this recipe, the toughness isn't a problem. Mutton is a fraction of the price of lamb or beef, making this great for when you're on a budget.

This recipe's also a perfect example of getting to know about different cuts and types of meat you can use to save you a bit of cash. The best place to get mutton, and also advice about different cuts of meat and how to cook them, is from your local butcher. So next time you're out shopping, pop in and don't be afraid to ask questions and try something new.

Preparation time: 5 minutes

Cooking time: 40 minutes

Serves: 1

Olive oil

½ onion, peeled and sliced

200 grams of minced mutton

½ carrot, peeled and cut into pieces

1 large potato, peeled and cut into small chunks

120 millilitres beef or lamb stock

Dash of milk

Butter

Salt and pepper

1 Preheat the oven to 200°C. Half fill a saucepan with water and put on the hob, full power, to bring to the boil.

2 Heat a glug of oil in a frying pan over a medium to high heat and add the onion.

3 Fry the onion for about 5 minutes or until it turns soft.

4 Crumble the minced mutton into the frying pan with your hands and add the chopped carrot. (Make sure you wash your hands before and after handling the meat.)

5 Break the meat up into small pieces with your spatula and fry until it turns a light brown colour.

6 By now the water should be boiling, so add a pinch of salt and then carefully add the chopped potato pieces.

7 Pour the stock into the frying pan. Mix well with the meat and everything else. Turn the heat down and simmer for about 10 minutes.

8 After 10 minutes, check the potatoes. If they're done, drain and add the potatoes back into the saucepan. Add a dash of milk and a chunk of butter and mash with a fork or potato masher until light and fluffy. If the mash starts to look too dry, add a tiny dash of milk. Add a bit of salt and pepper to give it some seasoning.

9 Get a heatproof dish and spoon in the meat mixture. Add the mashed potato on top, sealing in the meat. Place in the preheated oven for about 20 to 25 minutes or until the mash starts to turn a light golden-brown colour.

10 Remove from the oven and dig in.

Variation: *You can grill the shepherd's pie for the last 5 minutes of cooking to make the mash really crispy, but keep your eye on it because it's very easy to burn! Also, try swapping the carrot for some baked beans or frozen peas (they'll defrost during the frying and baking.)*

Per serving: *Calories 1028 (From Fat 581); Fat 64.5g (Saturated 24.0g); Cholesterol Trace; Sodium 974mg; Carbohydrate 64.8g, Dietary Fibre 6.6g; Protein 47.0g.*

Soy Sauce and Ginger Pork Chop

Add a bit of oriental flavour to an otherwise traditional pork chop by marinating it with some soy sauce and grated ginger. This is a great little recipe to remember and is very easy and quick to make.

Serve with some sweet potato mash (make it exactly the same as usual mash, but it'll take less time to cook). The sweetness of the potato goes really well with the sharp taste of the soy sauce.

Preparation time: *5 minutes*

Cooking time: *15 minutes*

Serves: *1*

1 pork chop
Couple of splashes of soy sauce

1 generous tablespoon peeled and grated ginger
Salt and pepper

1 Turn on the grill to a high heat.

2 Place the pork chop on a clean chopping board and carefully slash three slices in each side.

3 Place the slashed pork chop in a bowl and splash over some soy sauce. Turn over the chop and repeat.

4 Rub the grated ginger into the cuts in the pork chop. Season with some salt and pepper. Turn over and repeat.

5 Place under the hot grill and cook for 7 to 10 minutes on one side and then turn over. Cook until the middle of the chop has turned white and any juices that run out are clear.

Per serving: Calories 342 (From Fat 162); Fat 18.0g (Saturated 6.4g); Cholesterol Trace; Sodium 551mg; Carbohydrate 1.6g, Dietary Fibre 2.5g; Protein 43.4g.

Classic Lasagne

For some reason, lasagne takes on a mystical quality when you're at uni. Everyone loves lasagne, with the mere mention of the word sending people into drooling, hungry wrecks, loitering around your kitchen hoping for a slice of Italian goodness. You can see why it's a hit though. Lasagne tastes great and is a doddle to make.

White sauce is also known as *béchamel sauce,* named after Louis XIV's steward Louis de Béchamel (now you can impress your mates when that comes up on University Challenge). White sauce is made from mixing flour, butter and milk over a low heat to create a rich and smooth sauce. You can add cheese towards the end of cooking, or infuse the milk with chopped onions, bay leaves, carrots or celery before you add it to the other ingredients.

Preparation time: *20 minutes*

Cooking time: *30 minutes*

Serves: *1*

For the lasagne

Olive oil

½ an onion, peeled and chopped

Splodge of tomato purée

175 grams (a big handful) of minced beef

½ tin of chopped tomatoes

Big pinch of dried mixed herbs

Lasagne pasta sheets (about 3 or 4 should do, depending on the size of the dish)

For the white sauce	*100 millilitres of milk*
Small chunk of butter	*Salt and pepper*
Pinch of plain flour	*Handful of grated parmesan (optional)*

1 Preheat the oven to 180°C.

2 Heat a glug of olive oil in a frying pan over a medium heat and add the chopped onion. Fry the onion for about 5 minutes or until it starts to go soft.

3 Add a splodge of tomato purée to the onion and mix well.

4 Now add the minced beef, breaking it up with your hands as you put it in the pan. Use a spatula or wooden spoon to break it up a bit more when it's in the pan. Mix it well with the onion and tomato purée. Fry until the beef turns a light brown colour.

5 Add the chopped tomatoes and pinch of mixed herbs and mix well.

6 Now it's time to make the white sauce.

Chuck a chunk of butter in a saucepan over a low heat and add a pinch of flour. Using a wooden spoon, stir the butter until it melts and mixes in with the flour, forming a dry, rough paste. This is called a *roux* (pronounced *roo*). Add a little milk and stir until the milk is absorbed by the roux and turns into a very thick but slightly more liquid paste. Keep adding the milk gradually and stirring until the mixture turns into a thick and creamy sauce. If it starts to look a bit too wet, add a pinch more flour. If it's not getting thick, try turning up the heat a little. If it starts to look too dry, add a drop more milk. It may take a while to reach perfection (up to about 10 minutes), so keep stirring. Season with some salt and pepper towards the end and eventually you'll get a thick and creamy white sauce.

7 Get a heatproof dish and put a drop of olive oil at the bottom (this prevents the layer of pasta from sticking to the bottom of the dish). Add a layer of pasta and then spoon a thin layer of meat over it. Cover the meat layer with a layer of pasta. Keep layering until you've used up all the meat, finishing off with a pasta sheet on top. Spoon the white sauce all over the top lasagne sheet, sprinkle the parmesan over (if using) and put in the preheated oven for around 30 minutes.

8 Take out of the oven when the white sauce turns a golden-brown colour on top. (You can make it really nice by lightly grilling the top to make it crispy, but be careful it doesn't burn.)

9 Serve with some salad, garlic bread or whatever takes your fancy.

Variation: If you've made a lot of white sauce, try adding a layer on top of every pasta sheet. You'll end up with a creamier lasagne. Also, try adding some chopped sun-dried tomatoes in with the minced beef when you're frying it.

Per serving: Calories 1164 (From Fat 617); Fat 68.6g (Saturated 26.8g); Cholesterol Trace; Sodium 476mg; Carbohydrate 84.8g, Dietary Fibre 6.1g; Protein 51.8g.

Spaghetti and Home-made Meatballs

This recipe is a nice change from your usual spaghetti bolognaise. My variation uses (nearly) all the same ingredients, but is more fun to make, mainly because it involves getting your hands messy! This recipe may seem a little long but is actually very straightforward.

Make sure you have two frying pans and a saucepan; if you haven't, cook the tomato sauce first and then place in a bowl and leave to one side so that you can reuse the pan. Heat up the sauce in the microwave just before the end.

Preparation time: 15 minutes

Cooking time: 15 minutes

Serves: 1

For the meatballs

Glug of olive oil

1 clove of garlic, peeled and finely chopped

¼ onion, peeled and finely chopped

1 egg

200 grams (about a handful) of minced beef

Pinch of herbs – oregano, thyme or rosemary are good; fresh if you can, dried if you can't

Salt and pepper

Handful of plain flour

For the sauce and spaghetti

¼ onion, peeled and finely chopped

Splodge of tomato purée

½ tin of chopped tomatoes

100 grams of spaghetti (about half a fistful)

Olive oil

1 Heat a drop of oil in a frying pan and gently cook the garlic and onions over a medium heat until they turn brown.

2 Take the pan off the heat and leave to cool down.

3 Crack the egg into a bowl and whisk until smooth and yellowy.

4 Add the fried onion, garlic and raw meat, breaking the meat up in your (clean) hands as you add it to the egg.

5 Add the big pinch of herbs and a generous grind of the salt and pepper. Grab a large plate and sprinkle the plain flour over it, enough to coat it fairly thickly.

6 Wash your hands and get ready to get them messy! Mix the meat and egg mixture and shape into 5 to 7 meatballs. Aim to get them around the size of a ping pong ball. The trick is in the size: if you make them too big, they don't hold together in the pan or don't cook in the middle.

7 Roll your meatballs on the plate to coat them in flour. Leave them on the plate when you've used up all the meat and pop the plate in the fridge to chill the meatballs.

8 Right, now on to the spaghetti and the sauce. Half fill a saucepan with water and place on the hob, full power. Heat some more oil in a frying pan and fry the rest of your onion.

9 When the onion turns brown, add a big splodge of tomato purée and mix well with the onion.

10 Grab another frying pan and heat a drop of olive oil over a medium heat.

11 Take the meatballs out of the fridge and place them carefully in the hot oil. Fry them, turning them continuously until they turn golden brown.

12 Add the chopped tomatoes to the frying pan with the onions in it and turn the heat down to low.

13 By now, the water for the spaghetti should be boiling, so add a pinch of salt to the water and add the spaghetti. Keep turning the meatballs to ensure they cook evenly.

14 After 10 minutes, check to see if the spaghetti is done (by tasting it). Drain, tip onto a plate and add the sauce on top.

15 Check to see if the meatballs are cooked by cutting the largest one open. The meat should be brown inside, not pink. If it's pink, fry a bit longer. When the meatballs are cooked, add on top of your tomato sauce, season with salt and pepper and give yourself a high five!

Variation: Add some chopped chilli when you make the meatballs for a slightly spicier flavour.

Per serving: Calories 1696 (From Fat 828); Fat 92.0g (Saturated 23.1g); Cholesterol Trace; Sodium 467mg; Carbohydrate 145.2g, Dietary Fibre 10.2g; Protein 71.8g.

Making Fish Dishes Go Swimmingly

Fish is one of the most misunderstood ingredients when it comes to cooking at uni. Most people think it's expensive, hard to cook and worst of all, smelly, which couldn't be further from the truth. Full of protein and low on fat, with a delicate taste that just melts on your tongue and sends your tastebuds into overdrive, I love the stuff. Cooking a fillet of fish is one of the easiest things to do; so easy you can cook it in the microwave in under 5 minutes, or whack it in the oven for 20 minutes. Half the time you don't even need to prepare it, maybe just squeeze lemon juice or drizzle olive oil over it, and hey presto, the end result is a brilliantly healthy dish that's full of flavour and, most importantly, cheap as chips!

Fish is perfect when you're cooking for one because you can portion things up really easily. As a very general rule, one whole fish feeds one person. Mackerel, trout and tilapia are all great to buy whole; everything else you can ask the fishmonger to cut up for you, so you can have as much or as little as you want.

Freshwater fish (tilapia, Vietnamese cobbler, trout and so on) have a subtle taste and are more suited to curries and other dishes that give the fish a lot of flavour. Seawater fish (haddock, cod, mackerel and so on) are tasty enough to feature as the main part of the meal, and most of the time, need little flavour adding to them.

Smokin'!

Smoked fish are cooked or raw, depending on how they've been smoked. If the fish was *hot* smoked, it's been cooked in the smoking process. If it was *cold* smoked (the temperature was a lot lower during the smoking process) the fish isn't cooked, and you need to cook it fully. Ask your fishmonger if you're unsure whether the fish is cooked or not, or check the packaging if buying from a supermarket.

Many people are scared of eating bones when they eat fish, or think fish is difficult to prepare. In fact, your fishmonger does all the hard work for you, cleaning (getting rid of the guts) and boning the fish, making it ready for you to cook and eat.

This is my beginner's guide to fish. I give you some nice cheap recipes and end with dishes that are a little more of a treat.

Scales and tails: looking for good fish

The number one rule when it comes to buying fish is to try to use your local fishmonger, not your supermarket. Not only is your fishmonger more likely to give you a student discount, but they can also advise you on how to cook the fish you buy, and they can fillet and prepare it for you, so you have to do very little to it. Your fishmonger knows about where and how the fish was caught. Don't be afraid to ask questions, no matter how stupid you may think they are! Fishmongers are used to being asked for advice on how to cook fish.

Here's my guide to what to look for when buying fish:

✔ A fresh fish shouldn't smell of fish! It should have a lovely sea smell. Smoked fish should smell smoky.

✔ The eyes should look bright and the skin should be shiny and firm.

✔ Fishmongers and some smaller supermarkets have less selection on Monday because the fish merchants that deliver the fish are closed on Sunday. Tuesday to Saturday are the best days to shop for fish.

✔ Look out for and try other things that the fishmonger sells, like mussels, prawns or samphire, a delicious green edible plant. Many fishmongers also sell fish scraps. These are pieces of fish that they've cut off and are too small to sell individually. They're perfect for fish pies and cost next to nothing!

Storing and freezing fish

Follow these tips for storing and freezing your fish:

✔ As with meat, always store raw fish at the bottom of your fridge on a plate or tray. This stops any bits of raw fish or liquid dripping on to other food and prevents cross contamination.

✔ Fresh fish lasts around two to three days in the fridge. Store cooked fish that's ready to eat away from raw fish in the fridge.

✔ When freezing fish, wrap it in paper, then in a plastic carrier bag to stop *freezer burn,* when the surface of the fish comes into contact with the side of the freezer and damages the fish. Frozen fish is fine in the freezer for up to 4 months.

✔ The best method of defrosting fish is to place it in the fridge 24 hours before you need to cook it. You can defrost it in the microwave, but this isn't as good as letting it defrost slowly.

Finding ways to cook fish

One of the best things about fish is the variety of ways you can cook it. Fish is so versatile that you can cook it pretty much however you like, even in the microwave! Table 7-1 is a quick run through of some of the easiest ways you can cook fish and the best types of fish to use.

Table 7-1	Cooking Fish	
Method	*What It Means*	*Fish to Use*
Bake	Place the fish on a baking tray and put in a preheated oven, usually at around 200°C for about 20 to 25 minutes.	Smoked haddock
		Cod
	Alternatively, wrap the fish in tin foil and add a little water, white wine or lemon juice and then place it in the oven.	Salmon
Microwave	Place the fish and a bit of water and oil in a microwave-proof container. Cover tightly with cling film, pierce a few holes and place in the microwave, full power for around 5 minutes.	Coley
		Haddock
		Whiting
Grill	Coat the fish in olive oil and place under a grill on medium heat for about 15 minutes.	Mackerel
		Salmon
		Tuna steak
Poach	Cover and gently simmer the fish in milk or stock for about 15 minutes.	Trout
		Plaice
		Smoked haddock

Knowing when fish is cooked

Knowing if fish is cooked or not scares some people silly. Fish actually needs very little cooking to eat, and most people overcook their fish. If you were to seriously undercook your fish, you may get a slight tummy upset or feel ill for a few days, but this isn't as bad compared to the dangers of eating undercooked meat.

To help you know when your fish is cooked, here are a few guidelines for what to look out for:

✔ When fish is cooked, it should just fall apart when you gently pull at it with your fork. If it still seems too firm, cook for a bit longer.

✔ If the fish still looks a little moist inside, don't worry, that's a good thing. As long as it's hot all the way through and any juices run clear, then you've got a cracking bit of fish waiting to be devoured.

✔ If you poach or microwave fish, you can pour some of the hot juices or stock over the fish before you serve it, to add to the flavour.

In the next section are just a few recipes for fish dishes for one. Have a go; cooking fish is easier than you think!

Quick 'n' Easy Coley

Coley is a cheap alternative to cod or haddock, but is still delicious. This recipe shows how easy and quick cooking fish is in the microwave. Yep, the microwave.

Preparation time: *2 minutes*

Cooking time: *5 minutes*

Serves: *1*

1 portion of coley (ask the fishmonger to fillet it)	*Olive oil*
½ lemon	*Salt and pepper*

1 Wash the fillet under a trickle of cold water and pat dry with some disposable kitchen roll (or just gently shake over the sink.) *Don't* use a tea towel.

2 Slice the lemon and place at the bottom of a microwaveable dish.

3 Pour some olive oil onto a saucer or plate and coat both sides of the coley in it.

4 Place the fillet over the sliced lemon in the dish. Add a few drops of water over the fish and add a little bit in the dish.

5 Cover the dish tightly with cling film and pierce a few holes in the top with a fork to allow the steam to escape.

6 Place in the microwave and cook on full power for 3 minutes.

7 After three minutes, open the microwave door, but leave the dish inside with the cling film on top for another 2 minutes. The fish is still cooking because of the heat and moisture trapped in the dish.

8 After 2 minutes, carefully peel back the cling film (be careful – it'll be hot) and try to pull a bit of the fish away with a fork. If it comes off easily and is hot (taste it), then it's cooked. If it still looks a bit firm, pop the cling film over it again and cook for a further minute. You're looking for the point where the fish is *just* about to fall to bits, but it's still held together. If you're at all unsure, cook it for a further minute.

9 Take out the fish and place it on a plate. Squeeze a bit more lemon juice over the top and spoon some of the lemon liquid at the bottom of the dish over the fish. Season and serve with some new potatoes, green beans or whatever you fancy.

Per serving: *Calories 254 (From Fat 108); Fat 12.0g (Saturated 1.6g); Cholesterol Trace; Sodium 251mg; Carbohydrate Trace, Dietary Fibre Trace; Protein 36.6g.*

Tuna Pasta Bake

Tuna Pasta Bake is a classic hearty meal when you're dining for one. Remember, not all fish has to be fresh to be good for you – this recipe uses tinned tuna.

Preparation time: *10 minutes*

Cooking time: *25 minutes*

Serves: *1*

Olive oil

Mug of pasta (penne, conchiglie or whatever you have)

½ red onion, peeled and chopped

½ tin of chopped tomatoes

½ tin of tuna

2 spoonfuls of sweetcorn (tinned or frozen)

Salt and pepper

Handful of grated Cheddar cheese

1 Half fill a large saucepan with water and put on the hob to boil.

2 When the water in the saucepan is boiling, add a pinch of salt and pour in the pasta, giving it a quick stir to stop it from sticking to the bottom of the pan.

3 Heat a glug of oil in a frying pan over a medium heat and fry the chopped red onion until it turns soft and translucent.

4 Add the chopped tomatoes, tuna and sweetcorn to the onions in the frying pan, breaking up the tuna when it's in the pan. Season with salt and pepper and simmer for about 10 minutes, making sure the mixture doesn't go too dry. If it does, add a little boiling water and stir.

5 After 10 minutes, check that the pasta is cooked by tasting it. If it's cooked, drain in a colander and pour back into the saucepan.

6 Add the contents of the frying pan into the saucepan and mix everything together.

7 Put the pasta mixture into an ovenproof dish. Scatter the grated cheese over the top of the pasta bake and place under a hot grill for 5 minutes or until the cheese starts to melt.

8 When the cheese has melted, take it out from under the grill and dig in.

Variation: *Try adding a layer of breadcrumbs or crushed crisps before sprinkling the cheese over the top to give the pasta bake a slightly crunchier texture.*

Per serving: *Calories 1317 (From Fat 545); Fat 60.6g (Saturated 24.7g); Cholesterol Trace; Sodium 1150; Carbohydrate 125.6g, Dietary Fibre 3.3g; Protein 67.4g.*

Smoked Haddock Fishcakes

I love the flavour of smoked fish. It reminds me of childhood trips to Whitby in North Yorkshire and having smoked kippers for tea after a walk on the beach. Delicious . . . Anyway, smoked haddock is a little more expensive than the other fish in this chapter (not by much though), but as it's one of your recommended two portions of fish a week, just let that slide.

This recipe is perfect for using up any leftover mashed potato you may have from another meal in the week.

Preparation time: *5 minutes*

Cooking time: *20 minutes*

Serves: *1 (makes around 4 fishcakes)*

Olive oil (to coat baking tray)

1 small fillet of smoked haddock (check whether it's cooked or raw. If cooked, skip Steps 1 and 2; instead, wrap in some tin foil and place in the oven for 10 minutes to heat through.)

1 egg

1 potato, peeled, precooked and mashed

Salt and pepper

1 slice of lightly toasted bread, grated to make breadcrumbs

1 Preheat the oven to 200°C. Place the (raw) smoked haddock fillet on an oiled baking tray and place in the hot oven for 20 minutes.

2 When baked, remove the fish from the oven and allow to cool a little, then flake into pieces with a fork.

3 Break the egg into a small bowl and whisk until smooth.

4 Put the cooked mashed potato and smoked haddock into a different bowl and season with salt and pepper. Add a spoonful of the egg mixture. Mix together with a spoon, and shape into balls with your hands.

5 Dip a spoon into the egg mixture and drizzle a tiny bit onto the top and bottom of the fishcakes. Place the breadcrumbs onto a plate and dip each fishcake into the breadcrumbs to coat them. Place them onto the oiled baking tray you used for the haddock. Using a fish slice or the back of a spoon, gently press down on the fishcakes, to make them a flatter Frisbee shape.

6 Place in the oven on a lightly oiled tray and bake for 20 minutes or until they turn a light brown colour. Serve with some vegetables such as green beans or peas and a bit of tomato sauce.

Variation: *For a slightly cheaper alternative, use tinned tuna rather than haddock and add a couple of spoonfuls of sweetcorn at the mixing stage.*

Per serving: *Calories 605 (From Fat 171); Fat 19.0g (Saturated 3.7g); Cholesterol Trace; Sodium 1817mg; Carbohydrate 58.2g, Dietary Fibre 3.9g; Protein 50.3g.*

Fish Stew

I confess that Fish Stew doesn't sound particularly appealing, but don't judge a recipe by its name, and give this massively flavoursome dish a whirl. This stew uses a lot of spices to give the dish its flavour; you can pick up the spices at your local supermarket or nearest Asian food store.

 Spices keep for years, and a collection of herbs and spices really improves your cooking by adding subtle flavours to your dishes.

Preparation time: *5 minutes*

Cooking time: *15 minutes*

Serves: *1*

Olive oil

½ onion, peeled and chopped

1 clove of garlic, peeled and chopped

1 teaspoon of curry powder

1 teaspoon of ground cumin or cumin seeds

½ tin of chopped tomatoes

3 or 4 new potatoes, cut into quarters

150 millilitres of boiling water

Vietnamese cobbler fillet (or similar freshwater fish – ask your fishmonger for suggestions), cut into chunks

Juice from ½ a lemon

Salt and pepper

1 Heat a drop of oil in a large saucepan on the hob, over a medium heat.

2 When the oil is hot, add the chopped onion and garlic and fry for three minutes or until the onion softens.

3 Add the curry powder and ground cumin or cumin seeds. Fry until the smell of the spices is released.

4 Add the chopped tomatoes, potatoes and boiling water and mix well.

5 Simmer for around ten minutes or until the potatoes start to soften.

6 Add the fish chunks and mix well, ensuring that the fish is covered in the tomato mixture. If the stew looks a little dry at this point, add a bit more boiling water. Simmer for a further five minutes.

7 Squeeze in the lemon juice and mix again. Check that the fish is cooked – it should be soft and tender and fall apart easily.

8 Season the stew with some salt and pepper and serve with some couscous or rice.

Variation: Try stirring in a spoonful or two of honey five minutes before you serve for a slightly sweeter taste, or add some turmeric when you fry the onion and garlic.

Per serving: Calories 456 (From Fat 68.0); Fat 7.6g (Saturated 1.0g); Cholesterol Trace; Sodium 331mg; Carbohydrate 51.2g, Dietary Fibre 8.3g; Protein 45.7g.

Grilled Mackerel with Garlic and Cumin

This recipe sounds posh and exciting, doesn't it? *Grilled Mackerel with Garlic and Cumin* is essentially *Fish rubbed with a bit of spice and put under the grill,* so don't be put off by this recipe's fancy sounding title. Mackerel is one of my favourite fish. They always look amazing with their dark blue and black stripes glistening on the fishmonger's stall.

Ask the fishmonger to fillet the mackerel when you buy it.

Preparation time: 5 minutes

Cooking time: 12 minutes

Serves: 1

1 mackerel, filleted	1 teaspoon of cumin
Big chunk of butter	1 lime, cut in half
1 clove of garlic, peeled and finely chopped	

1 Turn on the grill to a medium heat.

2 Put the butter in a bowl and place in the microwave. Heat until the butter melts.

3 Carefully remove the bowl from the microwave and add the chopped garlic and cumin. Grate in some lime zest. Mix well.

4 Wash the mackerel fillets under a cold tap and dry with a bit of kitchen roll. If you haven't got any kitchen roll, gently shake most of the water off over the sink.

5 Place the mackerel on a clean chopping board (the one you use for meat and fish, not your veg one). Make slits with your knife, about 2 centimetres long and half a centimetre deep on each side.

6 Spoon the garlic and cumin mixture over the mackerel and rub it into the slits. Repeat with the other side.

7 Squeeze the lime over the mackerel and place under the grill. Grill the fillets flesh-side up for two minutes and then skin-side up for ten minutes.

8 When the mackerel is cooked and the skin is looking dark and crispy, take off the grill and serve with some new potatoes and peas.

Per serving: Calories 713 (From Fat 514); Fat 57.1g (Saturated 22.2g); Cholesterol Trace; Sodium 310mg; Carbohydrate 11.2g, Dietary Fibre 2.9g; Protein 38.5g.

Foil-Wrapped Trout

Wrapping fish in foil is a great way to cook fish. You can cook most fish in this way, and the fish absorbs the flavour of anything you add to the foil parcel.

You can use freshwater or sea trout for this recipe. Sea trout is more expensive but has a fantastic wild sea taste; freshwater trout is cheaper and more readily available, and still tastes great.

Preparation time: *5 minutes*

Cooking time: *25 minutes*

Serves: *1*

1 trout (gutted, with head and tail removed)

½ lemon, sliced

Olive oil

1 shallot, peeled and sliced

½ celery stalk, chopped

½ carrot, sliced

Half a glass of white wine or 75 millilitres of veg stock

1 Preheat the oven to 200°C.

2 Rinse the trout under a trickle of cold water from the tap. Dry with a kitchen roll or just shake off the excess water.

3 On a baking tray, roll out a sheet of kitchen foil that's big enough to wrap the trout in. Place the trout on the foil and stuff the slices of lemon inside the fish.

4 Drizzle the trout with olive oil and sprinkle the chopped vegetables over the top.

5 Fold up the edges of the kitchen foil and pour in the wine or vegetable stock. Seal the parcel.

6 Place the trout in the preheated oven and bake for 25 minutes.

7 Take the trout out of the oven and carefully unwrap the parcel. Be careful – the steam will be blistering hot. Check that the trout's cooked by pulling off a bit of the skin with your fork. If it comes off easily and the flesh is white and moist, your trout is beautifully cooked (if not, pop it back in the oven for a few minutes). Tuck in. Yum.

Per serving: *Calories 671 (From Fat 288); Fat 32.0g (Saturated 5.9g); Cholesterol Trace; Sodium 279mg; Carbohydrate 8.7g, Dietary Fibre 2.0g; Protein 87.0g.*

Salmon and Leek Parcel

This recipe has a posher name: *salmon en croute,* French for 'in pastry'. This parcel involves a bit of creativity and getting your hands messy, something all great recipes need! You make the parcel from puff pastry, which you roll out into squares. You simply place the fish on top and cover with another square to make a parcel. The parcel looks great when it comes out of the oven – tender salmon in a creamy leek sauce, which oozes out of a crispy pastry parcel. *Bon appétit!*

Preparation time: *15 minutes*

Cooking time: *35 minutes*

Serves: *1*

Olive oil	*¼ leek, cut into small pieces*
1 tablespoon of flour	*2 spoonfuls of crème fraîche*
Half a fillet of salmon	*90 grams (about 12 centimetres) of*
1 egg	*ready-rolled puff pastry (sold in the*
Butter	*freezer section of all supermarkets)*

1 Preheat the oven to 200°C and lightly oil a baking tray.

2 Scatter some flour over a chopping board and coat a rolling pin in flour (if you don't have a rolling pin, use a cylindrical bottle of wine or olive oil). Roll out the puff pastry until it's the size of a dinner plate.

3 Using a knife, cut out a square of pastry about 3 centimetres bigger than the half piece of salmon. Place the pastry square on the baking tray.

4 Place the half piece of salmon on the cut-out piece of puff pastry, skin side down. Cut out a square slightly larger than the last piece, about 3 centimetres bigger on all sides. Set aside.

5 Break the egg into a bowl and whisk until it turns into a light liquid. Again, set aside for now.

6 Melt a chunk of butter in a frying pan over a medium to high heat and add the chopped leek. Fry the leek for 2 minutes or until it turns slightly soft.

7 Stir the crème fraîche into the leeks. Turn the heat down and keep stirring for a minute or so until the crème fraîche forms a smooth sauce.

8 Take the pan off the heat and spoon the leek sauce over the salmon on the pastry on the baking tray. Brush or spoon some of the egg around the edges of the puff pastry.

9 Finally you come back to that bigger pastry square. Drape the second square over the salmon and leek sauce so that it covers the bottom layer of puff pastry too. Tuck in the edges so it's close to the salmon and then, using a knife, trim off any overlapping bits, leaving a 2-centimetre gap around the salmon. Gently press the edges together, sealing them tight – the egg you added will act like glue.

10 With a sharp knife, score a cross on top of the parcel and brush or spoon the egg over the pastry. The egg makes the pastry turn golden brown during cooking.

11 Place the baking tray in the preheated oven for 35 minutes or until the parcel turns golden brown.

12 Take out the oven and eat with your favourite vegetables.

Tip: If you have any leek sauce left over, heat it up, add a dash of lemon juice and pour over the leek parcel.

Per serving: *Calories 1338 (From Fat 965); Fat 107.2g (Saturated 43.2g); Cholesterol Trace; Sodium 548mg; Carbohydrate 55.4g, Dietary Fibre 3.2g; Protein 37.9g.*

Meals Minus the Meat: Veggie and Vegan Dinners for One

Even though I'm not vegetarian or vegan, I'm a massive fan of vegetarian food and often prefer it over meat dishes. Vegetarian dishes have so much flavour and colour, and you never feel bloated or over-full afterwards. Vegetarian and vegan meals are naturally cheap and very healthy, so make great meal choices when cooking for one.

The first few recipes in this section are low-budget and straightforward, leading on to some more special meals towards the end. And remember, although these dishes are designed for one, you can always double up the quantities if you want to share or feed yourself for two nights.

⟬Vegan Stir-Fry

Stir-fries are cheap and cheerful anyway, but when no meat's involved, they're incredibly cheap. Stir-fries are also a great way of using up any leftover vegetables you have hanging around.

If you're tight for time, you can swap the sauce for a ready-made vegan stir-fry sauce.

Preparation time: *10 minutes*

Cooking time: *15 minutes*

Serves: *1*

For the vegetables

Olive oil

¼ onion, sliced

1 clove of garlic, sliced

A selection of stir-fry vegetables such as carrots, broccoli and red pepper, finely sliced

Handful of cashew nuts

Small chunk of ginger, peeled and grated

1 block of noodles or 1 mug of rice

For the sauce

75 millilitres of vegetable stock

Dash of soy sauce

1 tablespoon of sweet chilli dipping sauce

1 Heat a glug of olive oil in a frying pan over a high heat.

2 Half fill a saucepan with water and put on the hob to bring to the boil.

3 When the oil in the frying pan is hot, add the onion, garlic and ginger and fry until the onion turns a light brown colour.

4 Add all the other vegetables and stir.

5 By now the water in the saucepan should be boiling, so add a pinch of salt and pop in the rice or noodles.

6 In a small bowl, mix together the vegetable stock, soy sauce and sweet chilli dipping sauce.

7 Pour the sauce into the vegetable stir-fry and mix together. Add the cashew nuts.

8 When the rice or noodles are cooked (taste to see), drain and pour onto a plate. Spoon the vegetables on top and eat.

Variation: If you're not vegan, you can swap the soy sauce or chilli dipping sauce for some honey.

Per serving: *Calories 1354 (From Fat 590); Fat 65.6g (Saturated 12.7g); Cholesterol Trace; Sodium 1623mg; Carbohydrate 145.0g, Dietary Fibre 24.4g; Protein 45.8g.*

⚲Pea and Mint Risotto

Risotto is made from arborio rice, rice that absorbs all the liquid it's cooked in. When you serve risotto, it doesn't look a lot, but is dead filling. This Pea and Mint Risotto is a fantastically flavoursome dish that goes great with a chunk of crusty bread. Have a go!

To make the risotto vegan friendly, leave out the grated parmesan (which is usually made with animal rennet) and swap the butter for olive oil.

Preparation time: *5 minutes*

Cooking time: *20 minutes*

Serves: *1*

Chunk of butter

½ onion, peeled and finely chopped

½ mug of arborio rice (roughly 70 grams)

¼ mug of frozen peas (roughly 50 grams)

700 millilitres of hot vegetable stock

2 teaspoons of chopped fresh mint, or 1 teaspoon of dried mint (not as good as fresh, but it'll do)

¼ mug of grated parmesan (roughly 50 grams)

1 Melt the butter in a saucepan over a medium heat. Add the onion and gently fry for 5 minutes.

2 Add the rice and mix well. Pour in a bit of the vegetable stock, just enough to cover the rice, and mix together. The idea is that you add the stock in gradually, just enough at a time for the rice to absorb it.

3 Add in a bit more stock and keep stirring until all the stock's been used up. Add in the peas and cook until the rice is soft and tender and the peas have defrosted and cooked through.

4 Add the chopped mint and parmesan and mix together until the parmesan melts.

5 Spoon onto a plate and serve with some salad or crusty bread.

Per serving: *Calories 1245 (From Fat 527); Fat 58.6g (Saturated 35.5g); Cholesterol Trace; Sodium 4384mg; Carbohydrate 113.9g, Dietary Fibre 16.6g; Protein 65.4g.*

⊙*Ratatouille*

Ratatouille is a traditional French dish made from aubergines, courgettes and other vegetables slowly cooked in chopped tomatoes. It's a lovely warming dish for a cold night. This dish is vegan.

Preparation time: *10 minutes*

Cooking time: *20 minutes*

Serves: *1*

Olive oil

½ onion, peeled and sliced

1 clove of garlic, peeled and chopped

Splodge of tomato purée

½ courgette, sliced

½ red pepper, sliced into pieces

1 tin of chopped tomatoes

Small aubergine, sliced then quartered

½ glass of red wine (optional)

140 millilitres of vegetable stock

Pinch of mixed herbs

Salt and pepper

1 Heat a glug of olive oil a large saucepan over a medium heat. Add the onion and garlic and fry for five minutes or until the onion softens.

2 Add a splodge of tomato purée and mix well. Then add the courgette and red pepper and fry for two minutes.

3 Add the chopped tomatoes, aubergines, red wine (if using), vegetable stock, mixed herbs and salt and pepper. Give everything a good stir and then simmer for 20 minutes.

4 After 20 minutes, check that all the vegetables are tender and serve with pretty much anything – some rice, a jacket potato or a big hunk of bread.

Per serving: *Calories 341 (From Fat 197); Fat 21.9g (Saturated 3.2g); Cholesterol Trace; Sodium 203mg; Carbohydrate 27.7g, Dietary Fibre 9.2g; Protein 8.2g.*

⌒Stuffed Red Peppers

This recipe calls for a mixture of couscous and fragrant chopped tomatoes, but you can stuff a pepper with loads of different things, so feel free to experiment. This vegan recipe is perfect as a light dinner with a bit of salad on the side.

Preparation time: *10 minutes*

Cooking time: *20 minutes*

Serves: *1*

1 red pepper, cut in half (horizontally rather than vertically), seeds removed	½ onion, peeled and chopped
	½ tin of chopped tomatoes
Olive oil	½ cup of chickpeas, drained and rinsed
Salt and pepper	½ cup of raisins
Cup of couscous	1 teaspoon of cinnamon (optional)

1 Preheat the oven to 180°C. Pop the pepper on a baking tray, drizzle with olive oil, season with salt and pepper and place in the hot oven.

2 Flick the kettle on. Pour the couscous into a bowl.

3 Heat a glug of oil in a frying pan over a medium heat and fry the onion until soft.

4 Pour just enough boiling water into the bowl to cover the couscous and place a clean tea towel over the bowl.

5 Add the chopped tomatoes and chickpeas into the saucepan with the onion and simmer for 10 minutes.

6 When the pepper has been in the oven for 20 minutes, take the baking tray out of the oven and allow the pepper to cool slightly.

7 Meanwhile, pour the couscous into the saucepan with the tomato mixture and add the raisins. Add the cinnamon (if using). Mix well and then spoon into the baked pepper shells. Eat.

Per serving: Calories 1546 (From Fat 161); Fat 17.9g (Saturated 2.2g); Cholesterol Trace; Sodium 283mg; Carbohydrate 293g, Dietary Fibre 26.9g; Protein 53.2g.

Sweet Potato and Spinach Curry

This vegan curry contains chickpeas and spinach, both high in protein, which is really important if you're on a vegan or vegetarian diet and don't get protein from meat. The spinach may seem like a lot, but shrinks down dramatically during cooking. This is a fantastic curry that's more mild than spicy.

Preparation time: *10 minutes*

Cooking time: *20 minutes*

Serves: *1*

Olive oil

½ onion, peeled and finely chopped

1 clove of garlic, chopped

2 teaspoons of curry powder

½ tin of chopped tomatoes

½ tin of chickpeas rinsed and drained

1 sweet potato, peeled and chopped into bite-size pieces.

150 grams spinach (2 big handfuls) cut or torn into small pieces

150 millilitres of hot vegetable stock (half a mug)

Salt

½ mug of rice

1 Half fill a saucepan with water and put on the hob, full power, to bring to the boil.

2 Get another saucepan and heat a glug of olive oil over a medium heat. When hot, add the onion and garlic and fry for five minutes.

3 Add the curry powder and mix well.

4 Add the chopped tomatoes, chickpeas, sweet potato, spinach and vegetable stock, mix and bring to the boil. When the curry starts bubbling, turn down the heat and simmer for 10 to 15 minutes or until the sweet potato softens.

5 When the water for the rice is boiling, add a pinch of salt and pour in the rice, giving it a quick stir to stop it from sticking to the bottom of the pan. Boil for about 10 minutes.

6 After 10 minutes, or when the rice is cooked, drain and spoon onto a plate. Serve the curry on the side (or on top of the rice) and enjoy.

Per serving: Calories 1932 (From Fat 319); Fat 35.4g (Saturated 4.2g); Cholesterol Trace; Sodium 1334mg; Carbohydrate 333.9g, Dietary Fibre 35.9g; Protein 69.5g.

⌒Vegetable Lasagne

I prefer this vegetable lasagne to its meatier cousin because it has so much flavour and is a lot cheaper.

Lasagne isn't vegan because you need milk and butter to make the white sauce.

Preparation time: *10 minutes*

Cooking time: *20 minutes*

Serves: *1*

For the lasagne

Olive oil

½ onion, peeled and chopped

½ green pepper, sliced

¼ courgette, sliced

2 small mushrooms, sliced

2 spoonfuls of tinned (or frozen) sweetcorn

½ tin of chopped tomatoes

75 millilitres of vegetable stock (¼ mug)

Pinch of mixed herbs

Lasagne sheets

Salt and pepper

For the white sauce

Small chunk of butter

1 tablespoon of plain flour

120 millilitres of milk

Salt and pepper

1 Preheat the oven to 180°C.

2 Heat some oil in a frying pan over a medium to high heat, add the onions and fry until soft.

3 Add the rest of the vegetables, the stock and mixed herbs. Mix well, turn down the heat to about halfway and let the sauce simmer for about 10 to 15 minutes.

4 While that's simmering, grab another saucepan and throw in a chunk of butter. Melt the butter over a medium heat and add a pinch of plain flour. Using a wooden spoon, mix together until you get a buttery, floury paste (officially called a *roux*, pronounced *roo*).

5 Pour a little milk into the paste, enough to turn it into a bit more of a sauce. Keep mixing. Keep adding in a bit of milk at a time and continue stirring until you get a thick white sauce. (Thicken a runny sauce with a pinch more flour or add a bit more milk to a dry sauce.) When the roux is at the right consistency, season with some salt and pepper.

6 Pour a drop of oil in a heatproof dish and add a lasagne sheet. Spread a spoonful of the vegetable mix on top and cover with another lasagne sheet. Repeat the layers until all the vegetable mix is used and finish with a lasagne sheet on top. Now pour or spoon the white sauce on top, ensuring all the pasta is covered.

7 Place in the preheated oven for about 35 minutes or until the top turns golden brown.

8 Take out, let it rest for a couple of minutes so it's easier to cut and then serve with some salad or whatever you fancy.

Per serving: Calories 858 (From Fat 392); Fat 43.5g (Saturated 16.5g); Cholesterol Trace; Sodium 797mg; Carbohydrate 94.2g, Dietary Fibre 8.4g; Protein 22.4g.

Spaghetti Puttanesca

Spaghetti Puttanesca has a delightful sounding name, but it actually means 'whore's spaghetti', although why it's linked to ladies of the night is a question for the university debating team. Thankfully, you don't have to be pimpin' yourself on street corners to make this. I've left out the anchovies that are in the traditional recipe so that it's suitable for vegetarians and vegans.

 Before you start throwing parmesan cheese on your pasta, stop! Parmesan cheese is *not* vegetarian. It contains *rennet*, an enzyme typically extracted from the stomach lining of calves. Search for vegetarian parmesan cheese instead.

Preparation time: *5 minutes*

Cooking time: *20 minutes*

Serves: *1*

Olive oil

½ onion, peeled and chopped

1 clove of garlic, peeled and chopped

One big pinch of dried chillies or chilli flakes

½ tin of chopped tomatoes

80 grams (small handful) of spaghetti

Salt and pepper

Handful of olives, chopped in half

Small handful of capers

1 Half fill a large saucepan with water and bring to the boil. This is for the spaghetti in Step 4.

2 Meanwhile, heat a glug of olive oil in a frying pan and add the onions and garlic. Fry for about 5 minutes.

3 Add the pinch of chillies, mix and then pour in the chopped tomatoes. Bring the heat down to a low simmer.

4 By now the water for the spaghetti should be boiling, so throw in a pinch of salt and then add the spaghetti. You'll find it easier to push in when the submerged bit of the spaghetti softens.

5 Add the olives to the tomato mixture and mix well. Gently cook for about 10 minutes.

6 Check the spaghetti. If it's done, drain and pour onto a plate.

7 Just before you serve the sauce, add the capers, making sure they're drained from the water or vinegar they were in, give the sauce a good season with salt and pepper and mix everything together one last time. Spoon the sauce over the spaghetti and eat it as seductively as possible. *Bellissimo!*

Per serving: *Calories 622 (From Fat 257); Fat 28.6g (Saturated 4.2g); Cholesterol Trace; Sodium 3000mg; Carbohydrate 75.3g, Dietary Fibre 9.0g; Protein 15.9g.*

Chapter 8

Eating the Right Food to Get You Going

In This Chapter

▶ Eating the right food to rev you up

▶ Feeding the little grey cells

▶ Building up your defences

*B*eing away from home for the first time is a great feeling, isn't it? You don't have to vacuum or change that perfectly good pair of four-day-old pants, and you can crawl back into your flat at five in the morning, knowing that you're not the last person in.

The trouble is, all this living to excess can take its toll on your health, particularly if your diet isn't too good. It's really easy to fall into a habit of rushing dinner or just grabbing a packet of crisps or a ready meal so you have more time to get ready for going out.

The truth is, at uni, contrary to what most people in society would have you believe, you can end up living a pretty active and busy life. In order to stay active and fight off the colds and flus that regularly sweep the campus, you need to eat the right food to keep your body topped up with everything it needs. So this chapter is all about meals that give you a boost, whether you need *energy* before a night out or a footie match, *brain food* for an exam or revision, or simply an all round *healthy option,* to keep you fighting fit when everyone around you isn't.

Best of all, these recipes are quick and straightforward to make. Aim to eat two of these dishes a week, and you'll be well on your way to living as full a uni experience as you can handle.

Eating Energy Food

Everyone needs a quick pick-me-up now and again, and instead of downing another energy drink, only to feel a caffeine crash later on, try going for one of these quick and healthy food fixes.

A lot of the dishes in this section are light meals. Big, heavy dishes can use a lot of energy to digest and can make you feel tired and sluggish. Lighter dishes keep you feeling full and alert.

ᘓSpinach and Chickpea Stew

If it's good enough for Popeye, it's good enough for you. Spinach, like many dark green vegetables, is stuffed with Vitamin B, which helps restore energy levels by replenishing vitamins used to fight stress. This is a great vegan meal but is also great for non-vegans too.

Don't worry if the amount of spinach seems like a lot; spinach is a most deceitful vegetable and shrinks dramatically when cooked.

Preparation time: 5 minutes

Cooking time: 15 minutes

Serves: 1

Glug of olive oil	2 handfuls of spinach, chopped
½ onion, peeled and chopped	1/2 mug of couscous
1 clove of garlic, peeled and chopped	Sprinkling of raisins (optional)
¼ tin of chickpeas, drained and rinsed	½ lemon
½ tin of chopped tomatoes	

1 Heat a drop of oil in a saucepan over a medium heat and, when hot, fry the onion and garlic.

2 When the onion softens, stir in the chickpeas, chopped tomatoes and spinach. Add the spinach one handful at a time – keep stirring until it shrinks into the tomato sauce.

3 While the mixture simmers, flick the kettle on and pour the couscous into a bowl. When the kettle's boiled, pour enough water over the couscous to cover it, and place a clean tea towel over the top of the bowl. The couscous will absorb the water and increase in size slightly.

4 After 10 minutes, check that the couscous has absorbed all the water. (No liquid should be left in the bottom of the bowl.) Fluff up the couscous with a fork and add the raisins, if using. (You can also drizzle some olive oil into it or fry the couscous in a little butter to make it more moist.)

5 Squeeze some lemon juice into the spinach and chickpea mixture and mix well.

6 Spoon the couscous onto a plate and then pour the spinach and chickpea stew over the top.

Per serving: Calories 1146 (From Fat 245); Fat 27.2g (Saturated 3.5g); Cholesterol Trace; Sodium 278mg; Carbohydrate 184.3g (Dietary Fibre 21.6g); Protein 41.1g.

Lamb and Sun-Dried Tomato Pasta

This is a delicious energy fix. Wholemeal pasta is a perfect energy booster, full of carbohydrates that are slowly broken down to release a stream of energy into your body.

Sun-dried tomatoes are a bit more expensive than usual tomatoes, but are so tasty, and really give this dish its flavour.

Preparation time: *5 minutes*

Cooking time: *15 minutes*

Serves: *1*

Glug of olive oil

½ onion, peeled and chopped

1 clove of garlic, peeled and chopped

200 grams of minced lamb (about 1 big handful)

1 mug of wholemeal pasta (penne or conchigli)

½ tin of chopped tomatoes

Small handful of sun-dried tomatoes, chopped

Pinch of dried mixed herbs

Salt and pepper

1 Fill a saucepan three-quarters full of water, pop the lid on and bring to the boil on the hob.

2 Heat the olive oil in a frying pan over a medium heat and fry the onion and garlic until the onion turns soft and translucent – about 5 minutes.

3 Add the minced lamb, breaking it up with your hands as you drop it in the frying pan. Using a spatula, keep breaking up the lamb in the pan until it's finely minced. Fry until it turns a light brown colour.

4 By now, the water should be boiling for the pasta. Add a pinch of salt and then add the pasta, giving it a stir to stop it sticking to the bottom of the pan.

5 Add the chopped tomatoes and sun-dried tomatoes to the lamb and mix everything together. Turn down the heat to halfway and gently simmer.

6 After 10 minutes, check to see if the pasta is cooked (by tasting a bit). If it is, drain through a colander and pour back into the saucepan.

7 Spoon or pour the lamb from the frying pan into the saucepan with the pasta in. Add a pinch of mixed herbs, some salt and pepper and mix well.

8 Spoon onto a plate and enjoy.

Variation: *You can use minced beef or pork rather than lamb for this recipe, and also add a dash of red wine to give a slightly richer flavour.*

Per serving: *Calories 1564 (From Fat 490); Fat 54.4g (Saturated 14.6g); Cholesterol Trace; Sodium 1975mg; Carbohydrate 191.4g (Dietary Fibre 28.7g); Protein 77.1g.*

Asparagus and Mushroom Risotto

Asparagus, like spinach, is a great energy food and is packed with loads of helpful nutrients your body needs. You can get hold of asparagus throughout spring and summer, but the best time to buy it is between May and June when it's picked in Britain.

Risotto is a thick and creamy rice dish. Some people think it's difficult to make, but I think risotto is dead straightforward. Follow this recipe, and I'll take you step by step to the perfect risotto.

 To prepare asparagus, chop off the white, slightly harder stem of the asparagus and carefully trim off any large sprouting leaves from the stalk.

Preparation time: *5 minutes*

Cooking time: *20 minutes*

Serves: *1*

Butter

½ onion, peeled and chopped

3 mushrooms, washed and sliced

700 millilitres of hot vegetable stock

1 cup of arborio rice

1 clove of garlic, peeled and chopped

4 asparagus spears, prepared and chopped in half

Pinch of dried mixed herbs

½ lemon

Salt and pepper

1 Heat a chunk of butter in a small saucepan over a medium heat. When melted, add the onions and mushrooms and gently fry.

2 When the onions have softened, pour in the rice, stir and then add just enough vegetable stock to cover the rice. Now, the trick is to keep stirring the rice to stop it from sticking to the bottom of the pan and to make sure that the rice absorbs the stock.

3 When the liquid in the saucepan starts to disappear, add in just enough to cover the rice again. Keep adding stock and stirring until you have only a small amount of stock left.

4 Grab a frying pan and melt another chunk of butter. Add the chopped garlic and fry for half a minute. (Remember to keep stirring the risotto in the other pan and adding stock when needed.)

5 After a couple of minutes, add the asparagus to the garlic and fry until the spears turn bright green and tender.

6 Back in the risotto pan, the stock should be completely absorbed into the rice and the rice should be nice and creamy. Add a pinch of mixed herbs and a squeeze of lemon juice, mix well and spoon onto a plate. Place the fried asparagus on top and tuck in.

Per serving: *Calories 876 (From Fat 242); Fat 26.9g (Saturated 15.7g); Cholesterol Trace; Sodium 3701mg; Carbohydrate 140.4g (Dietary Fibre 2.8g); Protein 18.0g.*

Lamb Fattoush

Fattoush is a Middle Eastern salad that uses up any leftover or stale pitta bread. I've added some cubed lamb to make it a slightly meatier dish that's more of a meal than a salad, but you can have it without, or swap the lamb for another kind of meat. Feel free to use a different selection of vegetables here too.

Preparation time: *10 minutes*

Cooking time: *20 minutes*

Serves: *1*

1 pitta bread, toasted and torn into small strips

150 grams (handful) of cubed lamb

¼ cucumber, chopped

6 to 8 cherry tomatoes, sliced in half

¼ red onion, peeled and finely chopped

Bunch of fresh parsley, finely chopped

Olive oil

1 Heat the grill to full power. Place the cubed lamb underneath and grill until brown on all sides and cooked all the way through (about 10 minutes). Check by cutting one of the thickest pieces open and seeing if the juices run clear.

2 While the lamb is grilling, mix all the other ingredients in a bowl except for the olive oil.

3 When the lamb is cooked, add it to the other ingredients in the bowl, mix well and drizzle with olive oil.

4 Pour onto a plate and eat.

Per serving: Calories 628 (From Fat 261); Fat 29.0g (Saturated 7.4g); Cholesterol Trace; Sodium 285mg; Carbohydrate 44.3g (Dietary Fibre 5.7g); Protein 47.5g.

⌣Sweet Potato and Red Onion Wrap

Sweet potatoes are packed full of vitamins, have antioxidant properties and also help aid in muscle recovery when you're working out. Oh, and they're pretty tasty too, which make them an ideal candidate for this wrap.

Preparation time: 5 minutes

Cooking time: 20 minutes

Serves: 1

Olive oil

½ red onion, peeled and chopped into chunks

1 sweet potato, peeled and chopped into chunks

1 spoonful of honey

1 cup of couscous

2 tortilla wraps

Handful of chopped coriander or mint (optional)

Small tub of Greek yogurt

1 Preheat the oven to 180°C. Drizzle a baking tray with olive oil and add the chunks of sweet potato and red onion. Drizzle a spoonful of honey over the pieces and place the baking tray in the oven.

2 After 10 minutes, pop the kettle on and put the couscous in a bowl. Pour over enough boiling water to cover the couscous, lay a clean tea towel on top and leave for 10 minutes so that the couscous can absorb the water. Give the potatoes and onions a quick stir and shake to stop them sticking to the baking tray.

3 When the couscous has absorbed all the water, fluff it up with a fork.

4 When the sweet potato and onion have cooked (about 20 to 25 minutes), heat the tortilla wraps according to the packet instructions and spoon the couscous into the middle of the wraps. Put the sweet potato and onion on top of the couscous.

5 Add the chopped coriander or mint (if using) to the Greek yogurt and drizzle over the tortilla filling.

6 Wrap and eat.

Variation: Try sprinkling cumin seeds over the sweet potato and onion before you roast them to give them a warm, aromatic flavour.

Per serving: Calories 1606 (From Fat 240); Fat 26.7g (Saturated 7.8g); Cholesterol Trace; Sodium 909mg; Carbohydrate 294.4g (Dietary Fibre 19.7g); Protein 46.9g.

Pork Stir-Fry with Brown Rice

Brown rice, like wholemeal pasta, is another great energy releaser, and with the pork's protein, makes this a good all round healthy meal.

I'm going to show you how to cook rice to make it fluffier and stickier than the rice we usually cook in Britain. This method involves adding only a small amount of water and steaming the rice rather than boiling it. White rice usually works best, but doesn't have the same fibre and energy content that brown rice has. Also, brown rice takes a lot longer to cook than white (30 to 40 minutes rather than 15 to 20 minutes), so if you choose white rice, halve the cooking time and add a bit less water.

Preparation time: 5 minutes

Cooking time: 20 minutes

Serves: 1

For the rice:

1/2 mug of brown rice

2 mugs of water

For the sauce:

2 teaspoons of cornflour

1 teaspoon of caster sugar

Soy sauce

For the stir-fry:

150 grams (big handful) of cubed pork

Selection of chopped vegetables (red pepper, celery, baby sweetcorn)

Groundnut oil

1 Pour the rice into a small saucepan and add the water, stirring once to make sure it's all mixed together. Put the lid on and bring to the boil.

2 When the water's boiling, turn down the heat to about 3 if you're using electric, or a very low heat if you're using gas. Keep the lid on and leave it alone. Limit the number of times you check on the rice because doing so lets out the steam and prevents the rice from cooking properly.

3 After about 10 minutes, add the cornflour, sugar and soy sauce into a bowl and add 3 spoonfuls of water. Mix together to create a sauce.

4 Heat a drop of groundnut oil in a frying pan over a medium to high heat and, when hot, add the pork. Fry the pork until it turns a light brown colour.

5 Add the other vegetables and then pour in the sauce. Stir and fry until the pork is cooked. (Check by cutting the thickest piece open and seeing if the juices run clear.)

6 Check to see if the rice is cooked 30 minutes after you put it in the saucepan. Hardly any water should be left in the pan, and the rice should be fairly fluffy and soft.

7 Spoon the rice onto a plate and add the pork and vegetables on top. Eat.

Per serving: *Calories 1085 (From Fat 188); Fat 20.9g (Saturated 5.1g); Cholesterol Trace; Sodium 1020mg; Carbohydrate 157.4 (Dietary Fibre 10.7 g); Protein 66.8g.*

Building Up Brain Food

Fish is pretty much the best brain food you can have, so a lot of the recipes in this section include, yep, you've guessed it, fish. Fish is full of omega-3 fatty acids, exactly what the brain needs to operate effectively, is high in protein and, unlike a lot of meat, low in fat.

Plus, fish is incredibly easy to cook. Most of the time, you can wrap the fish in foil and whack it in the oven, leaving it to cook while you watch a bit of telly.

I also include some tasty meat and vegan recipes to help you get through your exams and improve your, erm, memory.

Spiced Tilapia

Tilapia is a freshwater fish sold by most fishmongers. Like other freshwater fish, it doesn't have a strong fishy taste, but takes on the flavour of whatever you cook it with. So you're going to add some cumin to give it a really warming, aromatic flavour.

When you buy tilapia, ask your fishmonger to clean (gut) it and (if it freaks you out a bit) take the head off.

Preparation time: 5 minutes

Cooking time: 30 minutes

Serves: 1

1 tilapia, gutted	Sweet chilli dipping sauce
1 lime	Ground cumin
Olive oil	75 millilitres of hot vegetable stock

1 Preheat the oven to 200°C.

2 Cut a piece of kitchen foil big enough to wrap the fish in. Fold up the edges so that when you put the stock in it doesn't spill out and place on a baking tray.

3 Wash the fish out under a trickle of cold water and then score slits in each side of the fish.

4 Cut the lime into slices and place inside the fish.

5 Mix one teaspoon of olive oil with two teaspoons of the sweet chilli dipping sauce and a pinch of ground cumin. Spoon the mixture over both sides of the tilapia, rubbing some of it into the slits.

6 Place the fish on the foil and pour in the hot vegetable stock.

7 Seal up the foil parcel and place the baking tray in the oven. Bake for around 25 to 30 minutes or until the fish is cooked. To check, open up the parcel and pull a bit of the flesh away from the fish with a fork. If it comes off easily and the juices run clear, the fish is cooked. If not, put it back in the oven for 5 minutes longer.

8 Use a fish slice or spatula to lift the tilapia from the kitchen foil and onto a plate. Serve with some vegetables or rice.

Per serving: *Calories 326 (From Fat 79); Fat 8.8g (Saturated 2.3g); Cholesterol Trace; Sodium 475mg; Carbohydrate 20.3g (Dietary Fibre 4.3g); Protein 41.4g.*

Lemon and Chilli Haddock

Here's another recipe that adds a bit of a spicy kick to fish, although this time the taste is a bit more powerful! Haddock is a perfect replacement for cod, whose levels are falling due to over-fishing.

Preparation time: *5 minutes*

Cooking time: *20 minutes*

Serves: *1*

1 slice of bread (brown or white), grated into breadcrumbs (or gently whizzed in a food processor)

Zest of 1 lemon (grate a lemon to get the lemon zest)

Pinch of dried chilli flakes or chopped fresh chilli

1 fillet of haddock (you choose the size depending on how hungry you are)

2 spoonfuls of mayonnaise

Lemon juice

1 Preheat the oven to 200°C.

2 Mix the breadcrumbs, lemon zest and chillies in a bowl.

3 Rinse the haddock fillet underneath a trickle of cold water and dry with a kitchen roll or just gently shake off the excess water.

4 Spoon a layer of mayonnaise over the top of the haddock and then sprinkle the breadcrumb mixture over the mayonnaise. Don't pile on the breadcrumbs too thickly; you just need a light coating.

5 Place on a baking tray and pop in the preheated oven for 20 minutes or until the fish is cooked. (To tell if the fish is cooked, try gently pulling at the fish with a fork; if it starts to flake, it's cooked.)

6 Squeeze over some lemon juice and serve with some roast vegetables or whatever else you fancy.

Per serving: *Calories 447 (From Fat 221); Fat 24.6g (Saturated 3.7g); Cholesterol Trace; Sodium 424mg; Carbohydrate 15.7g (Dietary Fibre 0.6g); Protein 40.7g.*

Salmon with Mango and Yogurt Dressing

Low in calories, high in protein and stuffed full of omega-3 essential fatty acids, salmon is super good for you. Well, it's time to make it even tastier with a cool Mango and Yogurt Dressing. This is a delicious and refreshing meal for a spring or summer's evening and is good for a bit of brain food.

Preparation time: *5 minutes*

Cooking time: *15 minutes*

Serves: *1*

1 salmon fillet

Olive oil

½ mango, peeled and chopped (see nearby sidebar for how to do this)

3–4 spoonfuls of Greek yogurt

½ lime

1 Preheat the grill to a medium to high setting.

2 Spoon over or brush the salmon with a little olive oil and then place on the grill and cook for about 10 to 15 minutes.

3 While that's cooking, add the chopped mango to the Greek yogurt and mix together.

4 After 10 minutes, check on the salmon. It should be nicely cooked, and very tender to the touch, so that it pulls apart easily with your fork. Carefully place onto your plate.

5 Squeeze the lime over the salmon, and cover with the Greek yogurt and mango. Eat with some roast vegetables, couscous or salad.

Per serving: Calories 591 (From Fat 236); Fat 26.2g (Saturated 6.6g); Cholesterol Trace; Sodium 186mg; Carbohydrate 43.5g (Dietary Fibre 7.9g); Protein 45.3g.

Spaghetti al Tonno

This recipe is basically spaghetti with tuna. But how classy does *spaghetti al tonno* sound? This is another very simple and straightforward dish that uses tuna rather than the usual minced beef for a lighter and healthier dish.

Preparation time: *5 minutes*

Cooking time: *15 minutes*

Serves: *1*

Handful of spaghetti	½ tin of chopped tomatoes
Olive oil	Handful of olives, sliced in half
1 clove of garlic, chopped	2 teaspoons of capers (available from most supermarkets)
½ tin of tuna	Salt and pepper

1 Fill a saucepan three-quarters full of water and place on the hob to bring to the boil. When it's boiling, add a pinch of salt and the spaghetti.

2 Heat a drop of olive oil in a frying pan over a medium heat. When hot, gently fry the garlic for half a minute.

3 When the garlic is just about starting to turn brown, flake the tuna in and add the chopped tomatoes, olives and capers. Mix well. Gently simmer, just enough to reduce the excess liquid from the tomato sauce.

4 After 10 minutes, taste a bit of the spaghetti and if it's done, drain and put onto a plate. Add the sauce over the top of the spaghetti, season with salt and pepper and eat.

Per serving: Calories 571 (From Fat 124); Fat 13.8g (Saturated 2.1g); Cholesterol Trace; Sodium 2021mg; Carbohydrate 79.9g (Dietary Fibre 7.1g); Protein 31.7g.

TIP

Preparing a mango

Have you seen mangoes in grocers and supermarkets but not really known what to do with one? They're easy to prepare and eat, I promise. Choose a mango that's not rock hard and that smells really good. Prepare the mango by holding the mango on its side and slicing it vertically into three pieces, with the middle piece containing the stone. Now take one of the end pieces and carefully slice off the skin, leaving the yellow flesh. Now chop the yellow flesh into small cubes. Repeat on the other half, leaving the middle section until last. As for the piece with the stone in, there's no really easy way to do this, just chop and carve as much mango as you can get from around the stone.

Chilli Chicken Goujons

These chicken goujons (or strips) are coated in tongue-tingling chilli powder, then fried and served with a cooling avocado and red pepper salsa. This is a fantastic light dish that you can nibble on while you're revising.

See Chapter 5 for info on how to prepare an avocado.

Preparation time: *10 minutes*

Cooking time: *15 minutes*

Serves: *1*

2 teaspoons of plain flour

1 teaspoon of chilli powder

100 grams chicken goujons (about 4)

Olive oil

½ avocado, stone and skin removed, chopped into small pieces

½ red pepper, chopped into small pieces

2 spring onions, finely chopped

½ lime

1 Spoon the flour onto a plate and mix in the chilli powder. Dip the chicken goujons into the flour, coating them in the spicy mixture. Place onto a separate plate.

2 Heat a glug of oil in a frying pan over a medium heat and, when hot, add the chicken strips.

3 While they're frying, mix the avocado, pepper and spring onions in a bowl.

4 When the chicken's turned brown on one side, flip the pieces over and fry the other side.

5 When the chicken is cooked all the way through (around 15 minutes – check by cutting open the thickest piece – it should be white, with any juices running clear), put on a plate and add the salsa to one side. Squeeze over the lime juice and eat.

Tip: *If you can't get any chicken goujons, buy a chicken breast and lay it out on a clean chopping board (one you use for meat). Using a rolling pin, fist or some other heavy implement, bash the chicken breast until it is half as thick as before and slice it into pieces.*

Per serving: *Calories 753 (From Fat 474); Fat 52.7g (Saturated 8.6g); Cholesterol Trace; Sodium 655mg; Carbohydrate 45.8g (Dietary Fibre 8.3g); Protein 23.8g.*

⟋Baby Spinach and Beetroot Salad

Here's a great vegetarian salad for a pretty much instant brain boost. Beetroot and spinach have high levels of iron, which is good for keeping mentally alert. Plus, this salad is very quick to prepare and needs no cooking.

You can buy cooked beetroot in supermarkets (vacuum-wrapped and looking juicy).

Preparation time: *10 minutes*

Cooking time: *Nil*

Serves: *1*

½ bag of baby spinach (or 2 big handfuls)

2 cooked beetroot, chopped into cubes

1 apple, cored and chopped into cubes

4 cherry tomatoes, sliced in half

½ celery stalk, sliced

For the dressing

1 spoonful of honey

2 spoonfuls of olive oil

1 Mix all the dry ingredients in a bowl.

2 Combine the honey and olive oil in a cup and spoon over the salad. Yum!

Variation: *If you're not vegetarian, try adding some cooked chicken.*

Per serving: *Calories 374 (From Fat 188); Fat 20.9g (Saturated 3.0g); Cholesterol Trace; Sodium 156mg; Carbohydrate 42.4g (Dietary Fibre 7.3g); Protein 4.0g.*

Food to Fight Off Fresher Flu

With the onslaught of a fresh intake of students every September comes a wave of germs, making the annoying fresher flu as predictable as the fire alarm going off when you first use the toaster.

You need a neat arsenal of ultra-healthy recipes to fight off any infections and diseases milling around campus, and you can find them in this section. Many of the recipes here are vegetarian and vegan, because substituting meat for vegetables usually ends up being a healthier option, and an easy way of getting more nutritious goodness into your body.

⟳Roast Tomato and Aubergine Spaghetti

This spaghetti is a lot lighter than usual because it skips out a sauce and uses instead a selection of roast vegetables. This recipe is very easy to make because the oven and the hob do 90 per cent of the work while you can sit back and relax.

Preparation time: *5 minutes*

Cooking time: *25 minutes*

Serves: *1*

Olive oil

½ aubergine, cut into cubes

½ courgette, sliced

4 cherry tomatoes, sliced in half

Handful of spaghetti

Salt

Handful of mozzarella, sliced into small cubes

Small handful of chopped basil (optional)

1 Preheat the oven to 200°C.

2 Drizzle olive oil over a baking tray and scatter the courgette and cherry tomatoes onto it, coating them in the oil. Add the aubergines, a drizzle more oil and a light scattering of salt and place in the pre-heated oven.

3 After 10 minutes, fill a saucepan three-quarters full of water, put on the hob and bring to the boil.

4 Add a pinch of salt and the spaghetti. Cook the spaghetti for 10 minutes or until cooked.

5 Drain the spaghetti and pour back into the empty saucepan. Remove the roast vegetables from the oven and pour into the spaghetti. Add the chunks of mozzarella (and basil if you're using any) and mix together. Pour into a bowl and eat.

Per serving: Calories 849 (From Fat 386); Fat 42.9g (Saturated 17.1g); Cholesterol Trace; Sodium 492mg; Carbohydrate 79.4g (Dietary Fibre 7.7g); Protein 36.2g.

◌Vegetable Tagine

This vegetable dish is cooked in a rich tomato sauce. This is a great winter warmer, full of vegetable goodness and is a cheaper alternative to something meaty, such as a beef stew.

Preparation time: *5 minutes*

Cooking time: *20 minutes*

Serves: *1*

Olive oil

½ onion, peeled and sliced

½ aubergine, cut into cubes

½ courgette, sliced

½ tin of chopped tomatoes

½ tin of chickpeas

Pinch of mixed herbs

Salt and pepper

1 cup of couscous

1 Grab a saucepan and heat a glug of olive oil over a medium heat. Add the onion and gently fry.

2 When the onion softens, add the aubergine and courgette and fry. The aubergine absorbs a lot of the oil, so add a drop more if needed. Fry for about 5 minutes, or until the courgette starts to turn slightly brown.

3 Add the chopped tomatoes, chickpeas and mixed herbs, season, stir together and turn the heat down to a light simmer.

4 Put the couscous into a bowl and pour over boiling water, just enough to cover the couscous. Lay a clean tea towel over the top, trapping the steam in the bowl.

5 After 10 minutes, remove the tea towel and fluff up the couscous with a fork. Spoon it onto a plate, then add the vegetables and enjoy.

Variation: *Try roasting some pine nuts in a dry pan and adding them to the couscous. Or try sprinkling some cinnamon over the couscous and frying it in a little butter when it's cooked.*

Per serving: *Calories 1685 (From Fat 299); Fat 33.2g (Saturated 4.2g); Cholesterol Trace; Sodium 262mg; Carbohydrate 272.5g (Dietary Fibre 37.3g); Protein 74.0g.*

Healthy Chicken Curry

I'm a firm believer in the wonders of a good curry when you're bunged up with a cold. Thankfully, you don't have to make a trip to your local Indian restaurant or even pick up the phone for a takeaway, because this chicken curry is easy to make from scratch and works out a lot cheaper.

Preparation time: 10 minutes

Cooking time: 20 minutes

Serves: 1

½ mug of rice

Olive oil

½ onion, peeled and chopped

1 teaspoon of curry paste

1 chicken breast, cut into bite-sized chunks

1 carrot, peeled and sliced

3 or 4 florets of broccoli

150 millilitres of chicken stock

150 millilitres of coconut milk

1 teaspoon of hot curry powder

1 Pour the rice into a saucepan and add a mug of water. (If you've doubled the quantities of rice, make sure to double the quantity of water). Turn on the hob to full power to bring the water to boil.

2 Heat a glug of oil in a frying pan and add the onion. Fry until the onion turns soft and translucent.

3 Stir in the curry paste and then add the chicken pieces. Fry the chicken until it turns white.

4 By now, the water for the rice should be boiling. As soon as it starts boiling, put the lid on, turn the heat right down and let it boil away. Don't remove the lid during cooking because it'll let all the steam out.

5 Add the carrots and broccoli to the frying pan and fry for about a minute. Then add the chicken stock and coconut milk and mix together. Turn the heat down and simmer for 15 minutes.

6 After 15 minutes, stir in the hot curry powder and check on the rice. It should be nice and fluffy. (If it's still a little wet, keep cooking for a bit longer.) Check that the chicken is cooked by cutting the thickest bit open to see if it's completely white inside.

7 Spoon the rice onto a plate and add the chicken curry on top. Eat with some naan bread.

Per serving: Calories 1558 (From Fat 266); Fat 29.5g (Saturated 5.0g); Cholesterol Trace; Sodium 1098mg; Carbohydrate 230.0g (Dietary Fibre 10.5g); Protein 93.1g.

⟡Spicy Lentils

Lentils are a great vegetarian source of protein and are also high in potassium, fibre and all other sorts of good stuff. This spicy lentil recipe is relatively easy to make and goes nicely with a bit of chunky bread.

Preparation time: *10 minutes*

Cooking time: *25 minutes*

Serves: *1*

70 grams (about ¾ mug) of puy lentils

½ onion, peeled and chopped

Pinch of ground cumin

Pinch of paprika

2 spoonfuls of tomato purée

50 grams (handful) of feta cheese, crumbled

Handful of fresh coriander, chopped (optional)

Olive oil

1 Fill a saucepan three-quarters full of water and place on the hob to bring to the boil. When it's boiling, add the lentils, turn down the heat to a simmer and cover with the lid. Simmer for about 20 minutes, or until the lentils are soft.

2 After 15 minutes, add a drop of oil to a frying pan and fry the onion until soft. Add the ground cumin and paprika and fry for another couple of minutes.

3 By now the lentils should be cooked, so drain them in a colander and then add them to the frying pan. Add ¼ mug of water and the tomato purée and mix well.

4 Crumble in the feta cheese, add the coriander (if using) and spoon onto a plate. Serve with bread as a light dish, or with roast root vegetables for something more substantial.

Per serving: Calories 463 (From Fat 113); Fat 12.5g (Saturated 7.2g); Cholesterol Trace; Sodium 983mg; Carbohydrate 58.3g (Dietary Fibre 25.1g); Protein 29.3g.

Chapter 9

Mastering Microwave Cooking

*E*r, microwave cooking? Isn't this supposed to be a healthy student cookbook? You betcha. Microwaves are actually far healthier than you might think; it's the unhealthy ready meals you put in them that give microwaves a bad reputation. Microwaves cook food in a completely different way to conventional ovens, as I explain a bit later, and often keep more of the nutrients in food than when using other methods. Pretty much every student kitchen has a microwave, even if you're in catered accommodation, and it's an invaluable tool. You can do so much more with your microwave than simply reheat food. You can use that little box in the corner of the kitchen to cook vegetables, steam rice, bake a jacket potato and even cook fish. I also show you how to make some delicious puddings in the microwave.

So in this chapter, I give the humble microwave a bit of a renaissance. Far from being the enemy of healthy eating, microwaves are useful little appliances that can give you a helping hand when you're cooking on a budget in a really basic kitchen.

Delving Deeper into Microwave Cooking

Microwave cooking is a quick and practical way of cooking when you're pressed for time or just don't have any other alternatives – maybe a flatmate is using up all the hob rings, or maybe you don't even have an oven in your kitchen.

Microwaves cook food by emitting waves of oscillating electromagnetic energy. These waves primarily affect *polar molecules,* molecules that are negatively charged at one end and positively charged at the other. Water is a polar molecule, so microwaves work by basically heating the water molecules present in food. This is why plates and plastics don't heat in the microwave, because they're made up of non-polar molecules. How about that for technical jargon to impress your flatmates?

A brief history of the microwave oven

The microwave oven was invented almost by accident in 1946 when Dr Percy Spencer was testing a device called a *magnetron,* essentially a massive microwave without a door. After testing the magnetron, he noticed that the chocolate bar he had in his pocket had melted. Fast-forward a year, and Dr Spencer had created the first commercial microwave, a 6-foot monster of a machine that dominated kitchens and scared dogs. By the 1970s, microwaves had shrunk in size to the proportions we're used to today and become an established kitchen appliance.

Depending on what you cook, microwave cooking can be more healthy than normal cooking. Microwaves cook vegetables in only a small amount of water, so more of the vitamins and nutrients stay in the vegetable instead of being lost in the water when you boil them on the hob. Fish is the same. Steaming or microwaving fish keeps most of the goodness within the fish as opposed to grilling or frying.

Some items and food don't go well in a microwave:

✔ Never put a metal container in a microwave, because it can damage the oven.

✔ Don't hard-boil eggs in the microwave because they explode (not big, not clever).

✔ Be very careful when heating liquids. Often, they don't appear to be boiling, but when you move the bowl, they erupt and spill over.

✔ Grapes and other fruit are very dangerous when put in a microwave due to their high water content, although I can't work out why anyone would want to warm up some grapes. . . .

✔ Because of the way microwaves work, food sometimes heats unevenly in the microwave. Always make sure food is piping hot from the middle of the dish right to the edge.

Making Home-Made Microwave Mains and Snacks

Cooking a full-blown meal in the microwave is pretty difficult because of the small space (with the exception of pre-made ready meals) but knocking up snacks and side dishes like rice and veg is a doddle.

So here are a few recipes that show how easy cooking side dishes and snacks in the microwave is. All the recipe times are based on an 800W microwave oven.

All-in-One Chilli Con Carne

This is an ultra-easy recipe for chilli con carne, especially if you only have a microwave available (often the case if you're in catered accommodation).

 The key things to bear in mind are to keep stopping and stirring during the cooking process, and making sure that the meat is cooked at the end.

Preparation time: *5 minutes*

Cooking time: *25 minutes*

Serves: *1*

150 grams lean minced beef

½ small onion, diced

½ green pepper, sliced

½ tin of chopped tomatoes

1 splodge of tomato purée

1 teaspoon chilli powder

½ tin of kidney beans, rinsed

120 millilitres of beef stock (from a stock cube)

1 clove of garlic, peeled and finely chopped

1 spoonful of cornflour

1 spoonful of chopped fresh coriander (optional)

1 Place all the ingredients (except for the coriander) into a microwave-proof casserole dish and mix well.

2 Place the dish in the microwave and cook on high power for 3 to 4 minutes. Then carefully remove the dish from the microwave and stir well.

3 Cover with a lid or cling film (remembering to pierce the cling film) and continue to cook for a further 10 minutes, stopping after every 5 minutes to stir again.

4 After 10 minutes, remove from the microwave, add the coriander (if using), stir well for one last time and then leave to stand for 2 to 3 minutes before eating. Make sure that the meat is brown and hot all the way through before serving.

Per serving: Calories 1082 (From Fat 260); Fat 28.9g (Saturated 10.8g); Cholesterol Trace; Sodium 918mg; Carbohydrate 125.5g; Dietary Fibre 36.5g; Protein 79.9g.

Baked Fish with Tomatoes and Broccoli

One of the best ways to cook fish is in the microwave, because the fish retains its flavour so well; plus it's very quick too.

Choose a fillet of fish that fits in your microwave and your microwaveable dish!

Preparation time: *5 minutes*

Cooking time: *10 minutes*

Serves: *1*

2 florets of broccoli

Olive oil

½ small onion, finely sliced

1 clove of garlic, finely chopped

1 teaspoon fresh parsley or chives (optional)

Fillet of skinned white fish (haddock, coley and so on)

Squeeze of lemon juice

Salt and pepper

½ tin of chopped tomatoes, drained, but reserve the juice

Pinch of sugar

1 Place the broccoli in a shallow bowl with 1 teaspoon of water, cover with cling film (remembering to pierce it slightly) and microwave for about 2 minutes. When done, the broccoli should still be very firm. Place to one side.

2 Place the oil, onion, garlic and herbs (if using) into a shallow microwaveable dish. Cover with cling film (remembering to pierce it a few times again) and cook on high power for 2 to 3 minutes, until the vegetables are soft. Carefully remove from the oven and stir well.

3 Place the fish on top of the vegetables, squeeze the lemon juice over it and add some salt and pepper. Place the broccoli around the fish. Put the drained tomatoes in a bowl, add the sugar and stir well. Add some of the reserved juice to give a thick sauce consistency. Spoon this over the fish.

4 Cover the dish again with pierced cling film and cook on high power for 5 to 6 minutes until the fish is cooked – you should be able to pull the flesh away with your fork, and the juices should run clear.

5 When the fish is cooked, carefully remove the dish from the microwave and allow to stand for 1 minute. Serve and eat.

Variation: If you don't have any fresh herbs, you could add some dried herbs when making the tomato sauce. Try using thyme, oregano or just some mixed herbs.

Per serving: Calories 446 (From Fat 207); Fat 23.0g (Saturated 3.2g); Cholesterol Trace; Sodium 339mg; Carbohydrate 16.9g; Dietary Fibre 4.8g; Protein 42.9g.

Microwaved Kedgeree

Kedgeree is a very old Scottish dish, originally made in the eighteenth century. I bring it up to date by nuking it in a microwave – it tastes just as good though!

Preparation time: 2 minutes

Cooking time: 15 minutes

Serves: 1

150 grams skinned smoked cod or haddock (a large handful)

½ mug of rice

180 millilitres of hot chicken or vegetable stock

Olive oil

1 teaspoon turmeric

Pinch of garam masala or curry powder (or use curry paste)

1 hard-boiled egg

1 teaspoon of chopped fresh parsley

Small chunk of butter

Salt and pepper

1 Place the fish in a microwaveable dish. Cover with cling film (remembering to pierce a few holes in the top) and cook on a medium high heat for 3 minutes until the fish is almost cooked. The fish should just be starting to flake when pulled at with a fork. Remove from the microwave and place to one side.

2 Pour the rice into a large microwaveable dish. Pour the boiling stock into the dish and add the oil, turmeric and garam masala (or curry powder or paste). Stir it all together and cook in the microwave on high power for 10 minutes. Give the rice a quick stir every 3 minutes.

3 After 10 minutes, give the rice another stir, reduce the power to medium and cook for a further 5 minutes.

4 Flake the fish into large pieces and roughly dice the egg.

5 When the rice is cooked, stir in the butter, season and carefully add the egg, fish and parsley. Tuck in.

Per serving: *Calories 944 (From Fat 407); Fat 45.2g (Saturated 15.4g); Cholesterol Trace; Sodium 2657mg; Carbohydrate 83.2g; Dietary Fibre 0.3g; Protein 51.1g.*

Toasted BLT Sandwich

This recipe cheats slightly because you use a toaster as well as a microwave *(shock, horror!)* but it's still a minimum utensil way of making a snack. Who knew you could cook bacon in the microwave?

Preparation time: *2 minutes*

Cooking time: *3–4 minutes*

Serves: *1*

3 rashers of bacon (rind removed)	*1 tomato, sliced*
2 slices of bread	*1–2 crisp lettuce leaves*
Butter	*2–3 teaspoons of mayonnaise*

1 Place the bacon rashers side by side on a plate and cover with a bit of kitchen roll. Cook in the microwave on high power for 1½ minutes.

2 Meanwhile, toast and butter the bread.

3 After 1½ minutes, check on the bacon. Put it back in the microwave and cook for another 30 seconds if it isn't quite done.

4 When cooked, remove from the microwave and leave to stand.

5 Spread one side of the toast with the mayo and top with the lettuce and tomato. Pop the bacon on top, cover with the other slice of toast and eat.

Per serving: *Calories 752 (From Fat 528); Fat 58.7g (Saturated 16.3g); Cholesterol Trace; Sodium 1962mg; Carbohydrate 34.4g; Dietary Fibre 2.5g; Protein 21.6g.*

⏲*Microwaving Jacket Potatoes*

You may already pop your jacket potato in the microwave for a couple of minutes before putting it in the oven as a way to speed up the baking process, but you can also use the microwave to do all the work for you. Just remember to pierce the potato with a fork a few times before microwaving to allow some of the steam to escape from the potato during the cooking process.

Preparation time: *30 seconds*

Cooking time: *5–7 minutes (depending on size of potato)*

Serves: *1*

1 potato, washed and dried

1 Pierce the potato a few times with a knife or fork.

2 Place the potato on a bit of kitchen paper in the microwave and cook on full power for 5 minutes.

3 After 5 minutes, carefully take it out of the microwave and check that it's fully cooked by pushing a knife into the potato, which should feel soft in the centre. If it isn't, place it back in the microwave for another minute before checking again.

4 Allow it to stand for 1 minute before splitting it open to enable the flavour to improve. Then eat away.

Tip: *Try topping your potato with some tinned tuna mixed with mayo and sweetcorn, or strips of bacon and cream cheese. Check out Chapter 6 as well for more ideas on what to stuff in your spud.*

Per serving: *Calories 158 (From Fat 4.0); Fat 0.4g (Saturated Trace); Cholesterol Trace; Sodium 14mg; Carbohydrate 34.4g; Dietary Fibre 2.6g; Protein 4.2g.*

ᴗ*Microwaving Eggs*

Eggs can be very, very dangerous if you microwave them incorrectly. But if you know what you're doing, they can be a tasty eggy treat. The key is to never, ever microwave eggs in their shells. They explode. And no, that's not a cue for you to try it. THEY EXPLODE IN YOUR FACE AND HURT. A LOT.

 Microwave your egg on no more than 700 watts (a medium setting on a typical 800W microwave). If the power setting is too high, you end up with a very rubbery egg, and no one wants that.

Allow the egg to stand for at least one minute after cooking. The egg continues to cook during this minute.

Preparation time: *2 minutes*

Cooking time: *2 minutes*

Serves: *1*

Olive oil   *1 egg*

1 Lightly oil a plate with some olive oil.

2 Break the egg onto the plate and carefully pierce the yolk (the yellow middle) with a knife or fork prongs. Cover the egg with another plate.

3 Microwave on medium power for 30 seconds and then check. If the egg isn't cooked, pop it back in the microwave for another 15 seconds. Allow the egg to stand for 1 minute before eating.

Per serving: *Calories 135 (From Fat 105); Fat 11.7g (Saturated 2.6g); Cholesterol Trace; Sodium 84mg; Carbohydrate Trace; Dietary Fibre Trace; Protein 7.5g.*

⟲Scrambled Eggs in the Microwave

Scrambled eggs are a great speedy snack and are perfect for breakfast. Microwaving eggs this way rather than cooking them on the hob saves you washing up the pan with all the sticky burnt bits. . . .

Preparation time: *1 minute*

Cooking time: *2–3 minutes*

Serves: *1*

2 eggs	*Small chunk of butter (optional)*
1 spoonful of milk	*Salt and pepper*

1 Crack the eggs into a microwaveable bowl and add the milk. Beat together with a fork, add a little salt, pepper and butter (if using).

2 Cook in the microwave for 30 seconds. Take the bowl out and whisk it a bit more and then pop it back in the microwave for another 30 seconds. Keep doing this until the eggs turn light and fluffy.

Per serving: Calories 415 (From Fat 348); Fat 38.7g (Saturated 19.8g); Cholesterol Trace; Sodium 435mg; Carbohydrate 0.9g; Dietary Fibre Trace; Protein 15.7g.

⟲Microwaving Rice

Microwaving rice is really speedy and perfect if you've ordered a takeaway and want to save some money by cooking your own rice.

Preparation time: *1 minute*

Cooking time: *15 minutes*

Serves: *1*

65 grams (half a mug) of rice	*Salt and pepper*
150 millilitres of boiling water or vegetable stock	

1 Place the rice in a large casserole dish with the boiling water or vegetable stock.

2 Cover with pierced cling film. Microwave on high power for 3 minutes.

3 Reduce the power to medium and cook for a further 8 minutes, stirring the rice every 2 minutes.

4 Allow to stand for 5 minutes at the end before fluffing with a fork and eating.

Variation: *Try adding some spices or curry paste to the boiling water or stock for some extra flavour.*

Per serving: *Calories 243 (From Fat 5); Fat 0.5g (Saturated Trace); Cholesterol Trace; Sodium 816mg; Carbohydrate 54.1g; Dietary Fibre Trace; Protein 5.4g.*

◌*Microwaving Vegetables*

Vegetables cook really well in the microwave. They're very quick to prepare and retain a lot of their nutrients, as opposed to boiling or roasting them. Table 9-1 shows a run down of a few different vegetables and how to cook them. All the cooking times are based on an 800W microwave running at full power. Remember to cover each bowl with some pierced cling film.

Table 9-1	Guide to Cooking Vegetables in the Microwave	
Vegetable	*How to Cook It*	*Time in Microwave*
Frozen peas	Use 1–2 tablespoons of water per bowl of veg.	1½–2 minutes
Green beans	Use 1–2 tablespoons of water per bowl of veg.	4–5 minutes
Broccoli, cauliflower	Use 1–2 tablespoons of water per bowl of veg.	8–10 minutes

(continued)

Table 9-1 *(continued)*

Vegetable	How to Cook It	Time in Microwave
Carrots	Use 6 tablespoons of water per bowl of veg.	8 minutes
Swede, butter-nut squash	Use 6 tablespoons of water per bowl of veg.	10–12 minutes
Turnip	Use 6 tablespoons of water per bowl of veg.	7 minutes
Spinach	Use 1 teaspoon of water per bowl of spinach, poured evenly over the spinach.	1–2 minutes
Cabbage and other leafy vegetables	Use 2–3 tablespoons of water per bowl of veg.	4–6 minutes

Whipping Up Micro-Puds

Picture the scene. You've invited a few friends round for dinner and made them a huge lasagne. It's the end of term, and they haven't really eaten for a week. They devour the lot and give you a look that says, 'Where's dessert?' Which is exactly what you're thinking, because you haven't made one.

Thankfully, help is at hand. This trusty section shows you how to whip up a delicious pudding in a flash, simply by using your humble microwave. Your friends will swoon at your microwaveable ingenuity.

⟳5-Minute Microwave Sponge Pudding

This is a great little recipe for making a sponge pudding in five minutes (well, maybe six).

You need to get the exact ingredient quantities in order for this recipe to work. You also need a Pyrex bowl for the pudding to sit in (you can buy one from most hardware shops or supermarkets for a couple of quid).

Preparation time: 3 minutes

Cooking time: 3 minutes

Serves: 2–3

1 large egg	85 grams of self-raising flour
85 grams of margarine	60 millilitres of milk
85 grams of caster sugar	

1 Mix all the ingredients together and pour into a Pyrex bowl.

2 Cook on high power for 3 minutes.

3 Leave to stand for 2 minutes before turning out onto a dish, covering with custard or cream and eating.

Variation: For a chocolate pudding, replace 15 grams of the self-raising flour with cocoa. Or for a coffee pudding, try adding 2 teaspoons of very strong instant coffee diluted with a small amount of boiling water.

Per serving: *Calories 452 (From Fat 226); Fat 25.1g (Saturated 10.6g); Cholesterol Trace; Sodium 399mg; Carbohydrate 51.5g; Dietary Fibre 0.9g; Protein 5.1g.*

⟨⟩Microwaveable Bread and Butter Pudding

Bread and butter pudding is another very old recipe brought up to date by cooking it in that box of microwaveable magic. This dessert is a good way of using up any stale (that doesn't mean mouldy) bread.

Although the preparation and cooking time for this dessert is relatively quick, you have to leave it to one side for about 30 minutes to an hour, so try to start making this before you eat dinner. By the time you've polished off the main course, you just need to pop the pudding in the microwave.

Preparation time: 10 minutes (plus 30 minutes' minimum standing time)

Cooking time: 8 minutes

Serves: 3–4

Butter for greasing the dish

6–8 slices of buttered bread (cut off the crusts if you prefer)

80 grams of mixed fruit or sultanas

4 eggs

450 millilitres of milk

4 tablespoons of crème fraîche

75 grams of sugar

1½ teaspoons of vanilla extract (find it in the home baking section in the supermarket)

1 teaspoon of mixed spice or ground cinnamon

Big spoonful of apricot jam (optional)

1 Grease a microwaveable dish with the butter.

2 Cut each slice of bread into 4 triangles by cutting a big 'X' through it.

3 Place a layer of the bread, buttered side up, in the bottom of the dish and sprinkle with some of the dried fruit. Put a layer of bread on top of the fruit.

4 Continue to build up the layers until all the dried fruit and bread has been used up. Finish with a layer of bread.

5 Beat the eggs, milk, crème fraîche, sugar, vanilla and mixed spice or cinnamon together. Carefully pour it all over the bread.

6 Leave to stand for 30 minutes to 1 hour. This waiting time allows the bread to soak up the liquid.

7 After the waiting time, place the dish in the microwave and cook on a medium heat for 7 to 8 minutes until it begins to set at the edges. If the edges haven't set after this time, continue to cook, but check after every minute.

8 Keep the dish in the microwave, but turn off the power. Allow to stand for 5 minutes. (It continues to cook and set in the centre during this time.)

9 If you like, melt some apricot jam in the microwave and brush the top of the pudding before serving.

Variation: *For extra creaminess and richness, replace half the milk with double cream. Or for an extra twist, spread the buttered bread with marmalade before layering. You can also use wholemeal bread or croissants for this dish too.*

Per serving: *Calories 533 (From Fat 174); Fat 19.3g (Saturated 9.7g); Cholesterol Trace; Sodium 460mg; Carbohydrate 72.4g; Dietary Fibre 1.7g; Protein 17.3g.*

Microwaveable Chocolate Chip and Orange Pudding

This recipe requires a little bit of preparation beforehand, but when the cooking time is only six minutes, you can let that slide. Plus the finished result is delicious.

You need a 1-litre pudding bowl to serve four to six people. If you're only serving two (or just yourself!), get a 500-millilitre bowl. You can buy one in most supermarkets pretty cheaply.

Preparation time: 5 minutes

Cooking time: 6 minutes

Serves: 4–6

100 grams of soft margarine (plus a bit more for greasing the bowl)

2 oranges

150 grams of self-raising flour

100 grams of caster sugar

2 eggs, beaten

100 grams of chocolate drops or chips

1 Grease the inside of the bowl with some margarine.

2 Peel one of the oranges and slice it into layers. The best way to do this is if you slice across the segments. Arrange the sliced orange in the bottom of the bowl.

3 Sift the flour (by pouring it through a colander or a sieve) into a separate mixing bowl. Add the rest of the margarine, sugar and eggs.

4 Grate the rind of the other orange and then chop the orange in half. Add the grated rind to the bowl with the flour mixture in it and squeeze in the juice from the orange, making sure no pips get through (squeeze through a slightly cupped hand.) Whisk everything together until it's smooth and thoroughly mixed.

5 Stir in the chocolate drops or chips.

6 Spoon the chocolate-orange mixture on top of the oranges in the microwaveable pudding bowl and smooth the top over.

7 Cook on high power for 4–5 minutes.

8 Allow to stand for about 2 minutes before turning it over and removing the bowl.

Per serving: Calories 421(From Fat 185); Fat 20.5g (Saturated 9.3g); Cholesterol Trace; Sodium 280mg; Carbohydrate 52.8g; Dietary Fibre 2.3g; Protein 6.3g.

⚬*Pears in Chocolate Sauce*

Here's a super-quick and cheap recipe for you.

 You can use the chocolate sauce for other puddings – drizzled over ice cream or a cake, or maybe over some waffles. Mmmm. Waffles.

Preparation time: *2 minutes*

Cooking time: *5 minutes*

Serves: *4*

150 grams of chocolate

6 spoonfuls of golden syrup

8 tinned pear halves, drained (but keep some of the juice)

1 Break the chocolate into small pieces and put into a microwaveable bowl.

2 Add the golden syrup and mix together.

3 Cook in the microwave on high power for 30 seconds. Carefully stir the mixture and then pop back in for another 30 seconds. Repeat until the sauce has melted and is thick enough to coat the back of the spoon.

4 Place the pears in a serving dish and add a little of the reserved juice. Then pour over the hot chocolate sauce and tuck in.

Variation: *Try adding a couple of scoops of vanilla ice cream for an extra indulgent pud.*

Per serving: Calories 348 (From Fat 96); Fat 10.7g (Saturated 6.3g); Cholesterol Trace; Sodium 68mg; Carbohydrate 60.7g; Dietary Fibre 3.6g; Protein 2.1g.

↻Rice Krispie Crunch

You can't beat a bit of childhood nostalgia, and this recipe takes you back to the days when Saturday morning kids' TV was actually good. This Rice Krispie Crunch is one big slab of crunchy chocolate goodness rather than the little cakes, but nothing's stopping you from adapting it slightly and pouring the mixture into a bun tin.

Preparation time: *2 minutes*

Cooking time: *3 minutes*

Serves: *3*

55 grams of sugar

55 grams of block margarine (not the stuff in the tubs)

85 grams of golden syrup

140 grams of Rice Krispies

1 Line a baking tray (about 30 centimetres by 20 centimetres) with some greaseproof paper.

2 Mix the sugar, margarine and syrup in a large bowl and pop in the microwave at full power until melted (about 30 to 45 seconds).

3 Stir well, place back in the microwave and cook for a further 2 minutes.

4 Remove the bowl and add the Rice Krispies. Mix everything together, tip onto the lined baking tray, smooth out the mixture with the back of a spoon and leave to set for about 45 minutes. (If your baking tray is too big, instead of making one shallow layer, use half the tray to create one smaller, thicker portion.) Cut into squares and store in a plastic container or eat a piece now!

Variation: *Try adding a handful of small marshmallows in with the sugar, margarine and syrup for a chewier treat!*

Per serving: *Calories 480 (From Fat 133); Fat 14.8g (Saturated 6.4g); Cholesterol Trace; Sodium 251mg; Carbohydrate 83.6g; Dietary Fibre 0.8g; Protein 3.1g.*

Chapter 10

Making the Most of Time and Money

In This Chapter

▶ Concocting meals in a jiffy

▶ Using up leftovers

▶ Finding inspiration online

Recipes in This Chapter

○ Stir-Fry in a Flash

▶ Quick Salmon and Couscous

▶ Smoked Salmon and Courgette Omelette

▶ Pasta in a Flash-sta

○ Cracked Taco Salad

🦐 🧄 🍲 🌶 🌿 🥕

*E*veryone knows students are constantly short of money, but what about time? Well, after the mid-morning lie in, two-hour lecture, aimless wander around the library, afternoon pint and football/netball/World of Warcraft game, you have very little time left in your busy day, especially for making something to eat before you go out to the pub in the evening.

So in this chapter, I show how to cut down the money you spend at the supermarket and the time you spend in the kitchen. It's not hard to do as long as you know a few tips and tricks along the way.

Making Meals in Under 10 Minutes

Some days you don't have time to think, let alone cook, and although microwaveable ready meals may seem the answer, they soon make big holes in your bank account, not to mention your health, as many of them are packed full of fat and salt. So keep these recipes up your sleeve so that you can make a meal in minutes.

✎Stir-Fry in a Flash

Stir-fries are exceptionally quick to make. You chop. You stir. You fry. You eat.

This is a very straightforward recipe, made extra simple to keep it under the ten-minute mark.

Chapter 7 has a recipe for a vegan stir-fry, which takes slightly longer to cook, but is just as tasty.

Preparation time: *2 minutes*

Cooking time: *10 minutes*

Serves: *1*

Selection of vegetables (carrots, broccoli, baby sweetcorn and so on)

Vegetable oil

Ready-to-cook stir-fry noodles (ones that you can cook in the frying pan)

Soy sauce or sweet chilli sauce

1 Chop up the vegetables into thin strips and heat a drop of oil in a pan over a high heat.

2 When the oil is very hot, add the vegetables a few at a time and stir.

3 Add the noodles and cook according to the packet instructions.

4 When the vegetables are nearly cooked, add a good shake of the soy sauce or chilli sauce, stir a bit more and then serve.

Per serving: *Calories 911 (From Fat 201); Fat 22.3g (Saturated 5.3g); Cholesterol Trace; Sodium 1101mg; Carbohydrate 149.1g; Dietary Fibre 9.1g; Protein 28.5g.*

Quick Salmon and Couscous

My love of couscous continues with this absolutely delicious and quick recipe. Salmon is so simple to cook and has a naturally delicate and scrumptious flavour. This dish makes a great lunchtime meal or a healthy and light dinner.

You might think salmon is an expensive fish, but if you buy it from a fishmonger, you can buy as little as you want, and many supermarkets have special offers on salmon.

Preparation time: *1 minute*

Cooking time: *10 minutes*

Serves: *1*

½ mug of couscous

Small handful of raisins

1 salmon fillet

Olive oil

1 Turn the grill on to a high setting.

2 Boil the kettle and pour the couscous and raisins into a bowl.

3 When the grill is hot, place the salmon on the grill tray and pour over a drizzle of olive oil. Place under the grill.

4 Pour the boiling water over the couscous to just cover it. Cover with a clean tea towel and leave for 10 minutes.

5 After around 5 minutes, take the salmon out from under the grill and check that it's cooked. The fish should just flake away with a fork and should be a nice light pink colour. If you don't think it's cooked, put it back under the grill for a couple more minutes.

6 Fluff up the couscous with a fork. Spoon onto a plate and place the salmon on top. Enjoy!

Variation: *For a slightly sweeter taste to the couscous, try stirring in some melted butter or olive oil.*

Per serving: *Calories 1298 (From Fat 301); Fat 33.4g (Saturated 5.4g); Cholesterol Trace; Sodium 134mg; Carbohydrate 182.5g; Dietary Fibre 10.8g; Protein 66.9g.*

Smoked Salmon and Courgette Omelette

Omelettes are a student's best friend (unless you don't like eggs, of course). They're very quick to make, and you can add whatever's left in your fridge. Well, probably not that horseradish sauce. Or that jar of pickled onions.

People think that smoked salmon is an expensive, indulgent ingredient, but you can pick it up for about £2 from the supermarket, and it'll make three or four meals. Bargain!

Preparation time: *2 minutes*

Cooking time: *10 minutes*

Serves: *1*

2 eggs	*Salt and pepper*
Handful of smoked salmon, chopped	*Small chunk of butter*
Handful of grated courgette	

1 Crack the eggs into a bowl and whisk until they're light and smooth.

2 Add the salmon, courgette, salt and pepper and whisk again.

3 Heat the butter in a frying pan over a medium to high heat.

4 When the butter's melted, pour the omelette mixture into the frying pan and bring to a simmer.

5 Simmer until the mixture turns solid – shake the pan to see if the omelette slides about a bit. If it does, flip it over. (An easy way to do this is to put a plate over the top of the frying pan and then turn the pan over. Slide the omelette back into the pan, so the other side is facing up. If it doesn't slide about, you can also flip the omelette in half, then turn down the heat and let it cook on one side for about a minute, then flip it and cook the other side for a minute more.)

6 Fry again for another 2 minutes until slightly golden brown, then slide onto a plate and eat.

Per serving: Calories 536 (From Fat 352); Fat 39.1g (Saturated 17.8g); Cholesterol Trace; Sodium 2280mg; Carbohydrate 2.8g; Dietary Fibre 1.3g; Protein 43.3g.

Pasta in a Flash-sta

This dish is very straightforward to make and just borders on the 10-minute mark. It's fantastic before a footie match or stint at the gym.

Preparation time: 1 minute

Cooking time: 10 minutes

Serves: 1

Salt

1 mug of penne pasta

Handful of cooked chicken

3 spoonfuls of sun-dried tomato pesto

1 spoonful of mascarpone (optional)

1 Pour boiling water into a saucepan and put on the hob over a high heat. Add a pinch of salt and the pasta. Place the lid back on to bring back to the boil quickly and stir.

2 Cook the pasta for about 10 minutes and then drain through a colander.

3 Add in the cooked chicken, sun-dried tomato pesto and mascarpone, if using. Stir everything together, spoon onto a plate and serve.

Per serving: Calories 1036 (From Fat 317); Fat 35.2g (Saturated 10.7g); Cholesterol Trace; Sodium 780mg; Carbohydrate 113.5g; Dietary Fibre 1.9g; Protein 66.3g.

♻*Cracked Taco Salad*

This is a great dish for the summer months; a leafy green salad tossed with fresh vegetables and broken pieces of taco shells with no cooking involved.

Preparation time: 10 minutes

Cooking time: Nil

Serves: 1

1 taco shell, broken into pieces

Handful of lettuce leaves or a rocket salad

Half a cup of tinned cannellini beans

½ red onion, finely chopped

2 spoonfuls of tinned sweetcorn

1 tomato, chopped into chunks

Small piece of cucumber, diced (chopped into small chunks)

Combine all the ingredients together and eat.

Variation: Feel free to drizzle a bit of dressing over this. Mix some honey and lemon together with a drop of water, or mix a couple of tablespoons of mayonnaise with a tablespoon of white wine vinegar and drizzle it over the salad.

Per serving: Calories 287 (From Fat 95); Fat 10.6g (Saturated 3.7g); Cholesterol Trace; Sodium 283mg; Carbohydrate 37.8g; Dietary Fibre 4.5g; Protein 10.0g.

Making the Most of Leftovers

If you've just spent your last three quid on food to last you the week, you don't want to waste a single penny or morsel. Whether you have some leftover shepherd's pie or bread that's going a bit stale, chances are you can eke it out into another meal, meaning you spend less money the next week and end up using everything in your cupboards and fridge (very environmentally friendly!).

Short of rummaging through the bin, you'd be amazed at how much food you can re-use. In this section, I share a few tips to help you get the most out of your food.

Using up fruit and vegetables

Fruit and vegetables are very easy to use up. If you have any vegetables that are going a bit soft and past their best, one of the simplest ways to use them up and make enough lunches to last you a week is by turning them into a soup. You can find loads of great soup recipes in the other chapters in this book, but here's a quick recipe that you can use for a mix of soft vegetables:

1 Peel the vegetables and boil them in salted water for 20 minutes, or roast them in the oven at 180°C for 30 minutes.

2 Drain the vegetables and put them in a blender with 300–500 millilitres of vegetable stock and blend until thick. (If you don't have a blender, chop up the vegetables really finely and boil them in the vegetable stock. You may need to add some cornflour to thicken it up a little.)

Vegetables are good for blending into soups, and fruit is great for making into smoothies. Don't throw soft and bruised bananas away; blend them together to make a delicious smoothie. (Check out Chapter 4 for some cool recipes to try.)

Here's a recipe for how to use up any less-than-great bananas, strawberries, blueberries, kiwi fruit or blackberries you may have in a tasty smoothie:

1 Chuck the fruit in a blender.

2 Add a cup or two of orange or any other fruit juice.

3 Add a cup of ice cubes.

4 Add a little honey or brown sugar to sweeten things up a little.

5 Blend until smooth and then drink.

Using up leftover meat

One of the best ways to get the most out of meat is to buy a whole joint, cook and eat what you want in a roast dinner and then use the rest of the meat throughout the week. Talk to your butcher for recipe ideas, and here's a rough guide, with recipes you can try in the other chapters in this book.

Of course, cooked beef, lamb, pork and chicken always go nicely in a sarnie.

Chicken

Buy a whole chicken and roast it (check out Chapter 13 to find out how). Then choose one of these recipes to use up your leftover chicken:

- ✔ Honey and Tarragon Chicken on Toasted Ciabattas (Chapter 5).
- ✔ Chicken and Avocado Salad (Chapter 5).
- ✔ Healthy Chicken Curry (Chapter 8).

Beef

Several different joints of beef give you value for money (ask your butcher for the different options), but to get you started, take a peek at Chapter 13 and have a go at the Beef Brisket recipe.

Buy a bigger joint and have meat leftover to last you throughout the week using these recipes:

- ✔ Skint Shepherd's Pie (Chapter 7). Swap the mutton for leftover beef and, hey presto, you have a cottage pie.
- ✔ Beef Tortilla Wrap (Chapter 12). Use finely chopped beef.

Lamb

Take a look at the Lamb Shank recipe in Chapter 13 to have a go at cooking a joint of lamb and use the following recipes to make the most of any leftover meat:

✔ Lamb and Sun-Dried Tomato Pasta (Chapter 8).

✔ Lamb Fattoush (Chapter 8). Swap the cubed lamb for strips of cooked lamb.

Pork

Lucky Chapter 13 has roast pork recipes; have a go at the tasty Pork Shoulder, then use the rest of the pork up in Pork Stir-Fry with Brown Rice (Chapter 8).

Fish

You won't often have loads of fish left over unless you bought a whale, but if you do, use it in pies or fish cakes:

✔ Smoked Haddock Fish Cakes (Chapter 7). You don't have to have leftover smoked haddock to make these; they work well with any kind of fish.

✔ Fish Stew (Chapter 7).

✔ Smoked Fish Pie (Chapter 12).

Going online for inspiration

Loads of resources on the Internet can help you get the most out of your food (and money) and reduce the amount you throw away. Here's the best of the bunch:

✔ **www.lovefoodhatewaste.com.** This site is full of useful information about how to use any food you have leftover, including step-by-step recipes and videos. You can find sections on portion control, how to store food and how to save time and money.

✔ **www.stilltasty.com.** This is a fantastic website. Simply type in the food you have left over in the search bar, hit Enter and it tells you exactly how to store it, how long it keeps for, plus tips on how to make it last longer. The site also has a forum for asking and answering any questions you have, such as 'Does olive oil last longer if you store it in the fridge?' Interesting. . . .

✔ **www.frugalcooking.com.** Frugal cooking doesn't sound very exciting, but this is a useful blog from the States, regularly updated with recipes, hints and tips on making food last longer. One post was entitled 'Hedgehogs are tasty and frugal', so be careful. . . .

✔ **http://frugal-cooking.co.uk.** This British site has recipes divided into the usual categories – beef, chicken, lamb, vegetarian and so on. Plus you can send in your own recipes on how to eat on the cheap.

✔ **www.studentcooking.tv.** This site is my own simply outstanding (and award-winning) website. Packed full of recipes and videos on how to eat on the cheap at uni, and with an unbelievably witty blog, it's quite simply the best website ever to appear on the Internet. Fact.

Chapter 11

Decadent Desserts and Treats

In This Chapter

▶ Discovering decadent desserts

▶ Baking to win friends and influence people

▶ Enjoying fruity labours

*F*or some people, desserts are a quick afterthought; for others, they're the best part of a meal. Desserts can be a perfect end to a great dinner, that delicious sweet treat that leaves everyone's taste-buds lingering for more.

In this chapter, I cover the often overlooked area of making desserts and baking biscuits and cakes. Let me reassure you that you don't have to be part of the Women's Institute to fire off a few delicious brownies and a mean chocolate cake. Even if you're not a massive chocoholic or die-hard cake fan, I include plenty of recipes to tickle your tastebuds, whatever their preference may be.

When cooking, you can usually guesstimate and round quantities up and down, but for desserts, and baking in particular, you need to use exact quantities. It's worth investing in a cheap set of scales and a measuring jug.

So, clear away the empty plates and prepare for a few gasps of excitement and envy as you dish up dessert.

Naughty But Nice: Spoiling Yourself with Tempting Puddings

Welcome to full-fat, wall-to-wall tastebud blow-out, decadent with a capital *D* puddings, desserts and treats. Dig in.

⌒Chocolate Pots

They're pots (use ramekins or teacups). And they're full of chocolate. Need I say more?

Preparation time: *10 minutes*

Cooking time: *10 minutes (plus 3 hours in the fridge to set)*

Serves: *4*

1 orange, plus zest	*2 egg yolks*
300 millilitres of single cream	*2 tablespoons of Baileys, Cointreau or orange juice*
200 grams of plain chocolate, broken into small pieces	*20 grams of butter*

1 Finely grate the orange to produce the zest.

2 Cut the orange into quarters. Carefully remove the skin. Break off the segments of orange, placing two small pieces or one big piece into the bottom of each pot. If the pieces are too wet, place on a bit of kitchen roll first, to get rid of any excessive juice.

3 Heat a small saucepan on a low to medium heat.

4 Pour in the cream and heat it up, but don't allow it to boil.

5 Add the broken chocolate to the cream and heat until it melts. (The smaller the pieces, the quicker they melt.) Keep stirring until the mixture is smooth.

6 Add the egg yolks.

7 Pour in the alcohol or orange juice and lightly whisk to combine the ingredients.

8 Add in the butter and stir until it's completely blended in.

9 Pour the mixture into a jug and then carefully pour into each of your pots, over the orange segments.

10 Put the pots in the fridge for 3 hours (or better still, overnight) to set. Then serve.

Variation: *You can swap the orange for other fruit, such as raspberries, blueberries, sliced tinned pears or defrosted frozen summer fruits.*

Per serving: *Calories 514 (From Fat 344); Fat 38.2g (Saturated 21.5g); Cholesterol Trace; Sodium 69mg; Carbohydrate 35.1g; Dietary Fibre 1.3g; Protein 7.4g.*

⌀Apple and Rhubarb Cobbler

A cobbler is both a person who mends shoes and, in this case, a fruit pie with a scone top. Rhubarb is harvested in Britain during the autumn and winter months, so this is a great dish to warm the cockles on a cold winter's night.

You need a 9x9-inch ovenproof dish for this one.

Preparation time: *15 minutes*

Cooking time: *20 minutes*

Serves: *4*

350 grams of apples, peeled, cored, and chopped into bite-sized pieces

40 grams of sugar, plus extra for topping

200 grams of fresh rhubarb, chopped into bite-sized pieces

200 grams of self-raising flour

55 grams of butter or margarine, softened in the microwave

55 grams of caster sugar

100 millilitres of milk

Pinch of salt

1 beaten egg with 2 tablespoons of milk in a bowl or cup

1 Preheat the oven to 180°C.

2 Grab a saucepan and add a couple of tablespoons of water. Add the apple pieces and half of the sugar and place the saucepan over a medium to low heat. Gently cook the apples for 5 minutes.

3 Add the rhubarb pieces and the rest of the sugar and cook for a further 5 minutes, stirring occasionally and adding more water if needed to stop the mixture from burning. Cook until the rhubarb softens. Taste to check the sweetness, adding a little more sugar if required. If it's sweet enough, remove the pan from the heat and leave to one side.

4 Mix the flour and butter or margarine together in a bowl with your fingers until it's the consistency of breadcrumbs.

5 Make a well in the centre and add the caster sugar and milk. Carefully fold in the flour mixture to make a light, soft dough. The dough should be a little sticky, but not too wet.

6 Roll out the dough onto a lightly floured chopping board or clean surface until it's about a centimetre thick and is the size of your ovenproof dish.

7 Place the apple and rhubarb mixture into the ovenproof dish and lay the scone dough on top.

8 Brush on the beaten egg and milk mixture and sprinkle with some sugar.

9 Place in the preheated oven for 25 minutes until the dough turns golden brown. Serve with ice cream or custard.

Per serving: *Calories 453 (From Fat 132); Fat 14.7g (Saturated 8.4g); Cholesterol Trace; Sodium 319mg; Carbohydrate 72.1g; Dietary Fibre 3.6g; Protein 8.0g.*

Separating an egg

Some recipes call for egg yolk or egg white, so you need to somehow separate them. Crack open the egg over a bowl and keep pouring the egg between the two shells, catching the yolk in the shell as the egg white drains into the bowl. Or the messier version is to crack the egg open and pour it through your hand, keeping your fingers slightly open, so that the egg white drains through, but the yolk stays in your palm.

ꙨBanana and Blueberry Pancakes

If you and your mates are still hungry after dinner, pancakes are a great way to fill up and are super-quick to make. You don't need many ingredients, so you probably already have everything you need in your cupboard.

Preparation time: 10 minutes

Cooking time: 10 minutes

Serves: 4

100 grams of plain flour	3 bananas, peeled and chopped
2 eggs	2 big handfuls of blueberries
Pinch of salt	Olive oil
200 millilitres of milk mixed with 75 millilitres of water	4 scoops of vanilla ice cream (optional)

1 Sift the flour into a bowl by gradually pouring it through a sieve or colander and tapping the side to break up the flour as it falls through.

2 Make a well in the centre of the flour and break the eggs into it.

3 With a fork or a whisk, whisk the eggs together, gradually incorporating the flour.

4 Add the salt and a drop of the milk and water mixture and keep whisking everything together until the liquid is absorbed by the flour. Keep whisking in all the milk and water until you have a smooth liquid.

5 Heat a drop of oil in a pan over a medium heat. Pour in just enough pancake mix to cover the base of the pan. Swirl the mixture around so it coats the pan evenly.

6 Leave the liquid to set for a couple of minutes and then try sliding a spatula underneath to lift it from the pan. If the pancake comes up easily, then it's ready to flip and cook the other side.

7 Clear a big space, start a drum-roll and then give the pan a preliminary shake to build up the tension. Flip the pancake or, if you're nervous, place a plate over the pan and turn it upside down to put the pancake on the plate. Shuffle the pancake off the plate and back into the pan, cooked-side facing up.

8 Cook the other side for about 30 seconds until nice and golden and pop on a plate.

9 Before starting on the next pancake, add a drop more oil to lubricate the pan.

10 Repeat the whole process until all the batter is used up.

11 Place some of the chopped bananas and blueberries in the middle of each pancake. Fold the pancake in half. Place the ice cream on the side of the plate and serve.

Variation: Try drizzling golden syrup or honey over your pancake and dusting it with icing sugar before serving. Other good fillings are strawberries, summer fruit, raspberries, ice cream, almonds and pecans.

Per serving: Calories 497 (From Fat 165); Fat 18.3g (Saturated 9.4g); Cholesterol Trace; Sodium 153mg; Carbohydrate 69.9g; Dietary Fibre 2.6g; Protein 13.1g.

⌒Knickerbocker Glory

Knickerbocker glory has nothing to do with pants and is instead a pretty extravagant ice cream in a tall glass: layers of ice cream, fruit and jelly all topped off with a big mound of squirty cream. You could add a personal touch by making the jelly yourself (or take the easy route and buy it pre-made), but either way, be a bit creative with this dessert to make it look amazing.

Preparation time: 10 minutes

Cooking time: Nil

Serves: 4

2 small tubs of pre-made jelly

8 scoops of ice cream

300 grams of fruit (bananas, blueberries, raspberries, strawberries or defrosted frozen summer fruit)

100 grams of flaked almonds

Squirty cream

Strawberry or chocolate sauce

Alternate layers of jelly, ice cream and fruit in each tall glass and finish it off with a big squirt of the squirty cream, flaked almonds and a drizzle of the sauce.

Variation: Top it all off with a cherry!

Per serving: Calories 643 (From Fat 368); Fat 40.9g (Saturated 17.8g); Cholesterol Trace; Sodium 172mg; Carbohydrate 56.6g; Dietary Fibre 3.3g; Protein 12.2g.

⟳Eton Mess

Originating from Eton College in Berkshire, this bizarre sounding pudding is a mixture of meringue pieces, strawberries and cream. And jolly spiffing it is too.

Preparation time: *10 minutes*

Cooking time: *None*

Serves: *4*

400 millilitres of double or whipping cream

200 grams of strawberries

2–3 drops of lemon juice

1 tablespoon of caster sugar

4 meringue nests (you can find them in the supermarket)

Grated chocolate (optional)

1 Pour the cream into a bowl and whisk until it thickens and forms soft peaks. Cover it with cling film and place it back in the fridge.

2 Cut the strawberries into quarters and place in another bowl. Sprinkle with the lemon juice and caster sugar and carefully mix to ensure that all the strawberries are coated. Allow to sit for 15 minutes.

3 Break the meringues into bite-sized pieces.

4 Take the cream out of the fridge and gently mix in the chopped strawberries. Add the broken meringue.

5 Place into glasses or serving bowls and sprinkle chocolate over the top (if using) and serve.

Variation: *Although strawberries are the traditional fruit to use in an Eton Mess, nothing's stopping you using raspberries, blueberries or kiwi fruit instead.*

Per serving: *Calories 594 (From Fat 497); Fat 55.2g (Saturated 34.3g); Cholesterol Trace; Sodium 37mg; Carbohydrate 21.4g; Dietary Fibre 0.7g; Protein 2.8g.*

Baked Beauties: Delicious Cakes, Buns and Other Treats

Baking probably isn't the first activity you think of when you have a spare afternoon at uni, but it's a good laugh, especially when flatmates are involved, plus you end up with an enviable selection of cookies, cakes and biscuits.

With baking, get the quantities right, otherwise the recipes don't work – no one wants a half-baked cookie!

⌒*White Chocolate Chip Brownies*

Brownies: food of the Gods. These delicious squares go down nicely during revision or sneakily munched during a lecture.

For this recipe you need a baking tray about 1 centimetre deep and 18 centimetres across, and some greaseproof paper.

Preparation time: *10 minutes*

Cooking time: *40 minutes*

Makes: *10*

115 grams of butter

115 grams of plain chocolate, broken into small pieces

2 tablespoons of cocoa powder

115 grams of plain flour

250 grams of caster sugar

Pinch of salt

1 teaspoon of vanilla essence (you can find this in the supermarket, in the cake and bakery aisle)

2 eggs

100 grams of white chocolate chips or 50 grams of white chocolate chips and 50 grams of chopped walnuts

1 Preheat the oven to 180°C.

2 Grease an 18-centimetre tin and line it with greaseproof paper.

3 Half fill a small saucepan with water and bring to a gentle simmer over a medium heat.

4 Place the butter and plain chocolate in a small heatproof bowl and place over the saucepan of simmering water. Stir the chocolate and butter until melted and smooth.

5 Carefully remove the bowl from the saucepan and leave it to cool slightly.

6 Meanwhile, place the cocoa powder and flour into a colander or sieve and sift into a separate bowl.

7 Stir the sugar, salt and vanilla essence into the slightly cooled melted chocolate.

8 Add the eggs, one at a time, and stir until blended.

9 Add the sifted flour and cocoa and whisk or stir together until smooth.

10 Stir in the chocolate chips (or chocolate chips and nuts).

11 Pour the mixture into the lined tin and bake in the preheated oven for 40 minutes.

12 Leave to cool before cutting up into brownie pieces and eating.

Tip: *Pop a brownie into the microwave and eat warm with vanilla ice cream.*

Per serving: *Calories 374 (From Fat 161); Fat 17.9g (Saturated 10.6g); Cholesterol Trace; Sodium 136mg; Carbohydrate 48.7g; Dietary Fibre 1.0g; Protein 4.6g.*

Greased lightening

Line baking tins with greaseproof paper or grease them with a bit of butter before pouring in any cake mixture to stop whatever you bake from sticking to the bottom during the cooking process. Lining a tin with greaseproof paper means that you can more easily lift what you've baked out of the tin.

⌒*Ultimate Chocolate Cake*

This is a great cake for birthdays or parties, or if you're just desperate for a big slab of chocolate.

For this recipe you need two sandwich tins (you can pick these up very cheaply in a hardware shop or big supermarket) and some greaseproof paper.

Preparation time: *15 minutes*

Cooking time: *30 minutes*

Serves: *10–12*

225 grams of caster sugar

200 grams of self-raising flour

110 grams of margarine

2 tablespoons of drinking chocolate or cocoa (cocoa gives a stronger taste)

2 eggs

7 tablespoons of evaporated milk (buy in a tin from the supermarket in the home baking aisle)

1 teaspoon of vanilla essence

For the filling:

6 tablespoons of icing sugar

1 ½ tablespoons of drinking chocolate

85 grams of margarine

For the chocolate topping:

6 tablespoons of icing sugar

1½ tablespoons of drinking chocolate

1 Preheat the oven to 175°C.

2 Line the two sandwich tins with greaseproof paper.

3 With clean hands, rub together the caster sugar, flour, margarine and drinking chocolate or cocoa in a bowl until it resembles fine breadcrumbs.

4 In a separate bowl, mix together the eggs, evaporated milk, 3 table-spoons of water and vanilla essence. Add this to the chocolate mix. Whisk together until the mixture forms a smooth liquid.

5 Divide the mixture evenly between the two lined sandwich tins and place in the preheated oven for about 20 minutes.

6 To test if the cakes are cooked, push a knife or skewer into the middle of one of the sponges; it should come out clean. If it doesn't, pop the cakes back in the oven for another 5 minutes.

7 When the sponges are cooked, carefully remove them from the sandwich tins and place on the counter, in the greaseproof paper.

8 For the filling, mix the icing sugar with a few drops of water in a bowl and then add the drinking chocolate and margarine and mix together until it forms a thick paste.

9 When the sponges are cooled, place one sponge on a plate and cover with the filling. Place the other sponge on top.

10 For the topping, mix the icing sugar, a few drops of water and the drinking chocolate together (exactly the same as the filling, but without the margarine) and smooth over the top of the cake. Allow the topping to set slightly and then serve to your hungry housemates.

Variation: *Try crumbling a Flake over the top to add even more choco-latey kick!*

Per serving: *Calories 358 (From Fat 164); Fat 18.2g (Saturated 8.4g); Cholesterol Trace; Sodium 280mg; Carbohydrate 43.9g; Dietary Fibre 1.2g; Protein 4.6g.*

Ginger Biscuits

Ginger biscuits, or strawberry-blonde biscuits as they often prefer to be called, are a simple yet tasty treat to bake.

Preparation time: *10 minutes*

Cooking time: *15 minutes*

Makes: *15–18 biscuits*

110 grams of vegetable oil

110 grams of brown sugar

110 grams of caster sugar

1 egg, beaten

55 grams of flaked almonds

225 grams of plain flour

½ teaspoon of bicarbonate of soda

1 teaspoon of ground ginger

Pinch of salt

1 Preheat the oven to 200°C.

2 Line a baking tray with some greaseproof paper.

3 Combine the vegetable oil, brown sugar, caster sugar and beaten egg together in a bowl.

4 Add in the almonds, flour, bicarbonate of soda, ginger and salt and mix together to form a paste.

5 Using your hands, shape the paste into 15 to 18 biscuit shapes and place on the baking tray.

6 Place in the preheated oven for 15 minutes until cooked.

7 When cooked, remove and allow to stand for 2 minutes and then transfer to a cooling rack.

8 When the biscuits are completely cool, store in a Tupperware box or other airtight container.

Per serving: *Calories 174 (From Fat 75); Fat 8.3g (Saturated 1.0g); Cholesterol Trace; Sodium 42mg; Carbohydrate 22.4g; Dietary Fibre 0.6g; Protein 2.3g.*

⏾Oat-so Nice Biscuits

These scrumptious oaty biscuits (think home-made HobNobs) are perfect for dunking in a mug of tea.

Preparation time: 5 minutes

Cooking time: 15 minutes

Makes: 15–18 biscuits

340 grams of margarine

170 grams of caster sugar

170 grams of porridge oats

340 grams of plain flour

Icing sugar for coating

1 Preheat the oven to 180°C. Line the baking tray with the greaseproof paper.

2 Combine all the ingredients (except the icing sugar) in a bowl to form a paste.

3 Using a lightly floured rolling pin or bottle, roll out the paste on a clean chopping board or work surface to a 1-centimetre thickness.

4 Press a clean glass down onto the rolled-out mixture to cut out biscuit-shape circles. Re-roll any scraps to make a few more biscuits.

5 Place the biscuits onto the lined baking tray and prick with a fork.

6 Sprinkle the biscuits with icing sugar and place in the oven for 8 to 10 minutes, or until they turn a pale golden, but not brown, colour.

7 When cooked, remove from the oven and allow to cool on a wire cooling rack (or use one of the wire shelves from your oven or grill.)

8 To store, place in an airtight container.

Variation: *Try melting some chocolate and spreading it over the biscuits when they're cooked to make your own version of a chocolate digestive.*

Per serving: *Calories 281 (From Fat 145); Fat 16.1g (Saturated 6.7g); Cholesterol Trace; Sodium 179mg; Carbohydrate 31.0g; Dietary Fibre 1.3g; Protein 2.9g.*

↻Double Chocolate Chip Muffins

Spend your Sunday afternoon making these muffins and you'll have set up the following week's naughty snacks. Hide them away; otherwise, you find they mysteriously disappear from your cupboard.

You need a muffin tray and muffin cases for this recipe. You can find cheap ones in supermarkets and hardware shops.

Preparation time: *10 minutes*

Cooking time: *15 minutes*

Makes: *6*

200 grams of plain flour	125 millilitres of milk
2 teaspoons of baking powder	75 millilitres of vegetable oil or groundnut oil
Pinch of salt	
40-gram plain chocolate bar	50 grams of sugar
1 egg	50 grams of chocolate drops

1 Preheat the oven to 200°C.

2 Sift the flour and baking powder through a colander or sieve into a big bowl and add a pinch of salt.

3 Break the chocolate into chunks and put in a big microwave-proof bowl.

4 Put the bowl in the microwave and heat the chocolate in short bursts of 10 seconds at full power, stirring in between, until it melts.

5 Crack the egg into the melted chocolate and whisk together using a whisk or a fork.

6 Add the milk, oil and sugar and give everything a good stir.

7 Sift the flour mixture into the bowl with the chocolate mixture.

8 Mix everything into each other with a spoon. The trick is to get a rough texture for this; the rougher the better. As long as the flour is mixed in, your muffins will be fine.

9 Add the chocolate drops and mix again.

10 Get the muffin tray and place muffin cases in each of the dips. Using a spoon, carefully fill each muffin case to just below the top with the muffin mixture.

11 Place the tray in the oven and bake the muffins for 15 minutes. Don't open the oven door during cooking because the muffins can sag.

12 After 15 minutes, check if the muffins are done by carefully pushing a clean knife or skewer through the muffin. If it comes out clean, your muffins are cooked.

13 Hold yourself back for 5 minutes while the cakes cool down, otherwise your enjoyment will be marred by a burned mouth. Then tuck in.

Per serving: Calories 378 (From Fat 172); Fat 19.1g (Saturated 4.9g); Cholesterol Trace; Sodium 235mg; Carbohydrate 45.7g; Dietary Fibre 1.4g; Protein 5.9g.

Being Good: Eating Healthy Desserts

Don't think that puddings are always a lorry-load of calories, chocolate and sugar. You can still have a tasty and indulgent dessert that doesn't leave its mark on your waistline or force you to visit the gym for a week to work off its guilty pleasures.

The following recipes prove that you can have your (healthy) cake and eat it.

ᗒSexy Fruit Crunch

It's sexy, fruity and, erm, crunchy; it's the Sexy Fruit Crunch! Packed with fresh fruit and yogurt, this pudding even helps you to digest your main meal.

Preparation time: *10 minutes*

Cooking time: *Nil*

Serves: *2*

1 small tub of natural yogurt

6 HobNobs, broken into pieces

Selection of chopped fruit (kiwi fruit, strawberries, raspberries)

Bar of chocolate, grated

Pop a layer of yogurt in a wine glass followed by a layer of biscuit, then fruit. Keep going with the layers until you use up all your ingredients. Top with some grated chocolate and a whole strawberry or raspberry.

Per serving: *Calories 143 (From Fat 62); Fat 6.9g (Saturated 4.0g); Cholesterol Trace; Sodium 23mg; Carbohydrate 18.2g; Dietary Fibre 1.2g; Protein 2.0g.*

ᗒBananas with Butterscotch Sauce

You know a book's healthy when even the decadent desserts contain one of your five-a-day. One of your five-a-day that's covered in sugar, cream and golden syrup. . . .

The butterscotch sauce goes with many different puddings, especially sponges.

Preparation time: *10 minutes*

Cooking time: *10 minutes*

Serves: *4*

75 grams of butter

225 grams of brown sugar

140 millilitres of double cream

1 tablespoon of golden syrup

4 bananas, peeled and sliced in half lengthways

1 Melt the butter in a small saucepan over a low heat.

2 Add in the sugar and stir.

3 Pour in the cream and golden syrup.

4 When the sugar has dissolved after 2 or 3 minutes, bring the mixture to the boil and gently whisk until the mixture thickens and is as smooth as late-night jazz.

5 Remove from the heat and allow to cool slightly.

6 Place the sliced bananas onto a serving plate and spoon over the butterscotch sauce.

Variation: *Go wild by adding a scoop of vanilla ice cream on the side.*

Per serving: *Calories 666 (From Fat 311); Fat 34.5g (Saturated 21.6g); Cholesterol Trace; Sodium 148mg; Carbohydrate 86.7g; Dietary Fibre 1.3g; Protein 2.2g.*

Funky Flapjacks

These flapjacks qualify for the healthy category because of the fruit they contain. Plus, the oats are full of fibre, making you feel fuller for longer.

Preparation time: *5 minutes*

Cooking time: *25 minutes*

Makes: *10 flapjacks*

180 grams of butter

55 grams of caster sugar

2 tablespoons of honey or golden syrup

225 grams of rolled oats

50 grams of dried fruit, larger fruit chopped (sultanas, raisins, apricots)

1 Preheat the oven to 180°C.

2 Line a baking tray with greaseproof paper.

3 Place the butter, sugar, and honey or syrup in a saucepan and cook over a gentle heat. Stir until the mixture is all melted and the sugar is dissolved and then remove from the heat.

4 Add the oats and dried fruit and stir until they're coated with the mixture.

5 Spoon the mixture onto the baking tray and smooth everything out until it's the thickness of a flapjack (about 2 centimetres).

6 Place the tray in the preheated oven for 25 minutes and bake until golden brown.

7 Remove from the oven and, while hot, score where you're going to divide the mixture into individual flapjacks. Don't cut all the way through though. Allow the flapjacks to cool completely while still in the tray.

8 When cool, cut the flapjack into individual pieces, following the lines you made earlier on. To store, keep in an airtight container.

Variation: Add a mashed up banana when you add the oats to make banana flapjacks.

Per serving: Calories 269 (From Fat 152); Fat 16.9g (Saturated 9.7g); Cholesterol Trace; Sodium 114mg; Carbohydrate 26.4g; Dietary Fibre 1.7g; Protein 2.8g.

⌒Apple Strudel

This is another pudding with one portion of your five-a-day stuffed inside. Working with the filo pastry can be a little tricky, so leave this recipe until you feel really confident in the kitchen. The end result is lovely.

Preparation time: 15 minutes

Cooking time: 35 minutes

Serves: 4

1 packet of filo pastry, defrosted

400 grams of cooking apples, cored, peeled and chopped into small cubes

100 grams of brown sugar

Squeeze of lemon juice

100 grams of mixed dried fruit

75 grams of walnuts, roughly chopped into small pieces

1 teaspoon of mixed spice

1 beaten egg, mixed with 2 tablespoons of milk

1 Preheat the oven to 220°C and line the baking tray with greaseproof paper.

2 Grab a large saucepan and heat 2 tablespoons of water over a low heat. Add the apple pieces with half of the sugar and a squeeze of lemon juice and cook gently until the apples *start* to soften, but don't soften completely.

3 Remove from the heat and add the dried fruit, walnuts and mixed spice. Taste for the sweetness and spiciness, adding more sugar or spice if needed and leave to one side.

4 Carefully unwrap the filo pastry and cover with a clean damp tea towel (filo pastry dries out very quickly).

5 Take one sheet of filo and place it on the baking tray. Lightly brush it all over with the beaten egg mixture. Place the second sheet of filo pastry on top, halfway along the original piece, so that they create a length of around 36 centimetres. (Each sheet of filo is around 30 centimetres long, so the second piece should hang over the edge of the first one by about 6 centimetres.) Brush that with the egg and milk mixture.

6 Repeat this step (one sheet as normal, one overlapping) two more times, placing the next four sheets on top of the original two, making sure you brush them with the beaten egg each time.

7 Spoon the apple down the centre of the pastry, leaving approximately 6 centimetres clear at each end (for tucking the ends in).

8 Carefully fold the pastry over in half and then roll the strudel to make a sausage shape.

9 Carefully place the strudel on the baking tray with the seam underneath and place in the preheated oven for 25 minutes. It should look nice and golden when cooked.

10 Remove the strudel from the oven and allow to rest for 5 minutes before slicing the strudel into portions and serving with custard, ice cream or natural yogurt.

Per serving: *Calories 734 (From Fat 399); Fat 44.3g (Saturated 13.0g); Cholesterol Trace; Sodium 247mg; Carbohydrate 74.2g; Dietary Fibre 3.6g; Protein 9.5g.*

Part IV
Entertaining

'OK - you've tossed the salad enough, Joseph.'

In this part . . .

If the lads or lasses are coming over, you're going to
need something to feed them with. Part IV looks at how
to feed (what may feel like) an army of students, many of
whom have only eaten toast for the past month. With the
help of these chapters, throwing a party becomes a piece
of cake, literally. As does cooking for a date.

Plus, although not quite like a Sunday roast back with the
rents, you can create a cracking Sunday roast from the
comfort of your own student kitchen. How? Read on.

Chapter 12

Lads' and Girls' Night In

In This Chapter

▶ Putting together soups, skewers and wraps

▶ Enjoying Indian, Japanese and Italian dishes

▶ Picking the right tipple

*N*ights out with your mates are what uni life's all about. Crawling from pub to pub and catching up on the latest gossip from campus while slowly losing the ability to speak coherently is part of the very fabric of uni life. But it can get pretty expensive, even when it's pound-a-pint night down at the uni bar.

So have a break from the boozing and spend a quality night in with your mates. Nothing beats a quality catch up with your friends over a delicious home-cooked meal, or getting everyone round for some food when the footie's on. A lot of nights in are more memorable than trashed evenings in nightclubs, and you quickly build up a great circle of friends.

Cooking for a group doesn't have to be an expensive or difficult job. If everyone chips in a couple of quid, you soon have enough money to make something truly amazing, and why not get your mates to help you cook it? Antics guaranteed!

This chapter looks at some tasty dishes that you can pull together to feed your friends. I divide the recipes into 'Guys' and 'Girls', because, from my experience, guys seem to prefer full-bodied spicy dishes, and girls like things a little bit classier. But, of course, feel free to mix them around!

I end things on that all important topic, booze, specifically what wine or beer to choose for your dish. We're not getting into fancy wine-tasting territory here, just a straightforward guide to choosing the best type of wine or beer for your meal.

Food for the Footie

Footie, rugby, curling, it doesn't matter what sport's on the box (or even if it's a sport at all), these dishes are great to entertain a bunch of lads on a night in. Kicking and screaming with flavour, but dead easy to make, you don't spend all your time in the kitchen away from the action.

The first three recipes are starters; the rest are the mains.

⟡Spicy Sweet Potato Soup

This soup is a cheap and tasty starter that packs a bit of a kick.

 To cool things down a little and make the soup a bit creamier, leave out the chilli and add a touch of Greek yogurt or coconut milk towards the end.

Preparation time: *5 minutes*

Cooking time: *20 minutes*

Serves: *4*

Drop of olive oil

1 onion, peeled and finely chopped

1 clove of garlic, peeled and chopped

2 sweet potatoes, peeled and chopped into small cubes (chop into very small cubes if you don't have a blender)

Two big pinches of chilli powder

600 millilitres of vegetable stock (made with two stock cubes)

1 Heat a drop of oil in a big saucepan over a medium to high heat and add the onions, garlic and sweet potato. Fry for five minutes until soft and starting to turn brown.

2 Add the chilli powder and fry for another minute.

3 Pour the stock into the saucepan over the potatoes, stir and turn the heat down to a medium setting. Leave to simmer for about 15 minutes, or until the sweet potato has turned soft.

4 Leave the saucepan to one side to cool down a bit, then pour the sauce into a blender and blend until smooth before serving. If you don't have a blender, spoon the soup into four bowls and serve.

Per serving: Calories 154 (From Fat 11.0g); Fat 1.2g (Saturated 0.2g); Cholesterol Trace; Sodium 792mg; Carbohydrate 33.0g; Dietary Fibre 3.7g; Protein 2.8g.

⟨Roast Vegetable Skewers

These skewers are similar to shish kebabs, but not having any meat makes them a great starter dish. Don't be put off by the long cooking time; the oven does all the work, leaving you to chill out with your mates.

You need 8–12 skewers for this recipe.

Preparation time: *5 minutes*

Cooking time: *30 minutes*

Serves: *4*

Olive oil

1 red and 1 green pepper, deseeded and chopped into bite-sized chunks

1 red onion, peeled and sliced into chunks

8 cherry tomatoes

1½ aubergine, cut into chunks

1 courgette, cut into chunks

250 grams of mozzarella cheese, cut into chunks

1 Preheat the oven to 180°C.

2 Place the prepared vegetables in a bowl. Pour in 5 good glugs of olive oil to thoroughly coat the veggies and then season with some salt and pepper. Push them onto the skewers and place on a baking tray.

3 Roast the veggies for 30 minutes.

4 Take the baking tray out of the oven and leave for 2 minutes to cool down a bit.

5 Pop the cheese onto each end of the skewers and serve while still hot.

Variation: *Vary the vegetables however you like. Make this a main meal by adding some meat and serving with rice or couscous.*

Per serving: *Calories 224 (From Fat 125); Fat 13.9g (Saturated 8.9g); Cholesterol Trace; Sodium 254mg; Carbohydrate 11.0g; Dietary Fibre 3.0g; Protein 13.8g.*

⌖Home-Made Garlic Bread

You can't beat a bit of home-made garlic bread as a starter. Have fingerlickin' garlicky fun by making the butter as garlicky as you dare!

Preparation time: *5 minutes*

Cooking time: *10 minutes*

Serves: *4*

4 ciabattas

Butter or margarine

3 cloves of garlic, peeled and finely chopped

1 Turn the grill on to a medium heat.

2 Slice the ciabattas in half. Mix the garlic with the butter and spread on each ciabatta half. Now cut the ciabatta into strips about 2 centimetres wide.

3 Place the strips under the preheated grill and grill for just a minute or so until they're toasted.

4 Remove the bread pieces from the grill, leave until slightly cooled and then tuck in.

Variation: Add some chopped fresh chives or parsley on top to make it look a bit more fancy.

Per serving: Calories 234 (From Fat 45); 5.0 (Saturated 1.7g); Cholesterol Trace; Sodium 419mg; Carbohydrate 39.4g; Dietary Fibre 1.8g; Protein 7.8g.

Beef Tortilla Wraps

These wraps are fantastic – spicy beef stuffed inside a soft, floury tortilla wrap and topped with melted cheese. They'll disappear in a flash.

Preparation time: 10 minutes

Cooking time: 20 minutes

Serves: 4

Olive oil

1 onion, peeled and chopped

750 grams of minced beef (about 3 big handfuls)

3 big pinches of chilli powder

½ tin of red kidney beans, drained and rinsed

½ tin of sweetcorn, drained

Big squeeze of tomato sauce

4 tortilla wraps

Handful of grated Cheddar cheese

1 Heat a drop of oil in a frying pan over a high heat.

2 Add the chopped onion to the pan and fry until the edges start turning brown.

3 Crumble in the meat, breaking it up with your spatula when it's in the pan. Fry until the meat turns brown.

4 Add in the chilli powder, kidney beans, sweetcorn and a big squeeze of tomato sauce and mix everything together. Fry for another 5 minutes. Meanwhile, turn the grill on to full power.

5 Divide the mixture between the four wraps and wrap the tortillas up. Place the wraps in a heat-proof dish and scatter the cheese evenly over the top. Place under the grill until the cheese has melted and then eat.

Variation: If it's cheaper, or you fancy a different taste, try swapping the beef mince for pork.

Per serving: Calories 742 (From Fat 392); Fat 43.6g (Saturated18.9); Cholesterol Trace; Sodium 770mg; Carbohydrate 36.8g; Dietary Fibre 2.1g; Protein 50.5g.

Chilli Con Carne

A good chilli con carne is an amazing dish, and it doesn't even have to be 'blow your head off' spicy. Full of rich and warming flavours, and perfect in a bowl in front of the footie, this chilli con carne recipe is great. (Check out Chapter 9 for a microwaveable version.)

Preparation time: 10 minutes

Cooking time: 25 minutes

Serves: 4

Olive oil	1 tin of chopped tomatoes
1 onion, peeled and chopped	¼ bottle of red wine
Pinch of cumin seeds (optional)	1 tin of red kidney beans, drained and rinsed
2 cloves of garlic, peeled and chopped	Handful of sun-dried tomatoes, cut into quarters (optional)
750 grams of minced beef (about 3 big handfuls)	3 big pinches of chilli powder
1 big splodge of tomato purée	Salt
1 beef stock cube	2 mugs of rice

1 Heat a drop of oil over a medium to high heat in a frying pan and add the chopped onion (and cumin seeds if you're using them). Fry for a couple of minutes and then add in the garlic. Mix well and fry for a couple more minutes.

2 Crumble in the beef, breaking up the mince with your spatula in the pan. Mix and cook until the meat is a light brown colour.

3 Half fill a saucepan with water and put on the hob over a high heat to bring to the boil. This is for the rice.

4 Add the tomato purée to the pan and mix into the beef. Sprinkle the stock cube over the top and mix again.

5 Pour in the chopped tomatoes with their juice, red wine, kidney beans and sun-dried tomatoes (if using). Mix it all together and then add in the chilli powder and turn the heat down to medium to let the mixture simmer.

6 By now the water for the rice should be boiling, so add a pinch of salt and pour in the rice. Give it a quick stir to stop the rice sticking to the bottom and boil for about 10 minutes.

7 Check that the rice is cooked and then drain it through a colander. Spoon it onto plates and add the chilli on top.

Variation: Serve with nachos (check out Chapter 6) rather than rice.

Per serving: Calories 1187 (From Fat 307); Fat 34.1g (Saturated 13.4g); Cholesterol Trace; Sodium 1068mg; Carbohydrate 156.6g; Dietary Fibre 10.9g; Protein 63.5g.

Creamy Chicken Curry

This recipe won't quite beat a cracking curry from your local curry house, but it comes a close second, especially when money's a bit tight.

This is a good curry recipe to master before moving on to more complicated ones.

Preparation time: 10 minutes

Cooking time: 25 minutes

Serves: 4

Groundnut or vegetable oil

1 onion, peeled and chopped

4 teaspoons of curry paste

1½ spoonfuls of ginger, peeled and finely chopped

1 green chilli, finely chopped

1 red pepper, cut into small pieces

4 chicken legs, skin removed

500 millilitres of chicken stock

1½ mugs of long grain rice (basmati's also good to use for curries, but has a longer cooking time; check the packet instructions)

1 head of broccoli, chopped into florets

½ mug of peas

4 teaspoons of curry powder

4 spoonfuls of natural yogurt

Handful of raisins

1 Heat a drop of oil in a frying pan over a medium to high heat. Add the onion, curry paste and ginger and mix well. Fry for about 5 minutes.

2 Add the chilli, red pepper, chicken legs and curry powder and fry until the meat turns brown.

3 Pour 1½ mugs of rice into a dry saucepan and then pour in double the quantity (3 mugs) of water, so that the water just covers the rice. Turn on the heat to full power.

4 Pour the hot chicken stock into the frying pan with the chicken thighs and add the broccoli and peas.

5 Turn the heat down to halfway so that the stock simmers gently for 10 minutes or until the stock reduces by about a third.

6 By now the water in the saucepan should be boiling. Wait until craters appear in the rice and then turn the heat down to low (about 2 or 3 if you're using electric) and cover the saucepan with a lid. Don't open the lid for another 10 to 15 minutes, otherwise the steam escapes and the rice takes a lot longer to cook.

7 Add the raisins and yogurt to the curry and give it all a good stir. Simmer for another 5 minutes.

8 Check on the rice. The water should have practically gone and the rice should be nice and fluffy. Spoon the rice onto plates and add the curry to the side. Enjoy with a few naan breads and cold beers.

Variation: Add a few fresh coriander leaves when you add the raisins to give the curry a more authentic taste.

Per serving: Calories 836 (From Fat 85); Fat 9.4g (Saturated 2.2g); Cholesterol Trace; Sodium 806mg; Carbohydrate 141.2g; Dietary Fibre 7.5g; Protein 46.6g.

Smoked Fish Pie

Here's a bit of brain food for half-time analysis. This fish pie is high on taste and low on cost, especially when spread between four friends. The fish is cooked twice – first poached, then baked, so you can be absolutely sure you're not eating anything raw or half cooked!

 You can choose any fish you like really, but a good selection is half smoked and half white fish. White fish like coley, whiting and haddock are cheap; have a look at what smoked fish your fishmonger has.

Don't be put off by the number of steps in this recipe – it's not as complicated as it looks!

Preparation time: 10 minutes

Cooking time: 45 minutes

Serves: 4

½ onion, peeled and chopped

2 carrots, peeled and chopped

1 mug of peas (frozen are fine)

2 fillets of white fish (coley, haddock or whiting are good), chopped into bite-sized pieces

2 fillets of smoked fish (smoked haddock, smoked mackerel, smoked salmon), chopped into bite-sized pieces

Mug of milk (275 millilitres)

1½–2 baking potatoes, chopped into quarters

Big chunk of butter

Handful of plain flour

3 teaspoons of wholegrain mustard (optional)

1 Preheat the oven to 200°C and place an ovenproof dish into the oven to warm up.

2 Place the onion, carrots, peas and fish in the bottom of a saucepan and pour over enough milk to just about cover everything. Stir and turn the heat right up to bring the milk to the boil. As soon as it's boiling, turn off the heat, put the lid on the saucepan and leave the pan where it is.

3 While the fish is being poached gently in the milk, grab another saucepan, fill it two-thirds full of water and bring it to the boil. When it's boiling, add a pinch of salt and add the potatoes. Cook them for about 15 minutes, drain through a colander and place back into the saucepan.

4 Pour the fishy mixture through a colander into a bowl. You end up with the fish and vegetables in the bottom of the colander and the milk sauce in the bowl.

5 Add a bit of the butter and a spoonful of the milk mixture to the potatoes and mash them. Just before the potatoes are completely mashed, add a bit of salt and pepper and carry on mashing.

6 Place the lid back on the saucepan over the mash and put it to one side. So by now, you have the mash in one saucepan, the fish in a colander and the milk in a bowl.

7 Clean out the saucepan that had the fish in it, put the rest of the butter (about 2 teaspoons) in the bottom and melt over a low heat. Add two big pinches of plain flour and mix the melted butter and flour together. Add a couple of spoons of the fishy sauce and stir well. Keep adding the sauce and keep stirring until you get a smooth sauce (3 to 4 minutes). Stir in the wholegrain mustard (if using) and mix the fish and vegetables into the sauce.

8 Carefully take the dish out of the oven and pour in the fish mixture. Spoon the mashed potato on top, sealing down all the corners. Place the dish in the oven for 25 to 30 minutes.

9 Finally, place the dish underneath a hot grill and cook until the mash goes crispy on top. Serve with some crusty bread to mop up the creamy sauce and a big dollop of tomato sauce.

Variation: *Try adding prawns rather than some of the smoked fish.*

Per serving: *Calories 456 (From Fat 110); Fat 12.2g (Saturated 6.2g); Cholesterol Trace; Sodium 1289mg; Carbohydrate 35.9g; Dietary Fibre 5.4g; Protein 50.6g.*

Nosh and a Natter

Girls tend to go for something a little classier when they're entertaining and, dare I say it, are often a little better than the blokes in the kitchen. So the following recipes push the boat out a bit and are perfect companions to a bottle of wine and a group of friends for a night of films and gossip.

⟡Tomato and Mozzarella Bites

These classic Mediterranean morsels bring a bit of the continent to our grey shores at any time of the year. This recipe is super-quick to prepare and very tasty.

Preparation time: *10 minutes*

Cooking time: *5 minutes*

Serves: *4*

1 baguette, chopped into chunks

3 cloves of garlic, peeled and chopped in half

2 250-gram packets of mozzarella, sliced

Fresh basil (optional)

3 tomatoes, sliced

Olive oil

Pepper

1 Preheat the grill.

2 Grill the pieces of bread until they're lightly browned (keep an eye on them because they won't take long).

3 When the bread is toasted, take out from under the grill and gently rub the garlic clove halves over the toasted side.

4 Top with a slice of mozzarella, then a basil leaf (if using), then a slice of tomato. Place on a plate. Repeat for all the other bites.

5 When they're all on a plate, drizzle a bit of olive oil over them, grind pepper over them and then serve.

Per serving: *Calories 431 (From Fat 261); Fat 29.0g (Saturated 17.8g); Cholesterol Trace; Sodium 657mg; Carbohydrate 15.4g; Dietary Fibre 1.3g; Protein 27.1g.*

Avocado Wrapped in Smoked Salmon

This is a quick and very healthy starter that's delicious with a glass of white wine – and no cooking involved!

Preparation time: *20 minutes*

Cooking time: *Nil*

Serves: *4*

2 avocados	*1 lemon, cut in half (for juicing)*
2 fillets of smoked salmon	*Pepper*

1 Cut the salmon into strips about 1½ centimetres wide by 4 centimetres long.

2 Cut the avocado in half, separate the two halves and prise out the stone with a teaspoon.

3 Slice the skin away until you're left with the green flesh. Chop the flesh into cubes.

4 Roll the avocado cubes in the salmon strips and press a cocktail stick into them to hold them together. Repeat until you use up all the avocado and salmon.

5 Squeeze the lemon over the bites, grind a little pepper over them and serve immediately.

Per serving: *Calories 285 (From Fat 172); Fat 19.1g (Saturated 3.9g); Cholesterol Trace; Sodium 1885mg; Carbohydrate 1.4g; Dietary Fibre 2.6g; Protein 26.8g.*

○Vegetable Tempura

Tempura is a Japanese dish of crispy deep-fried vegetables. Even when Japanese food is deep fried, it seems to taste healthy and delicious. Tempura is great finger food and goes nicely dipped in a little dish of soy sauce.

Preparation time: 15 minutes

Cooking time: 10 minutes

Serves: 4

For the vegetables:

2 carrots, peeled and cut in half and then into thin strips

1 courgette, cut in half and then into strips

1 small head of broccoli, cut into bite-sized florets

Vegetable or groundnut oil

Salt

For the batter:

200 grams of self-raising flour

250 millilitres of cold sparkling water

1 Place all the vegetables on a plate and sprinkle over a bit of the flour, coating all the vegetables in a light dusting.

2 Sift (pour through a sieve) the rest of the flour in a bowl and slowly pour in the sparkling water, whisking together to make a light batter.

3 Pour an inch of oil into a large saucepan and place on a high heat. Leave for about 3 minutes to heat up, but keep an eye on it. Hot oil can be very dangerous, so don't leave the room while it's heating up.

4 After 3 minutes, drop a bit of bread into the oil. If it turns brown pretty much instantly the oil is ready; if not, it needs a bit longer.

5 Dip the vegetables in the batter and then carefully place a few in the oil and deep fry. The courgettes and broccoli cook the quickest at roughly 3 minutes, while the carrot takes 4 minutes. When they're cooked, fish them out with a fork or slotted spoon and place on a plate lined with kitchen roll.

6 Repeat with the rest of the vegetables. Sprinkle some salt over the vegetables and then serve with a saucer of soy sauce to dip them into.

Per serving: *Calories 375 (From Fat 125); Fat 13.9g (Saturated 1.8g); Cholesterol Trace; Sodium 227mg; Carbohydrate 55.2g; Dietary Fibre 5.3g; Protein 7.3g.*

Bacon and Gorgonzola Gnocchi

Gnocchi is an Italian potato dumpling, but looks and tastes like pasta. Most supermarkets sell it or if not, have a look in a deli or world food shop.

Gnocchi is very filling, so you don't need a lot to feed a crowd. This dinner's dead quick to make, so you don't have to spend too long in the kitchen.

Preparation time: *5 minutes*

Cooking time: *10 minutes*

Serves: *4*

1 tin of chopped tomatoes

2 big handfuls of spinach, roughly chopped

Salt

400-gram pack of gnocchi

300 grams of Gorgonzola, crumbled into bits

120 grams of pre-cooked bacon, cut into strips or pieces

Ground black pepper

1 Fill a saucepan three-quarters full of water and place on the hob to bring to the boil.

2 Heat a frying pan over a medium heat and, when hot, pour in the chopped tomatoes. Fry for a minute.

3 Add the spinach to the tomatoes and gently fry for about 5 minutes, until most of the excess liquid has evaporated.

4 By now the water for the gnocchi should be boiling, so add a pinch of salt and then carefully add the gnocchi. Boil for 5 minutes; they should float to the top when they're done.

5 Just before the gnocchi has finished cooking, stir the bacon and Gorgonzola into the tomato and spinach mixture. Then drain the gnocchi through a colander.

6 Pour the gnocchi back into the empty pan and pour the tomato mixture over the gnocchi.

7 Add plenty of black pepper and then divide between four plates.

Variation: Add some torn basil at the end, or swap the Gorgonzola for mozzarella.

Per serving: Calories 585 (From Fat 305); Fat 33.9g (Saturated 19.0g); Cholesterol Trace; Sodium 1313mg; Carbohydrate 42.0g; Dietary Fibre 4.0g; Protein 28.0g.

The World's Best Spag Bol

This recipe is a student classic that raises the bar with some succulent sun-dried tomatoes and a generous glug of full-bodied red wine. Prepare to find yourself with a lot of new friends the morning after this meal. . . .

Preparation time: *10 minutes*

Cooking time: *25 minutes*

Serves: *4*

Olive oil

1 onion, peeled and chopped

2 cloves of garlic, peeled and chopped

650 grams of minced beef

1 beef stock cube

A few splashes of Worcestershire sauce

2 big handfuls of spaghetti

Splodge of tomato purée

1 tin of chopped tomatoes

1 glass of red wine

1 small tub of sun-dried tomatoes, chopped into small pieces

Pinch of mixed herbs

6 fresh basil leaves, torn into smaller pieces

Salt and pepper

1 handful of grated Parmesan cheese

1 Heat a glug of olive oil in a frying pan over a medium to high heat and, when hot, add in the chopped onion. Fry for 5 minutes and then add in the chopped garlic. Fry for another 2 minutes.

2 Fill a saucepan three-quarters full of water and put it on the hob, full power, to bring to the boil.

3 Crumble the minced beef into the frying pan, breaking it up with your spatula in the pan. Fry the beef until it turns brown.

4 Sprinkle over the beef stock cube and shake in a few splashes of Worcestershire sauce. Mix it all together.

5 By now, the water should be boiling, so add a pinch of salt and the spaghetti. Wait until the bottom half of the spaghetti softens and then push the top half into the water.

6 Add the tomato purée to the frying pan and mix it into the beef. Pour in the chopped tinned tomatoes, red wine, sun-dried tomatoes and mixed herbs, stirring everything together. Turn the heat down and simmer for 10 to 15 minutes, until most of the liquid has reduced and the spaghetti is cooked.

7 Taste the spaghetti to see if it's cooked and then drain it in a colander. Shake the colander a bit and drizzle a little olive oil over the spaghetti. Shake it one more time.

8 Mix the basil leaves into the bolognaise and season with some salt and pepper.

9 Divide the spaghetti onto four plates and spoon the bolognaise on top.

10 Sprinkle the grated Parmesan on top and eat immediately.

Tip: *Use the Home-Made Garlic Bread recipe from the lads' section and serve with the spag bol.*

Per serving: *Calories 671 (From Fat 272); Fat 30.2g (Saturated 12.6g); Cholesterol Trace; Sodium 1233mg; Carbohydrate 54.2g; Dietary Fibre 5.4g; Protein 45.6g.*

Salmon and Rocket Tagliatelle

This dish is perfect for slyly showing off your culinary skills to your friends. And the best bit is, you don't have to be a good cook because it's so easy to make!

Preparation time: *10 minutes*

Cooking time: *35 minutes*

Serves: *4*

3 salmon fillets (about 5 centimetres square)	*200-gram bag of rocket (torn into bite-sized portions)*
Handful of cherry tomatoes	*4 spoonfuls of crème fraîche*
Salt	*4 teaspoons of capers*
350 grams of tagliatelle (roughly 4 handfuls)	*Ground black pepper*
	1 lemon, cut in half

1 Turn the grill on to full power and, when hot, put the cherry tomatoes underneath the grill. Grill for 5 minutes, then add the salmon and continue grilling for another 5 to 10 minutes, until the salmon is cooked (the salmon should flake easily when pulled with a fork).

2 Place the salmon and tomatoes to one side to cool down. While they're cooling, fill a large saucepan three-quarters full of water and put on the hob, full power, to bring to the boil. Add a pinch of salt and then the tagliatelle. Cook for about 10 minutes or until the pasta starts to soften.

3 When cooked, drain the tagliatelle through a colander and pour back into the empty pan.

4 Break up the salmon with a fork (leaving the skin to one side) and put in the saucepan with the tagliatelle. Add in the rocket, crème fraîche, capers and grilled tomatoes, and stir well.

5 Grind black pepper and squeeze some lemon juice over the pasta. Mix one final time and then spoon into four bowls and serve with a cold glass of white wine.

Per serving: Calories 647 (From Fat 228); Fat 25.3g (Saturated 7.5g); Cholesterol Trace; Sodium 230mg; Carbohydrate 61.5g; Dietary Fibre 3.7g; Protein 43.4g.

Chicken Wrapped in Parma Ham

This classic dish is still a firm favourite. The succulent chicken is wrapped in crispy Parma ham, and you can serve it with salad, fresh vegetables or whatever you fancy to be honest. Give this dish a try; it's dead easy.

Preparation time: *10 minutes*

Cooking time: *20 minutes*

Serves: *4*

4 chicken breasts	*Lemon juice*
200 grams of mozzarella, sliced	*Black pepper*
8 slices of Parma ham	

1 Preheat the oven to 180°C.

2 Place the chicken breasts on a clean chopping board (the one you use for meat) and slice each one open, almost cutting it in half.

3 Place a slice of mozzarella inside the cut chicken.

4 Wrap two slices of Parma ham around each chicken breast so that the ends meet underneath the chicken.

5 Squeeze over some lemon juice and grind some pepper over each one.

6 Place on a baking tray and put in the preheated oven for 25 to 30 minutes or until the chicken is cooked. (Check by pressing a knife in and making sure any juices run clear.)

Per serving: *Calories 516 (From Fat 188); Fat 20.9g (Saturated 9.8g); Cholesterol Trace; Sodium 908mg; Carbohydrate 0.2g; Dietary Fibre Trace; Protein 81.7g.*

Choosing Beers and Wines

Sparing a thought about what you're going to drink with a slap-up meal for your mates can make a real difference to the food, so don't just choose the first alcoholic liquid you see on the supermarket shelf.

Fortunately, choosing a good beer or wine isn't all about swilling the drink round in a glass and making weird sucking noises as you drink it (unless you really want to); it's about drinking something to complement the taste of the meal.

So here's a brief guide to different beers and wines and the food they go with.

Selecting beer

It's pretty hard to go wrong when choosing beer. A cool refreshing beer or lager goes well with any kind of meal, but beverages like white beers and stout can be a better choice than a typical lager with some meals. Here's a quick rundown of what to drink when you eat:

✔ **Stout.** Stout is often seen as an old man's drink and, to be honest, that's mostly true! But I think stout is a deliciously rich alternative with far more variety of flavour than a run-of-the-mill lager. Stout is a dark beer brewed with roasted malts or barley. Its rich and hearty flavour goes well with traditional British and Irish dishes, such as stews and pies.

Good stouts include Guinness and Old Peculiar. Look out for locally brewed stouts.

✔ **Ale.** Ale, like stout, has an unfair image as the bearded, sandal-wearing man's tipple of choice. Yeah, ale's a bit old-fashioned, but tastes great. Ales are brewed from malted barley, using a top-fermenting type of yeast. This yeast ferments the beer quicker and gives it a sweet taste, but is slightly heavier than a lager. Ales go well with lamb and turkey; meat that has a more subtle flavour than, say, beef.

Ales are good to cook with. You can cook (or braise) joints of meat in ale, allowing the flavour of the beer to seep into the meat. Yum.

Try Bishop's Finger, Speckled Hen, Newcastle Brown Ale and any locally brewed ales you can find.

✔ **Cider.** Cider is made from the fermented juices of apples (and sometimes pears). In the kitchen, cider goes great with pork; its sharp, zingy, appley flavour really complements the taste of the meat. Like ale, you can also cook with it.

Look out for Magner's, Brother's and independent cider manufacturers that produce great quality cider.

✔ **Wheat Beers.** Also known as *white beers,* these are beers brewed with a high proportion of wheat, resulting in a slightly tangy but smooth drink, which is usually less gassy and sharp than the usual lager. If you're not a fan of wine, wheat beers are a good choice for fish dishes and white meat.

Good wheat beers are Hoegaarden and Kronenbourg 1664 Blanc.

Picking the right wine

Wine isn't just a cheap way to get drunk quickly – whenever you have your friends round for a meal, or if you're eating out, picking the right wine really makes a difference to the food.

As a general rule, white wine goes best with fish and poultry and red wine with meat dishes such as steaks, burgers and even meat-based pasta dishes like spaghetti bolognaise.

Here's a very brief guide to just some of the varieties of red and white wine available on the market:

Varieties of red wine include:

✔ **Merlot.** (Pronounced *mer-low.*) Not as strong as some other red wines, merlot has quite a mellow taste and is a great match for beef and pasta dishes, especially spag bol.

- **Rioja.** (Pronounced *ree-ocka*.) Rioja has quite a strong taste and goes well with steak and other dishes that are full of flavour.

- **Cabernet Sauvignon.** (Pronounced *cabernay so-vinyon*.) Cabernets have a rich blackcurrant taste. They're traditionally aged in oak, so can take on a delicious oaky vanilla flavour. Cabernet goes well with beef, lamb and chocolate. . . .

After something a little more refreshing? Then white wine it is. Try:

- **Pinot Grigio.** (Pronounced *peen-oh grijee-oh*.) A really light and refreshing wine that goes very nicely with fish or chicken dishes, or cool salads in the summer.

- **Sauvignon Blanc.** (Pronounced *so-vinyon blonk*.) Sauvignon Blanc is usually a very light wine and tends to be crisp and acidic, making it ideal for drinking with heavy foods such as stews or risottos.

- **Chardonnay.** (Pronounced *shar-donnay*.) Chardonnay is one of the cheapest wines to buy, but still tastes great. Chardonnay goes best with poultry or seafood, such as lobster or scallops.

Chapter 13

Pulling Together a Sunday Roast

*A*lthough it won't be as good as your mum's home-cooked roast (what does she put in there to make it taste so nice?!), pulling together a roast at uni isn't as hard as it sounds. And if you get your mates involved, cooking a roast is guaranteed to brighten up any dull, hungover Sunday. The key to perfect roast dinners is timing. Ensuring that all the meat, vegetables and trimmings are ready at the same time is the hardest part. Crack the timing, and the rest is a breeze.

So this chapter is dedicated to the good ol' British Sunday Roast, and how you can cook one in a student kitchen. Yes, it is possible, and when you've cracked the first one, don't be surprised to find a few new faces loitering around your kitchen next time.

Roasting Poultry

Roasting a chicken is probably the easiest out of all the meats, and a good one to start with if you've never cooked a roast before.

You can use any leftover roast chicken in a curry or in roast chicken sandwiches for the next few days (see Chapter 8 for the chicken curry recipe). Cut off all the meat you can from the chicken and place on a plate to cool down to room temperature. (Put an upturned colander or some kitchen roll over it to stop any flies or other students nibbling it.) When the chicken pieces are at room temperature, pop them in the fridge.

Large joints of meat need time to *rest* after cooking. When meat is cooked, it tightens and shrinks slightly, squeezing moisture out of the hot areas into areas that aren't as hot (such as the middle of the joint). Resting for between 15 minutes and up to half an hour gives the meat time to relax and allow the moisture to redistribute through the meat again.

Roast Chicken with the Works

Okay, time to roll up your sleeves and get stuck into a proper roast dinner. Remember the saying 'too many cooks spoil the broth'? Well, forget it, and get your mates to help you cook. It gives you a bit of company in the kitchen and is more fun. Especially if you have a bottle of wine on the go too. . . .

Check the weight of the bird when you buy it and allow 40 minutes of cooking time per kilogram of meat, then an extra 10 minutes at the end. A chicken big enough to feed four takes roughly an hour and a half in the oven.

Be a true pro and place the plates in the oven for two minutes before dishing up, so they're nice and hot and keep the food warm when served.

Preparation time: 30 minutes

Cooking time: 2 hours

Serves: 4

For the chicken:

1 chicken (giblets removed, look on the packaging or ask the butcher)

½ lemon

Big chunk of butter

For the vegetables:

3 baking potatoes, peeled and cut into roast potato-sized chunks

3 carrots, peeled and sliced

1 bowl of peas (frozen are fine)

Salt

Olive oil

Other stuff:

Gravy granules (not stock cubes)

Bread sauce mix

Mug of milk (275 millilitres)

1 Turn the oven on to 200°C.

2 Place the chicken on a clean plastic chopping board, the one you use for meat.

3 Cut any strings or elastic bands from the legs. Give the chicken a quick rinse under some gently running cool water. Dry with a bit of kitchen roll (don't use a towel or you contaminate it with raw meat).

4 Place your half lemon inside the chicken (in the hole between the legs). When it's cooking, the lemon gives off a lovely aroma, infusing the chicken skin.

5 Melt the butter in the microwave and pour or brush over the chicken to help turn the skin slightly crispy during cooking.

6 When the oven is at the right temperature, place the chicken on a roasting tray and place it in the oven for 30 minutes, making sure enough room is underneath it to put a baking tray in.

7 After 30 minutes, fill a large saucepan with water and put it on the hob, full power, until the water is boiling.

8 Add a pinch of salt and then drop in the chopped potatoes. Leave them to boil for 5 minutes.

9 While the potatoes are boiling, get a baking tray and pour olive oil on it, making sure the tray is all lightly coated in the oil. Place this in the oven to make it hot for when you put the potatoes on it.

10 After 5 minutes, drain the potatoes through a colander and let them sit for a moment so they dry more.

11 Take the baking tray with the olive oil out of the oven and carefully pour the potatoes onto the hot oil. Using a spoon, turn the potatoes over a couple of times, making sure they're coated in the oil. Place them back in the oven, on the oven shelf underneath the chicken, and cook them for 15 minutes.

12 After 15 minutes, give the potatoes another shake, turning them over and coating them again in the hot oil. Put them back in the oven to roast for about 20 minutes.

13 Flick the kettle on and make the gravy according to the packet instructions. Doing this now saves you a bit of time at the end, so when made, leave it to one side and reheat it at the end of cooking. (See the nearby sidebar if you want to make your own gravy.)

14 After 20 minutes, get the saucepan again, fill it full of water and place it on the hob, full power, to bring to the boil. When it's boiling, drop in the carrots.

15 Now it's time to check the chicken, which should have been cooking for about an hour and a half. Carefully take the chicken out of the oven on the roasting tray and place on a heatproof surface (a big wooden chopping board works well, or place on the hob if you have enough room). Push the blade of a long sharp knife into the thickest part of the chicken, usually the thigh. This is the place that's cooked the least. Lever the knife to the side a bit and look at the juice on the knife. There should be no blood, and the juices should appear clear. If this part, the thickest part of the chicken, is cooked, you know that the rest of the meat is cooked. If it isn't cooked, pop the bird back in the oven for another 10 minutes or so and repeat the testing process.

16 When the chicken is cooked, place it to one side to rest while you sort everything else out.

17 Add the peas in with the carrots and boil for another 5 minutes. Now on to the bread sauce. Empty the contents of the sachet into a saucepan (over a low to medium heat) and pour in a little milk. Stir until the milk has mixed in and then gradually stir in the rest of the milk. Let the bread sauce simmer while you move on to the next step.

18 Drain the carrots and peas in a colander and divide evenly between four plates.

19 Take the potatoes out of the oven and check that they're cooked by sticking your knife in them; it should go all the way through. If not, pop them back in the oven for another 5 minutes. When they're cooked, distribute the roast potatoes between the four plates. The bread sauce should be done by now, so take the saucepan off the heat.

20 Now it's time to carve the chicken. Pull the legs and wings off and put them on a separate plate. Then simply slice the chicken off in strips, making sure the knife runs along the length of the breast. The slices don't really have to be neat, just edible. Split the pieces between the four plates.

21 Heat up the gravy on the hob and then pour into a jug, place a dollop of the bread sauce onto each plate and serve.

Variation: *Feel free to choose your own vegetables.*

Per serving: *Calories 818 (From Fat 210); Fat 23.3g (Saturated 9.2g); Cholesterol Trace; Sodium 1111mg; Carbohydrate 56.9g; Dietary Fibre 8.7g; Protein 95.2g.*

Christmas Turkey

You don't have to wait until December for a good Christmas dinner. Get a few friends to club together, buy a turkey and have a proper Christmas dinner in your flat.

(This recipe is just for cooking the turkey. You can use the vegetables from the roast chicken recipe or choose your own.)

Preparation time: *5 minutes*

Cooking time: *2 hours 30 minutes*

Serves: *4*

1 turkey (about 3 kilograms, giblets removed)

150 grams of butter, softened for a few seconds in the microwave

Salt and pepper

Couple of sprigs of fresh thyme

1 lemon

1 Preheat the oven to 190°C.

2 Wash the turkey under a trickle of cold water to remove any dirt from the skin and then pat dry with a bit of kitchen roll. Place the turkey on a roasting tray and loosen the skin a little by running your hands between the skin and the flesh.

3 Wash your hands and then season the softened butter with salt and pepper. Pick a small piece up between your fingers and slide it underneath the skin of the turkey, smothering the flesh underneath. Repeat until you've used all the butter.

4 Wash your hands and cut the lemon in half and place inside the turkey with a few sprigs of thyme.

5 Wrap some kitchen foil around the turkey, folding the edges underneath the edges of the roasting tray. Place the turkey in the preheated oven and cook for 2 hours.

To get an even tastier turkey, try *basting* the bird every 30 minutes. To do this, remove the turkey from the oven (closing the oven door behind you to keep in the heat), lift up some of the foil and spoon some of the juices at the bottom of the pan over the turkey. This enriches the flavour of the meat. Yum!

6 After 2 hours, remove the turkey from the oven and turn up the temperature to 220°C. Take the foil off the turkey (put to one side because you need it later) and, when the oven's hot enough, put the turkey back inside and cook for another 30 minutes until the skin turns golden.

7 After 30 minutes, check if the turkey is cooked. Place a knife in the thickest part of the bird and gently prise the meat open. The meat should appear white and any juices should run clear. If it doesn't appear white, place back in the oven for another 15 minutes.

8 Take the turkey out of the oven and place on a clean plastic chopping board, place the foil loosely over the turkey and allow to rest for about 10 minutes before carving.

9 To carve the turkey, remove the wings then carefully pull the legs apart and cut through the skin between the leg and the body. You should now be able to pull off the legs easily.

10 Run your knife down the bone that runs down the middle of the bird, cutting off half of the breast meat in one big piece. Repeat for the other side. With the white side of the breast meat facing down, slice the meat into layers and serve.

Per serving: Calories 672 (From Fat 331); Fat 36.8g (Saturated 21.4g); Cholesterol Trace; Sodium 247mg; Carbohydrate 0.2g; Dietary Fibre Trace; Protein 85.0g.

Home-made chicken gravy to make you drool

If you want to make your own chicken gravy, crumble a chicken stock cube into a jug and add 300 millilitres of boiling water. Pour in some of the chicken juices and scrape up the caramelised bits from the roasting tray and add a drop of white wine. Pour in a spoonful of cornflour dissolved in two spoonfuls of cold water to thicken the gravy and mix well. Voilà. Home-made chicken gravy.

Cooking Red Meat

Red meat is meat that's (surprise, surprise) red before it's cooked, such as beef, lamb and pork.

Red meat is delicious, especially when it's cooked slowly so that it becomes tender. Don't be put off by the rather fancy-sounding recipe titles in this section; these are the forequarter cuts of an animal. This means cuts of meat from the front half of the animal, like the neck, shin and shoulder. These are typically cheaper than rear cuts of meat because they're a little bit tougher and need more cooking time. Most of these recipes need about 3 hours in the oven, but don't be put off by this – it doesn't mean you have to be stuck in the kitchen for 3 hours; you can go off and do something else while it's cooking.

As always, go to your local butcher to get your meat for these roasts. Some supermarkets are starting to stock these cuts of meat, but they won't be able to give you the advice or discounts that a local, independent butcher can. And, remember, butchers won't laugh at you if you ask them loads of questions; it's all part of their job.

So, get stuck in and try some of these amazing red meat roasts, and fill your student kitchen with the warm, homely smell of a proper roast dinner.

Roast Shoulder of Pork

If you think of pork as being fatty or tough, you need to try shoulder of pork. It's a very cheap cut that you cook for a long time on a low heat so the end result is a really tender piece of pork with beautifully crispy crackling, infused with a tangy cider aroma. Oh, and the smell you get in your kitchen is amazing. . . .

Weight-wise, you need about 2 kilograms to feed 4 to 6 people. However, if you buy a slightly bigger piece or if you end up with loads left over, remember that you can use the rest of it throughout the week in sandwiches or in other meals (see Chapter 10 for some ideas.)

Preparation time: *30 minutes*

Cooking time: *3 hours*

Serves: *4–6*

For the pork:

2 kilograms of boneless pork shoulder

Oil

Salt and pepper

Whole cloves from 1 bulb of garlic, not peeled or chopped

1 onion, peeled and sliced

250 millilitres of cider

250 millilitres of hot vegetable stock

Few sprigs of rosemary (optional)

Spoonful of cornflour (optional)

For the vegetables:

2–3 potatoes, peeled and cut into cubes

4 carrots, peeled and cut into quarters

3 turnips, tops and bottoms removed, and cut into pieces roughly the same size as the carrots (don't bother peeling them)

Chunk of butter

Splash of milk

1 Preheat the oven to 230°C.

2 Rinse the pork under a trickle of cold water from the tap, just to wash off any dirt from the skin. Dry with a bit of kitchen roll. Don't use a tea towel or it will be contaminated with raw meat.

3 Place the pork in a roasting tin with fairly deep sides. Score the skin of the pork (if it hasn't already been done) by cutting lines in it with a sharp knife.

4 Drizzle a bit of oil over the skin and rub it in. Sprinkle and rub a generous amount of salt over and into the lines of the skin. This draws the moisture out of the meat and makes the skin a little crispier.

5 Turn the meat on to its side, so the meaty part faces up. Sprinkle salt and pepper over this part and rub it in. Turn the pork back over so that the skin side is facing up.

6 Place the pork in the preheated oven, leaving enough room to put a baking tray on the oven shelf underneath, and cook for 30 minutes.

7 After 30 minutes, take the pork out of the oven and turn the temperature down to 160°C. Lift the pork onto a clean plastic chopping board or a baking tray. Pour the fat from the roasting tray into a bowl. Leave to one side until the fat solidifies and then chuck in the bin.

8 Put the whole garlic cloves (don't bother peeling them) and the sliced onions in the bottom of the roasting tray. Pour in the cider and hot vegetable stock. Carefully place the pork back in the roasting tray, sprinkle over the rosemary (if using) and cover with kitchen foil. Place back in the oven for another 2 hours.

9 After 2 hours, take the pork out of the oven and turn the temperature back up to 220°C. Remove the foil and place the pork back in the oven for another 30 minutes.

10 After 25 minutes, put two pans of water on to boil and when the water's boiling, add the potatoes to one pan and the carrots and turnips to another.

11 Carefully remove the pork from the oven, take out of the roasting tray and place onto a clean chopping board. Turn the oven off and put some plates in to warm up. If you want to make your own gravy, read on; otherwise, move on to Step 12. Pour the remaining juices in the roasting tray into a small saucepan and bring to the boil. While that's coming to the boil, mix one spoonful of cornflour with 2 spoonfuls of water in a cup and then pour into the saucepan to thicken the liquid into a gravy.

12 Slice the crackling (the hard stuff on top) off the pork by carefully running your knife underneath and prising it away from the meat. Slice the pork in layers and place on the plates. Cut the crackling into strips and place on top of the pork.

13 Drain the vegetables and mash the potatoes with a little butter and a splash of milk (if needed). Take the plates out of the oven and spoon on the vegetables.

14 Pour the gravy through a sieve into a jug (to catch the garlic and onion) and serve with the roast pork and veg. Smile, you've just cooked shoulder of pork, you legend!

Variation: Try swapping half of the potato with some celeriac, a sweet tasting (and pretty odd-looking vegetable) to make celeriac mash. The sweetness of celeriac goes really nicely with pork. Also, if you like your crackling really crunchy, pop it back in the oven for 10 minutes after you've cut it, to crisp it up a little more.

Per serving: Calories 634 (From Fat 244); Fat 27.1g (Saturated 10.0g); Cholesterol Trace; Sodium 781mg; Carbohydrate 27.2g; Dietary Fibre 8.0g; Protein 70.4g.

Braised Lamb Shanks with Boulangère Potatoes

Uh oh. Fancy title territory. In fact, lamb shank is a really cheap cut of meat from the top of the leg and far from being fancy stuff. *Braised* means cooking it slowly in some liquid; in this case, alcohol. See, it's already starting to sound like a student roast dinner. . . .

Don't worry about the long cooking time (3–4 hours); the oven does all the work to make the lamb so tender that it just falls off the bone by the time you come to eat it.

Boulangère potatoes are basically sliced potatoes cooked in the oven. So, this is an incredibly easy meal to make.

If you don't have one large roasting tin, divide all the ingredients between two smaller tins.

Preparation time: *10 minutes*

Cooking time: *4 hours*

Serves: *4*

3 carrots, peeled and quartered	Few sprigs of thyme
3 parsnips, peeled and quartered	Olive oil
1 bulb of garlic, cloves broken off, but still in their skins	4 lamb shanks
	2 tins of chopped tomatoes
Few sprigs of rosemary	½ bottle of red wine

For the boulangère potatoes:

2 baking potatoes, peeled and thinly sliced

1 onion, peeled and thinly sliced

300 millilitres of vegetable stock

½ mug of milk

Chunk of butter

For the gravy:

2 teaspoons of cornflour

_1_ Preheat the oven to 180°C.

_2_ Get a large, deep roasting tin and add the carrots, parsnips and garlic.

_3_ Cover with the rosemary and thyme, saving a bit of rosemary for the Boulangère Potatoes.

_4_ Grab a large saucepan and heat a glug of olive oil in it over a hot heat. When hot, add the lamb shanks one at a time, turning them to brown each side of the meat. You may need to add a drop more oil after you've browned the first two.

_5_ Place the lamb shanks in the roasting tin on top of the vegetables and herbs.

_6_ Pour over the chopped tomatoes and red wine, and then carefully place in the preheated oven for an hour.

_7_ After an hour, turn the heat down to 160°C and cook for another hour.

_8_ Turn over the lamb shanks in the roasting tray and place back in the oven for a third hour.

_9_ Take the roasting tray out of the oven and place the lamb shanks on a clean plate. Carefully pour the liquid through a colander and into a small saucepan. Place the vegetables and herbs in the colander back into the roasting tray and place the lamb shanks on top. Spoon about a third of the liquid back over the shanks and pop the shanks back in the oven.

_10_ Place a layer of the sliced potatoes in another roasting tray and scatter with a few sliced onions. Keep layering the sliced potatoes and onions, finishing with a layer of sliced potatoes. Mix the vegetable stock with milk in a jug and pour over the potatoes, just enough to half-fill the roasting tray. Cut up the butter into small cubes and place over the potatoes. Sprinkle the rest of the rosemary over the potatoes. Place in the oven on the shelf above the meat and cook for an hour.

_11_ After 50 minutes, bring the saucepan of red wine juices to the boil. When boiling, put the 2 teaspoons of cornflour into a cup and add 4 teaspoons of cold water. Mix and then pour into the gravy. Whisk it with a whisk or a fork until the gravy thickens and pour into a jug.

12 Put four plates into the oven to warm up for a couple of minutes.

13 The lamb shanks should be really nice and tender now and just falling off the bone. Take them and the vegetables out and put them on
the plates. Add a couple of spoonfuls of the potatoes and pour the
gravy on. Yum.

Variation: Use blade side shoulder rather than lamb shanks. It is similar
to lamb shank but slightly cheaper. You cook it in exactly the same way,
so try asking your butcher for it.

Per serving: Calories 1101 (From Fat 445); Fat 49.4g (Saturated 23.0g); Cholesterol Trace;
Sodium 509mg; Carbohydrate 93.8g; Dietary Fibre 15.6g; Protein 70.3g.

Beef Brisket with Newcastle Brown Ale Gravy

Brisket is a cheap cut at the very top of the leg above the
shank and is a thick round shape.

You braise this joint in a good old drop of Newcastle Brown
Ale to give the meat a really nice flavour.

Preparation time: 10 minutes

Cooking time: 3 hours 30 minutes

Serves: 4

Oil (groundnut or vegetable, not olive oil)

1 kilogram of beef brisket

2 carrots, peeled and sliced

2 parsnips, peeled and sliced

1 onion, peeled and chopped

2 bottles of Newcastle Brown Ale

Salt

2 baking potatoes, peeled and cut into pieces

2 teaspoons of cornflour

1 Turn the oven to 180°C and place a roasting tin or casserole dish
with fairly deep sides inside for five minutes to warm up.

2 Heat a glug of oil in a large saucepan over a medium to high heat and
add the beef brisket. Fry the brisket until each side has turned
golden brown (4 to 5 minutes per side).

3 Remove the casserole dish from the oven and place the carrots, parsnips and onion inside. Place the browned beef brisket (try saying that when you're drunk) on top of the vegetables.

4 Pour over the Newcastle Brown Ale until the liquid fills about two-thirds of the roasting tin or casserole dish. Tightly cover with some kitchen foil and place in the oven for 30 minutes.

5 After 30 minutes, turn the oven down to 140°C and cook for an hour.

6 After an hour, carefully remove the pan from the oven and uncover the foil. Carefully turn the beef over. Cover again with the tin foil and place back in the oven for another hour.

7 After an hour, fill a large saucepan three-quarters full of water and place on the hob to bring to the boil. When boiling, add a pinch of salt and add in the potato pieces. Cook the potatoes for 5 minutes.

8 Meanwhile, pour some oil on a baking tray and put it in the oven to heat up. When the potatoes have been boiling for 5 minutes, drain through a colander and carefully pour them onto the hot baking tray. Put them in the oven.

9 Remove the kitchen foil from the casserole dish and cook the uncovered beef and the potatoes for a final hour, bringing the cooking time up to 3 and a half hours.

10 Remove the beef from the pot and place on a clean chopping board (one you use for meat). Let that rest while you make the gravy.

11 Pour the liquid through a sieve into a saucepan, catching the vegetables in the sieve and put them onto warmed plates. Bring this liquid to the boil. Mix the cornflour with 3 teaspoons of cold water in a cup and pour into the juices to thicken it and make it into a gravy.

12 Remove the potatoes from the oven and place them onto the plates with the vegetables.

13 Slice the beef into layers and arrange on the plate with the vegetables. Pour the gravy into a jug and serve.

Per serving: Calories 879 (From Fat 445); Fat 49.4g (Saturated 19.1g); Cholesterol Trace; Sodium 224mg; Carbohydrate 56.4g; Dietary Fibre 8.1g; Protein 52.2g.

Chapter 14

Food to Impress: Cooking for a Date

In This Chapter

▶ Sensuous salads

▶ Mouth-watering mains

▶ Setting the mood

So you've invited that special someone to come round tonight for a romantic meal for two. You're wearing clean pants, you've lit some candles and turned on the Barry White; and now it's time to start cooking. You look in your cupboards and suddenly come to the conclusion that serving up a bowl of cheesy chips isn't really the best way to impress.

You need something with a bit more va-va-voom to really show your feelings, so in this chapter I share the best recipes for lurve. In this chapter you can find some sexy starters that are perfect for sharing before strutting on to the mains, all of which need just a little time in the kitchen to get maximum results. And you only have to turn to Chapter 11 to find a gorgeous dessert to finish things off.

Creating Sexy Starters

Starters are perfect for dates. Your date won't expect anything other than a main course, so when you bring out a
starter, it's a subtle way of showing how much you care. Plus,
if you've made finger food, it gives you the chance to be a bit
playful and show your generous side by leaving the last piece
to your date. Or you could just show who's boss and wolf it
all down.

Warm King Prawn Salad

Prawns are a classic starter, and this decadent dish is sure to
impress.

If you're using frozen prawns, place them in a dish
covered with cling film and defrost overnight in the
fridge. When the prawns are defrosted, pour out any
water and drain the prawns on a bit of kitchen roll.

Preparation time: *15 minutes*

Cooking time: *5 minutes*

Serves: *2*

Handful of green beans	6 large prawns, shelled
3 handfuls of mixed salad, rinsed and drained	Small chunk of butter
¼ red onion, finely sliced	1 clove of garlic, crushed
Olive oil	2 teaspoons of chopped chives
10 cherry tomatoes	Salt and pepper

1 Put a small saucepan of water on to boil over a high heat and, when
   boiling, add a pinch of salt and the green beans.

2 When the green beans are cooked, drain them and then run them
   under the cold water tap for a minute until they're cool.

3 Place the salad in a bowl and add the finely sliced red onion.

4 Pour a drop of the olive oil into the frying pan and heat over a
   medium heat. When hot, fry the cherry tomatoes until they soften
   and then add them to the salad.

5 Add a drop more oil to the pan and turn the heat down to low. Add the prawns and cook for about 2 minutes or until they turn pink. Turn them over in the pan and add a chunk of butter and the crushed garlic. Continue cooking for a further 3 minutes and then turn off the heat and stir in the chopped chives.

6 Drizzle some olive oil over the salad and toss lightly with your hands, making sure the salad is evenly coated in the oil.

7 Arrange the green beans around the edge of the plate and place the salad in the centre. Top with the garlicky prawns and serve.

Variation: *To make a very simple dressing for the prawns, mix 2 spoonfuls of mayonnaise with 2 spoonfuls of tomato sauce and lightly season with pepper.*

Per serving: *Calories 272 (From Fat 194); Fat 21.5g (Saturated 9.2g); Cholesterol Trace; Sodium 142mg; Carbohydrate 6.5g; Dietary Fibre 3.2g; Protein 13.0g.*

Warm Chicken Salad with Baby Spinach and Mozzarella

Salads don't always have to be lettuce-based affairs. Some of the best salads, such as this one, are made from fresh, tasty spinach. The spinach here is topped with succulent chicken breasts and crispy bacon. This salad is rather good with some warm crusty bread.

Preparation time: *15 minutes*

Cooking time: *10 minutes*

Serves: *2*

For the dressing:
Olive oil
Juice from ½ lemon
Salt and pepper
For the salad:
½ an avocado
Juice from ½ lemon
3 slices of bacon

2 chicken breasts, cut into 12 strips
¼ red onion, peeled and finely sliced
2 handfuls of baby spinach
6 sun-dried tomatoes (optional)
1 big ball of mozzarella
Salt and pepper
Olive oil

1 To make the dressing, mix 4 glugs of oil in a bowl with the lemon juice. Mix well and season with a little salt and pepper.

2 Preheat the grill to a medium setting.

3 Peel the avocado and then slice and place in a bowl. Squeeze over the other half of the lemon and mix carefully. (The lemon juice stops the avocado from turning brown.)

4 Place the bacon under the grill and cook until crispy, turning when necessary. Meanwhile, heat a frying pan with a drop of olive oil and gently fry the chicken strips until browned. Add the red onion slices and cook for a further minute.

5 Add the baby spinach and sun-dried tomatoes (if using) to the frying pan with the chicken and turn off the heat. Start stirring everything together; the spinach should start to wilt and shrink slightly. Break the mozzarella into bite-sized pieces and place in the pan. Season with a little salt and pepper.

6 Remove the bacon and place on a clean plastic chopping board. Carefully slice into strips.

7 Divide the chicken and spinach mixture between two plates, placing the avocado slices round the edge. Then place the bacon slices on top and drizzle over some dressing. Serve immediately.

Per serving: Calories 885 (From Fat 373); Fat 41.4g (Saturated 14.2g); Cholesterol Trace; Sodium 2356mg; Carbohydrate 36.8g; Dietary Fibre 9.9g; Protein 91.3g.

⌕*Lentil Stuffed Courgettes*

This dish is a great choice for a special vegetarian friend (you can make it vegan by leaving out the cheese). You can pre-cook the lentils before the special guest arrives and then just pile them into the prepared courgettes and whack them in the oven.

Preparation time: *25 minutes (plus 40 minutes to cook the lentils)*

Cooking time: *15 minutes*

Serves: *2*

For the lentils:
½ mug of green lentils
200 millilitres of vegetable stock
For the courgettes:
2 small to medium-sized courgettes
Olive oil

Salt and pepper
½ onion, peeled and chopped
1 clove of garlic, finely chopped
Small handful of chopped walnuts
Handful of grated cheese

1 Preheat the oven to 180°C.

2 Wash the lentils and place in a pan with the vegetable stock. Heat over a low heat and simmer for 30 to 40 minutes or until the lentils soften. (You may need to top up the stock a little during this time.)

3 After 15 minutes, cut the courgettes in half lengthways and carefully scoop out the centre with a teaspoon. Lightly drizzle with olive oil and season with salt and pepper. Place on a lightly greased baking tray.

4 Check on the lentils; if they're cooked, drain them and leave to one side.

5 Heat a little oil in a frying pan over a medium heat and gently cook the onion until it starts to turn golden. Add the chopped garlic, drained lentils, walnuts and add a little salt and pepper. Moisten with a drop more olive oil if needed. Fry for 5 minutes.

6 Now fill each courgette with the lentil mix. Top with the grated cheese and place in the preheated oven for 20 minutes until the cheese starts to melt. (You can finish the cheese off under the grill to give it a slightly glazed effect.)

7 Use a spatula to place each courgette onto a plate, drizzle with a little olive oil and serve.

Per serving: *Calories 601(From Fat 340); Fat 37.8g (Saturated 12.9g); Cholesterol Trace; Sodium 901mg; Carbohydrate 33.5g; Dietary Fibre 7.2g; Protein 31.6g.*

Prawn and Horseradish Salad

This tasty starter comes with a bit of a kick, so make sure that your date likes fairly strong flavours.

 If you're using frozen prawns, make sure you defrost them thoroughly before using. Place in a bowl, cover with cling film and allow to defrost in the fridge for 24 hours before you need them. Squeeze out any excess moisture before using.

Preparation time: *15 minutes*

Cooking time: *Nil*

Serves: *2*

2 handfuls of cooked and shelled prawns

6 spoonfuls of mayonnaise

2 teaspoons of horseradish sauce

2 teaspoons of chopped chives

Salt and pepper

2 small handfuls of mixed leaf salad, washed and drained

1 Place the prawns, mayonnaise and horseradish sauce in a bowl and carefully mix together. Add one teaspoon of the chopped chives and mix.

2 Neatly arrange the salad on two plates and top with the prawn mixture.

3 Sprinkle the remaining chives over in a fancy fashion and serve.

Per serving: *Calories 435 (From Fat 329); Fat 36.5g (Saturated 5.6g); Cholesterol Trace; Sodium 292mg; Carbohydrate 2.5g; Dietary Fibre 1.0g; Protein 24.0g.*

⏍Melon with Green Peppercorn and Orange Dressing

This recipe sounds a bit posh, but is actually very simple to make. You can find peppercorns in the supermarket. They're not the hard peppercorns you grind over food, but small soft green berries.

Like the Prawn and Horseradish Salad recipe, no cooking's involved in this one.

Preparation time: *10 minutes*

Cooking time: *Nil*

Serves: *2*

1 teaspoon of soft green pepper-corns, drained

1 tablespoon of mayonnaise

1 tablespoon of orange juice

½ melon (honeydew, galia or canteloupe)

½ orange, peeled and evenly sliced into 6 slices

½ kiwi fruit, peeled and evenly sliced into 6 slices

1 strawberry, cut in half through the green stem (don't remove the green top, it looks better with it on)

1 Place the peppercorns on a chopping board and gently crush them with the back of a kitchen knife and scoop them into a bowl.

2 Add the mayonnaise and stir. Add in ½ tablespoon of the orange juice. Mix together and taste, adding more orange juice if needed.

3 Cut the ½ melon in half again lengthways.

4 Skin the melon by running your knife between the rind and flesh, following the natural contour of the fruit. The melon should just fall away.

5 Carefully cut the melon into slices lengthways.

6 Neatly arrange the slices of melon onto the plate, with one point of each melon in the centre of the plate, and the rest circling out like clock hands.

7 Arrange the orange and kiwi fruit to overlap each other (3 slices of each fruit per plate). Add the strawberry.

8 Carefully drizzle the dressing across the melon with a teaspoon and serve.

Variation: *If the sauce doesn't sound like your thing, serve the melon on its own, or place a little dollop of crème fraîche on the side.*

Per serving: *Calories 222 (From Fat 57); Fat 6.3g (Saturated 0.9g); Cholesterol Trace; Sodium 90mg; Carbohydrate 38.0g; Dietary Fibre 4.9g; Protein 3.2g.*

Ham and Leek Risotto

Risottos don't just make great main meals; you can serve them as starters too. Just make sure that you don't serve too much because risotto is very filling.

Risottos also require you to be with them while they cook because you need to constantly stir them, which means they're better off for someone you've been with for a while, instead of a first date. The pay off is how good they taste though!

Preparation time: 5 minutes

Cooking time: 20 minutes

Serves: 2

Chunk of butter

1 leek, sliced

3 slices of ham, cut into strips

Handful of mushrooms, sliced

1 mug of arborio rice

500 millilitres of hot chicken stock

Chunk of Parmesan, grated

Pinch of freshly chopped parsley (optional)

Salt and pepper

1 Heat the butter in a saucepan over a medium heat until melted. Add the leeks and fry until softened.

2 Add the ham and mushrooms and cook for about 3 minutes until they're lightly browned.

3 Pour in the arborio rice and mix well with the other ingredients.

4 Pour in just enough chicken stock to cover the rice and then give the rice a stir. Keep stirring the rice, and every time it absorbs most of the stock, pour in a bit more. Keep going for about 30 minutes until all the stock is used up or the rice becomes soft and creamy.

5 Grate the Parmesan into the saucepan and mix well, so that the heat starts to melt the Parmesan. Season with salt and pepper and sprinkle with fresh parsley to serve.

Per serving: Calories 539 (From Fat 203); Fat 22.5g (Saturated 12.6g); Cholesterol Trace; Sodium 1477mg; Carbohydrate 63.7g; Dietary Fibre 3.4g; Protein 20.4g.

Making Foolproof Main Courses

Okay, so the starter's gone well, you're halfway through the first bottle of red and now it's time to pull out all the stops for the mains.

Coming up are the essential, foolproof main meals that you can make to really impress your date. Packed full of flavour, these little beauties will get you some serious Brownie points.

Braised Beef and Guinness with Olive Mash

This is a full-bodied and hearty meal, perfect for snuggling up on a winter's night. Also, due to the slow cooking of this dish, it allows you to enjoy another glass of wine or two while it braises.

Chuck steak is a thick (usually about an inch) steak from the shoulder of a cow. It's sometimes known as *braising steak,* and is ideal for long, slow cooking.

 You can make the steak and the sauce (but not the mash) up to two days in advance. This actually improves the flavour. Reheat it in the oven until everything in the dish is piping hot.

Preparation time: 15–20 minutes

Cooking time: 2 hours

Serves: 2

For the beef:

Olive oil

½ large onion, sliced

1 tablespoon of plain flour (plus a pinch for dusting the beef)

2 x 200-gram chuck steaks (or braising or stewing steak)

½ can of Guinness

1 tablespoon of tomato purée

400 millilitres of beef stock (from two beef stock cubes)

Salt and pepper

For the potatoes:

2 potatoes, peeled and cut into chunks

6 glugs of olive oil

Chunk of butter

1 Place a casserole dish in the oven and preheat to 170°C.

2 Heat a little oil in a saucepan over a medium heat and, when hot, add the sliced onion and cook until soft and golden.

3 While the onion is cooking, scatter a pinch of flour on a large plate and lightly press the steaks into the flour to coat them.

4 By now, the onion should be done, so carefully take the casserole dish out of the oven and pour the onion into it. Add a drop more oil to the pan.

5 When the oil is hot, add the steaks and cook until they're well browned on both sides. Place the steaks in the casserole dish.

6 Reduce the heat in the pan and add the Guinness and tomato purée. Cook for about 5 minutes until the Guinness reduces by half. Add the tablespoon of flour and stir well.

7 Add the stock a bit at a time, stirring the stock into the flour to make a sauce. Continue until you've used all the stock and then bring to a simmer, season and pour into the casserole dish with the steak and onion.

8 Cover the casserole dish with a lid or some kitchen foil and place in the oven for 2 hours.

9 Try a bit of the meat to see if it's nice and tender. It should just fall apart when you pull it with a fork. Turn the heat down to about 50°C and put two plates in the oven to warm up.

10 Fill a saucepan with water, bring to the boil over a high heat and add the peeled and chopped potatoes. Boil for 15 minutes or until soft and then drain and mash with the olive oil and a chunk of butter.

11 Remove the casserole dish from the oven and spoon the mash into the centre of each plate, top with a steak and pour over the sauce. Mmm, braised steak with olive mash.

Per serving: *Calories 1242 (From Fat 778); Fat 86.4g (Saturated 21.6g); Cholesterol Trace; Sodium 1233mg; Carbohydrate 50.0g; Dietary Fibre 3.7g; Protein 66.0g.*

Chicken in Cream and White Wine Sauce

The flavour from the white wine in the sauce goes perfectly with the chicken in this delicious recipe. Feel free to swap the spinach for some mashed potato if you're not a fan of the green stuff.

Preparation time: 15 minutes

Cooking time: 2 hours

Serves: 2

2 chicken thighs (skin on, with or without bones)

2 chicken breasts (skin on), cut in half widthways

Salt and pepper

Big chunk of butter, plus a bit more for the sauce

1 small clove of garlic, crushed

½ leek, finely diced

½ onion, finely diced

½ celery, finely diced

125 millilitres of white wine

125 millilitres of double cream

½ lemon (optional)

2 teaspoons of chopped chives

4 handfuls of spinach (this seems like a lot, but it shrinks when cooked)

1 Season the chicken with salt and pepper. Melt most of the butter in a large saucepan over a medium heat and add the chicken. Cook until just about to brown; about 7 minutes on each side.

2 Add the garlic and vegetables, stir and then cover and gently cook for about 30 minutes until the chicken is cooked. Check by cutting a piece open – the flesh should be white, and any juices should run clear.

3 Preheat the oven to 50°C. Remove the chicken from the saucepan and place on a baking tray. Place in the oven, along with a couple of plates, to keep warm while you make the sauce.

4 Drain off any fat from the pan, keeping the vegetables in the pan. Turn up the heat a little and add the wine to deglaze the pan (loosen any cooked bits that are clinging to the side of the pan) and allow the wine to reduce (evaporate away) a bit.

5 Pour in the cream, bring to the boil and then turn the heat back down and simmer for about 2 minutes. The sauce should start to thicken.

6 Add the remaining bit of butter and stir. Grab a separate frying pan and melt a chunk of butter over a medium heat. When melted, add the spinach in handfuls and cook until it wilts.

7 Take the chicken and plates out of the oven and place half of the spinach on each plate. Place the chicken on top.

8 Squeeze the lemon into the sauce (if using), add the chives, mix together and then carefully spoon over the chicken. Serve and watch your date's eyes light up!

Per serving: Calories 906 (From Fat 581); Fat 64.5g (33.8); Cholesterol Trace; Sodium 472mg; Carbohydrate 10.7g; Dietary Fibre 4.1g; Protein 70.7g.

Minted Lamb Chops with Roast Vegetables

This is a relatively quick meal to knock up, despite the apparently long cooking time; most of this time is for the vegetables roasting in the oven. The minted lamb chops are gorgeous.

Preparation time: *10 minutes*

Cooking time: *40 minutes*

Serves: *2*

Olive oil	*Salt and pepper*
¼ red, green and yellow pepper (each cut into 8 segments)	*Couple of pinches of chopped fresh mint*
½ courgette, sliced at an angle	*4 lamb chops*
¼ red onion, peeled and thickly sliced	

1 Preheat the oven to 230°C.

2 Pour a couple of glugs of olive oil onto a baking tray and place in the oven to warm up. When hot, add the vegetables, season with some salt and pepper and place back in the oven to roast until soft.

3 Mix the mint with some olive oil in a bowl and brush or spoon over the lamb chops. Season with salt and pepper and place back in the bowl to marinate for 25 minutes while the vegetables are roasting, so sit back with your date for a bit.

4 After 25 minutes, turn the grill on to a medium setting. Place the lamb chops under the grill and cook for 5 minutes on each side.

5 Place the roast vegetables in the centre of each plate and top with a lamb chop.

Variation: *You could add a few new potatoes or some leafy green vegetables to this meal.*

Per serving: Calories 1009 (From Fat 849); Fat 94.3g (Saturated 33.1g); Cholesterol Trace; Sodium 127mg; Carbohydrate 6.8g; Dietary Fibre 2.0g; Protein 33.3g.

Pork Fillets in Cider

Pork fillets are a really tasty cut of meat, coming from the lower back of a pig. The cider adds a delicious zesty tang to the meat. I've put some red cabbage with this dish as a very tasty accompaniment.

Preparation time: *10 minutes*

Cooking time: *30 minutes*

Serves: 2

For the pork:

4 pork fillet medallions

Olive oil

120 millilitres of dry cider

1 teaspoon of soft green peppercorns, drained and crushed on a board with the back of a knife

120 millilitres of double cream

Small chunk of butter

For the cabbage:

Big chunk of butter

2 handfuls of finely shredded red cabbage

½ apple, peeled and chopped into very small cubes

1 tablespoon of brown sugar

1 Preheat the oven to 190°C. While that's heating up, brush or spoon the pork fillets with a little olive oil. Place on a baking tray and, when the oven is hot, place in the oven for 20 to 25 minutes.

2 While the pork is cooking, you can prepare the cabbage accompaniment. Melt the butter in a saucepan over a medium heat and add a little water.

3 Add the cabbage, apple and sugar, stir, and then cover with a lid and cook for 20 minutes until the cabbage softens. Keep checking on it to make sure the pan doesn't dry out (if it does, add a bit more water).

4 After 10 minutes, grab another saucepan and pour in the cider. Turn the heat up to full and boil for about 7 minutes until the cider reduces by two-thirds.

5 Add the peppercorns, then the cream, stir and bring to the boil. Reduce the heat and simmer for 5 minutes until the mixture thickens.

6 By now the pork and the cabbage should be cooked, so remove the pork and let it rest on a clean chopping board for 2 minutes.

7 Spoon the cabbage onto a couple of preheated plates, place the pork on top and spoon the sauce over everything.

Per serving: Calories 855 (From Fat 530); Fat 58.9g (Saturated 30.8g); Cholesterol Trace; Sodium 302mg; Carbohydrate 15.2g; Dietary Fibre 3.0g; Protein 65.9g.

Salmon Fillet with Basil and Olive Oil Dressing

Fish is always a really refreshing and light dish, and this salmon fillet won't disappoint. It's perfect on a spring or summer's night with a glass of cool white wine.

Preparation time: *15 minutes*

Cooking time: *15 minutes*

Serves: *2*

For the dressing:

Olive oil

½ onion, peeled and finely chopped

1 clove of garlic, peeled and crushed

Pinch of sugar

1 splodge of tomato purée

6 tomatoes, skinned and chopped (see the nearby sidebar for a preparation tip)

75 millilitres of chicken, vegetable or fish stock

3 fresh basil leaves, finely chopped

Salt and pepper

For the salmon:

2 salmon fillets (ask the fishmonger to skin them)

4 big handfuls of baby spinach

Olive oil

1 In a saucepan, heat a little oil over a medium heat and cook the onion and garlic until they turn soft. Add a pinch of sugar.

2 Stir in the tomato purée and chopped tomatoes. Add the stock and gently simmer for 10 to 15 minutes.

3 Meanwhile, turn on the grill to a medium setting, drizzle some olive oil over the salmon pieces and then place on a tray under the pre-heated grill. Cook for 10 to 15 minutes.

4 While they're under the grill, melt a little oil in another frying pan and when hot, fry the spinach off in batches until wilted.

5 To check if the salmon is cooked, try pulling a bit away with your fork. It should just fall apart when cooked; if it doesn't, place it back under the grill.

6 Place the spinach onto some pre-warmed plates and then place the salmon on top.

7 Check on the dressing. If it seems too thick, add a touch of boiling water; then stir in 50 millilitres of olive oil and the chopped basil, add some salt and pepper and pour over the salmon and spinach. Serve.

Per serving: Calories 689 (From Fat 447); Fat 49.7g (Saturated 7.8g); Cholesterol Trace; Sodium 486mg; Carbohydrate 14.3g; Dietary Fibre 5.2g; Protein 46.0g.

Tricks with tomatoes

To skin tomatoes, submerge them in a bowl of boiling water for 5 minutes. Carefully spoon them out and cut a cross on top of the tomatoes. You should be able to pull the skins off very easily.

Warm Duck Salad with Orange

Duck is always a real treat, so cooking it on a date sends some really good signals to your partner. Some people find duck a little fatty, but it works really well here when served with a salad.

This recipe also includes fennel, a vegetable that looks like a white bulb with green stalks coming out of the top. You can find it in the vegetable section in most supermarkets.

Preparation time: 10 minutes

Cooking time: 45 minutes

Serves: 2

For the duck:

1 fennel bulb, trim the top, remove the bottom, slice in half and cut into large chunks

½ red onion, cut into large slices

2 duck breasts, skin on (you can find these in the supermarket)

3 handfuls of mixed leaf salad

10 cherry tomatoes

2 oranges, peeled, cut in half and sliced

2 handfuls of precooked bacon, sliced into strips

2 glugs of olive oil

Salt and pepper

For the dressing:

4 glugs of olive oil

Bit of juice from the sliced oranges

1 tablespoon of balsamic vinegar

2 pinches of chopped fresh chives

1 Preheat the oven to 200°C.

2 Drizzle a couple of glugs of olive oil onto a baking tray and place in the oven until hot.

3 When hot, chuck on the fennel and onion and roast for about 40 minutes, shuffling the tray occasionally to keep the vegetables coated in the oil. Cook until they turn a dark, even colour and become soft.

4 Meanwhile lightly score the skins of the duck breasts. Heat a frying pan over a medium to high heat and, when hot, add the duck breast, skin down. (You don't need to add any oil because the fat comes out of the duck as it cooks.)

5 After about 15 to 20 minutes when the skin has turned a dark golden colour, turn the duck over onto the flesh side and cook until the flesh is lightly browned; it doesn't need to be fully cooked because you finish it off in the oven. (You may need to drain away some of the fat from the pan.)

6 By now, the fennel and onion should be roasted, so remove them from the oven and set aside. Put the duck on the baking tray and place in the oven for 10 minutes.

7 While that's cooking, whisk all the dressing ingredients together in a bowl.

8 Place the mixed leaf salad in a separate bowl and add the tomatoes, roast fennel and onions. With clean hands, mix them into the salad.

9 When the duck is cooked (it should still be a little pink in the middle – this is fine, but cook it for a bit longer if you want to), remove from the oven and place on a clean chopping board. Leave it to rest for 2 minutes and then season the duck with a little salt and pepper.

10 Carefully carve the duck breast into neat slices.

11 Add the orange slices and half the dressing to the salad, carefully combine and then place onto plates. Lay the duck on top and cover with the rest of the dressing and scatter over the bacon.

Variation: *Try rubbing some Chinese five spice (available in most super-markets) into the duck breast before cooking for a slight tang to the flavour.*

Per serving: *Calories 1521 (From Fat 1096); Fat 121.8g (Saturated 32.4g); Cholesterol Trace; Sodium 291mg; Carbohydrate 26.7g; Dietary Fibre 6.6g; Protein 79.4g.*

Stuffed Tomatoes with Rice

This is a great main meal for a vegetarian date. The stuffed tomatoes look great and show that you've gone to some effort to make them. You can also do most of the cooking (up to step 7) before your date comes, meaning you just have to pop the tomatoes in the oven before you're ready to eat. (Keep them in the fridge until you're ready to cook them.)

This is quite a light main meal, so if you're both feeling hungry or haven't had a starter first, double up all the ingredients.

If you don't have fresh herbs, dried will do.

Preparation time: *20 minutes*

Cooking time: *45 minutes*

Serves: *2*

Olive oil

½ onion, peeled and finely chopped

1 clove of garlic, peeled and crushed

50 grams of long grain rice

130 millilitres of vegetable stock

Salt and pepper

2 large beef tomatoes

1 big handful of mushrooms, sliced

1 ball of mozzarella, broken into pieces

3 big pinches of chopped fresh basil

3 big pinches of chopped fresh chives

1 Preheat the oven to 180°C.

2 Grab a high-sided saucepan and add a glug of oil over a medium heat. Fry the onion until soft and then add the garlic.

3 Stir in the rice and pour in the stock. Bring things to a simmer, add a little salt and pepper, cover and entertain your date while it gently cooks for 15 minutes.

4 After 15 minutes, check the rice, which should be nice and soft. If so, remove the pan from the heat and put it to one side.

5 Wash the tomatoes, then cut the tops off and keep them to one side (you use them later). Carefully scoop out the flesh of the tomatoes with a spoon, keeping the sides of the tomato intact.

6 Heat another frying pan with a little oil and fry the mushrooms over a high heat until golden brown.

7 Add the mushrooms, chopped herbs and mozzarella to the rice and carefully mix together. Stuff the tomatoes with the filling, put the tops back on and place onto a lightly oiled baking tray.

8 Drizzle the tomatoes with a little olive oil, season with salt and pepper and place in the preheated oven for 25 minutes.

9 After 25 minutes, take out the tomatoes and let them cool down (so they're not red hot!) for a couple of minutes. Place onto a plate and serve with roast vegetables, salad or crusty bread.

Variation: *You can leave out the mozzarella to make this a vegan meal.*

Per serving: *Calories 405 (From Fat 234); Fat 26.0g (Saturated 9.2g); Cholesterol Trace; Sodium 255mg; Carbohydrate 29.1g; Dietary Fibre2.8; Protein 13.7g.*

Getting Everything Else Ready

By now you should have your cooking sorted and be confident that your date will be seriously impressed with the food you're about to serve up.

But what about everything else that goes along with the date? Time to slip into something more comfortable and work through the checklist below to make the night perfect.

Choosing the best wine

If you've put in the time and effort to make a cracking meal, you want to finish things off with a well chosen bottle of wine. It doesn't have to be expensive, but choose something to go well with the meal. Spending a couple of quid more can push a mediocre wine up to a good one. A general rule is to drink red wine (merlot, rioja, cabernet sauvignon) with red meat and white wine (pinot grigio, sauvignon blanc, chardonnay) with fish and poultry dishes. For a more in-depth guide to wine, check out Chapter 12.

As well as alcoholic drinks, make sure you have tea, coffee, milk and sugar for after the meal.

Setting the mood

Getting the right mood or atmosphere is really important to ensuring the evening's success. Follow these tips:

- **Clean the flat.** First impressions are everything, so if your date has to struggle getting past a bike or laundry basket in the hallway, you're not giving off quite the right impression. It's hard to feel romantic in a dirty kitchen too, so make sure that you clear away all the used pans and dishes.

- **Dim the lights.** That classic trick of turning down the lights to create a softer, more romantic atmosphere makes a real impression and shows your date that you want him or her to have a great night.

- **Light scented candles.** Try lighting a few candles to give it more of a wow factor, and to mask any burning smells from the oven. . . .

- **Choose some decent relaxing music.** You can not only show your date your good taste in music, but also music can provide a great talking point and helps to make your date relax and unwind.

- **Wash your hands after cooking.** Passing raw chicken from your fingers onto your date's face or hair may not go down too well, so make sure that you wash your hands thoroughly. You might also need to change your clothes if they smell of cooking.

Turn to Chapter 11 for some great dessert recipes, and you have a fantastic romantic evening ahead of you!

Chapter 15

Getting into the Party Spirit

* *

In This Chapter

▶ Tiny, tasty treats

▶ Lip-smackin' finger food

▶ Tips and tricks to ensure a great party

* *

1 doubt very much that you need a guide to throwing a party when you're at uni. But what about cooking for one? Rustling up a few tasty treats for your friends to nibble on can make any party that bit more special.

In this chapter, I look at the best party and buffet food to make for people to really tuck in and enjoy. Plus, I look at how to throw a great party and still save a few pennies so that you can eat for the rest of the week.

Anyone can throw a decent party. But not everyone can create some amazing food to go with it. . . .

Recipes in This Chapter

↺ Garlic Breaded Mushrooms

↺ Spicy Chips

↺ Mini Carrot Wraps

↺ Vegetable Samosas

▶ Mini Roast Beef and Yorkshire Puds

↺ Baby Baked Potatoes

↺ Tomato and Mozzarella Bruschetta

▶ Pigs in Blankets

▶ Sticky Chicken Drumsticks

↺ Root Vegetable Crisps

▶ Home-Made Pizza

▶ Cheese and Ham Quiche

↺ Potato Salad

▶ Chicken Dippers

Cooking for a Party

The best party food is stuff that's just as tasty eaten hot or cold. There's no point making an extravagant and delicious stir-fry for only three eager ravers to enjoy before it gets cold.

Finger food is perfect for parties. It's easy to pick up and eat, and party-goers can mix and match it with the other food on the table. Having a selection of home-made dips on the table is a great little touch. Check out Chapter 6 for some easy ones to try.

For a colourful twist to the dips, add in a few drops of food colouring (picked up in the baking section of the supermarket). Works brilliantly at Halloween!

Right, time to get down to some good ole' cooking before the party gets its groove on. Roll up your sleeves, start your carefully crafted 90s pop mega mix and let's make this buffet bangin'. . . .

⟲Garlic Breaded Mushrooms

These mushrooms are a great little nibble and go really nicely dipped in some mayo. They're delicious hot or cold.

Preparation time: 10 minutes

Cooking time: 10 minutes

Makes: 1 bowl

2 slices of bread, crusts removed

2 cloves of garlic, peeled and chopped (garlic powder works well if you can get it)

Salt and pepper

2 eggs, beaten

3 handfuls of button mushrooms, cut in half

¼ mug of plain flour

Oil (groundnut or vegetable, not olive oil)

1 Grate the bread into breadcrumbs or blitz in a blender.

2 Put the breadcrumbs into a bowl and add the chopped garlic. Mix together and season with salt and pepper.

3 Crack the eggs into a separate bowl and whisk until light.

4 Place the mushrooms on a plate and sift (pour through a sieve) some flour over them. Carefully dip a mushroom into the egg, then into the breadcrumbs. Place onto a separate plate. Repeat until all the mushrooms are coated in the breadcrumbs.

5 Pour oil into a small saucepan until it's about 3 centimetres deep. Heat over a high heat.

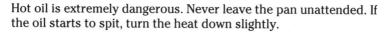

Hot oil is extremely dangerous. Never leave the pan unattended. If the oil starts to spit, turn the heat down slightly.

6 Carefully fry the mushrooms in the oil, a few at a time, until the breadcrumbs turn golden brown. Repeat until all the mushrooms are done.

Variation: *Try swapping the chopped garlic for chilli or curry powder for a spicy alternative.*

Per serving: *Calories 54 (From Fat 32); Fat 3.5g (Saturated 0.8g); Cholesterol Trace; Sodium 56mg; Carbohydrate 3.2g; Dietary Fibre 0.3g; Protein 2.3g.*

⌒Spicy Chips

This dish is hardly a recipe, more of a tip. Thin-cut chips or French fries rather than chunky chips work best here, because they taste okay even when they're cold.

Preparation time: *30 seconds*

Cooking time: *20 minutes*

Makes: *1 big bowl*

3 big handfuls of frozen chips

4 big pinches of hot paprika or chilli powder

1 Cook the chips, following the instructions on the back of the packet.

2 When they're done, sprinkle them generously with hot paprika or chilli powder.

Per serving: *Calories 28 (From Fat 9); Fat 1.0g (Saturated 0.1g); Cholesterol Trace; Sodium 45mg; Carbohydrate 4.2g; Dietary Fibre 0.3g; Protein 0.5g.*

◌*Mini Carrot Wraps*

This recipe is a bit of a global food mash-up. The tortilla wraps are Mexican and the filling is a simple Middle Eastern dish – grated carrot with yogurt – with a complicated name: *sarimsakli havuc sote*. (Try saying that after a vodka Slush Puppy.) The combination of the two is great and makes wicked finger food. You need some short wooden skewers for this recipe (you should be able to find some in your supermarket).

Preparation time: *10 minutes*

Cooking time: *20 minutes*

Makes: *1 plate of mini carrot wraps*

Olive oil	Pinch of salt
6 carrots, peeled and grated	Fresh parsley, chopped (optional)
2 cloves of garlic	3 tortilla wraps
½ mug of yogurt	

1 Heat the olive oil over a medium heat and fry the grated carrot for about 10 minutes until soft. When done, take off the heat and leave to cool.

2 Crush (or very finely chop) the garlic and mix with the yogurt. Pour the yogurt over the carrots in the cooled pan and mix together well. Throw in a pinch of salt and mix again. Top with the chopped parsley, if using.

3 Warm the tortillas according to the packet instructions.

4 Spoon a thick line of the grated carrot mixture in the middle of each tortilla and then tightly wrap up.

5 Slice the tortilla wraps into pieces and skewer each piece so the skewer holds the wraps together. Serve cold on a plate.

Variation: *Try adding a few peas in with the carrot mix. Also, you can always serve the grated carrot on its own rather than in the wraps.*

Per serving: *Calories 101 (From Fat 36); Fat 4.0g (Saturated 0.9g); Cholesterol Trace; Sodium 129mg; Carbohydrate 13.6g; Dietary Fibre 1.6g; Protein 2.7g.*

⟲*Vegetable Samosas*

Here's another global snack that makes great finger food. You can buy pre-made samosas (spicy vegetables wrapped in pastry) in the supermarket, but they're never as tasty as home-made ones. Plus, you can choose exactly what you want to put in your samosas and make them as spicy or as mild as you like.

Preparation time: *20 minutes*

Cooking time: *20 minutes*

Makes: *1 plate of samosas (about 15 to 20)*

1 potato, peeled and quartered	*½ mug of frozen peas*
Oil (vegetable or groundnut)	*2 carrots, cut in half, then grated*
3 teaspoons of curry powder	*2 teaspoons of chilli powder*
1 teaspoon of turmeric (optional, but worth using)	*Pinch of fresh, finely chopped coriander (optional, but worth using)*
1 onion, peeled and finely chopped	*1 pack of filo pastry*
Small piece of ginger (about half the size of your thumb), peeled and finely chopped	*Saucer of melted butter*

1 Preheat the oven to 200°C.

2 Half fill a saucepan with water and bring to the boil. When hot, add a pinch of salt and the potatoes. Boil for 5 minutes and then drain. Don't worry about cooking them completely; you fry them in a second.

3 Run the potatoes under cold water and, when the potatoes are cool, cut them into pea-sized pieces.

4 Grab a frying pan and heat a drop of oil in the pan over a medium heat. When hot, stir in the curry powder and turmeric (if using).

5 When they've dissolved and are releasing a lovely, warming aroma (after about 30 seconds), chuck in the chopped onions and ginger and fry for about 5 minutes or until they turn brown.

6 Now add the potato pieces and fry for another 5 minutes.

7 Add the peas and carrots and sprinkle the chilli powder and coriander over the mixture. Fry for about 3 minutes or until the peas defrost and turn bright green and then take the pan off the heat.

8 While that's cooling down, place 3 sheets of the filo pastry onto a clean chopping board. Brush or spoon a bit of the melted butter over each sheet, layer them on top of each other and then cut them into squares. They need to be about as big as a beer mat (about 5 centimetres by 5 centimetres).

9 Have a cup of water handy. Pop a teaspoon of the mixture from the frying pan into one corner of the filo square and fold the other corner over to cover it, making a triangle.

10 Dab your fingers in the cup of water and seal down the edge of the samosa. Place on a lightly oiled baking tray and brush with butter. Repeat this process until all the filling is used (you may need to use up to 9 sheets of filo pastry in all).

11 Repeat until the rest of the mixture and pastry is used up. Then place the baking tray of samosas in the oven for 10 to 15 minutes until they crisp up.

12 Place on a plate and eat. They taste good hot or cold.

Per serving: Calories 212 (From Fat 115); Fat 12.8g (Saturated 4.1g); Cholesterol Trace; Sodium 108mg; Carbohydrate 20.2g; Dietary Fibre 2.8g; Protein 4.1g.

Mini Roast Beef and Yorkshire Puds

Honey, I shrunk the roast beef! Here's a classic British dish that gets miniaturised. Little Yorkshire puddings are filled with roast beef and horseradish sauce – Sunday dinner in the palm of your hand.

You need a muffin tray for the Yorkshire puddings.

Preparation time: *10 minutes*

Cooking time: *25 minutes*

Makes: *1 plate of Mini Roast Beef and Yorkshire puds*

2 eggs	Chunk of butter
100 grams of plain flour	2 slices of cooked roast beef
Pinch of salt	Couple of spoonfuls of horseradish sauce
250 millilitres of milk	

1 Preheat the oven to 200°C.

2 Crack the eggs into a large bowl and add the flour and salt. Add a drop of milk and whisk together. Keep adding the milk in and whisking until you get a light batter.

3 Rub a little butter around each hole in the muffin tray to stop the Yorkshire puds sticking to the tray when they're cooked.

4 Pour the batter into each hole in the muffin tray, filling it half full.

5 Place the tray in the oven and cook for 20 minutes.

6 Remove the tray from the oven and allow each Yorkshire pudding to cool on a wire rack (if you don't have one, use the tray from the grill, but take it out before you turn the oven on so it's not hot).

7 While they're cooling, slice the roast beef into squares small enough to place inside each Yorkshire pudding. Pop inside the Yorkshire puddings, top with a teaspoon of horseradish sauce and serve.

Variation: *Try adding little chipolata sausages rather than the roast beef for little Toad in the Holes.*

Per serving: Calories 107 (From Fat 50); Fat 5.5g (Saturated 2.8g); Cholesterol Trace; Sodium 84mg; Carbohydrate 9.5g; Dietary Fibre 0.4g; Protein4.8.

⌒*Baby Baked Potatoes*

The miniaturisation of food will stop soon, trust me, but in the meantime, enjoy these mini baked potatoes, which you can eat in one go. These taste best when they're hot, but aren't bad cold either, and are simple to make because the oven does all the cooking.

Preparation time: *2 minutes*

Cooking time: *20 minutes*

Makes: *1 plate of Baby Baked Potatoes*

Olive oil	*1 bag of new potatoes*
Salt	

1 Place a baking tray in the oven and preheat it to 180°C.

2 Pour 5 glugs of olive oil in a big bowl and add a generous pinch of salt.

3 Add the potatoes and mix well, coating them all in the olive oil and salt.

4 Carefully remove the baking tray from the oven (it will be hot) and pour the potatoes and remaining olive oil on it. Place the tray in the oven for 20 minutes.

5 Remove the tray from the oven and place the potatoes on a plate. Leave to cool slightly before serving so that people don't burn their fingers or mouths.

Tip: *Try serving these with a dollop of mayo or some of the dips from Chapter 6 – try the Garlic and Chive Dip or the Tomato and Red Onion Salsa.*

Per serving: *Calories 106 (From Fat 29); Fat 3.2g (Saturated 0.4g); Cholesterol Trace; Sodium 15mg; Carbohydrate 17.2g; Dietary Fibre 1.3g; Protein 2.1g.*

⟡Tomato and Mozzarella Bruschetta

Bruschettas are typical Italian fare – simple and delicious. I go for a classic tomato and mozzarella recipe for a taste sensation, although you could be a little more adventurous and add a fresh basil leaf on top of the tomato or swap it for a slice of Parma ham.

Preparation time: *10 minutes*

Cooking time: *5 minutes*

Makes: *1 plate of Tomato and Mozzarella Bruschettas*

2 ciabattas	*5 tomatoes*
4 cloves of garlic, peeled and chopped in half	*Pepper*
	Olive oil
2 mozzarella balls	

1 Preheat the grill to a medium to high setting.

2 Cut the ciabattas in half and lightly toast under the grill. Take them out before they turn too dark.

3 Rub a clove of garlic over each half and then cut the ciabattas into squares.

4 Cut the mozzarella into pieces that will nicely cover the ciabatta squares and slice the tomato into slices.

5 Place a piece of mozzarella over each square and then top with a piece of tomato. Grind over a light sprinkling of pepper and drizzle lightly with olive oil.

6 Place on a plate and serve.

Per serving: Calories 125 (From Fat 54); Fat 6.0g (Saturated 3.1g); Cholesterol Trace; Sodium 190mg; Carbohydrate 11.7g; Dietary Fibre 0.9g; Protein 6.1g.

Pigs in Blankets

Most people usually have Pigs in Blankets (chipolata sausages wrapped in bacon) with their Christmas dinners, but in our house we eat them as a snack beforehand. They're simple, more-ish party food. You need some cocktail sticks on hand for this recipe.

Preparation time: *2 minutes*

Cooking time: *45 minutes*

Makes: *1 plate of Pigs in Blankets*

2 handfuls of chipolata sausages   *5 to 6 rashers of bacon*

1 Cook the sausages according to the packet.

2 Fry the bacon for about 7 minutes – don't let it turn crispy.

3 When both are cooked, leave the bacon to cool slightly and then slice into strips and wrap each sausage in a strip, making sure the join is at the bottom.

4 Skewer each 'pig' with a cocktail stick and place on a plate.

Per serving: Calories 86 (From Fat 65); Fat 7.2g (Saturated 2.5g); Cholesterol Trace; Sodium 379mg; Carbohydrate Trace; Dietary Fibre Trace; Protein 5.4g.

Sticky Chicken Drumsticks

You can buy chicken drumsticks very cheaply from the market (or supermarket). Coating them in this sticky sauce makes them even tastier.

Preparation time: *5 minutes*

Cooking time: *35 minutes*

Makes: *12 drumsticks*

6 teaspoons of cornflour	*6 teaspoons of soy sauce*
4 teaspoons of caster sugar	*12 chicken drumsticks*

1 Preheat the oven to 200°C.

2 Put the cornflour, caster sugar and soy sauce in a bowl and mix with 2 teaspoons of water to form a runny paste.

3 Coat each chicken drumstick in the sauce and place them on a baking tray.

4 Pop the tray in the oven and bake the drumsticks for 35 minutes.

5 Leave to cool slightly before serving.

Tip: If you have any leftover dipping sauce, drizzle it over the drumsticks halfway through cooking to make them even tastier.

Per serving: Calories 325 (From Fat 157); Fat 17.4g (Saturated 4.8g); Cholesterol Trace; Sodium 345mg; Carbohydrate 3.5g; Dietary Fibre Trace; Protein 38.7g.

❍Root Vegetable Crisps

These crisps go really nicely with some of the dips in Chapter 6. Just be careful when you're cooking them because the hot oil can be dangerous.

Preparation time: *5 minutes*

Cooking time: *10 minutes*

Makes: *1 bowl of Root Vegetable Crisps*

Selection of root vegetables (parsnips, sweet potato, beetroot, carrots)

Groundnut or vegetable oil

Salt

1 Peel and thinly slice the vegetables. The easiest way to do this is to use a vegetable peeler, but press a little harder as you're peeling so that you get a thicker peel.

2 Pour about 3 centimetres of oil in a small saucepan and heat over a high heat.

3 While that's heating up, line a plate with some kitchen roll.

4 After 2 minutes, drop a small bit of bread in the saucepan. If it quickly turns brown and crispy, the oil's hot enough, if not, keep heating the oil for a bit longer.

5 Place a couple of the vegetables in the oil and fry until they turn brown and crispy (about 4 minutes). Then remove with a slotted spoon, drain off any excess oil and place on the kitchen roll to absorb any extra oil. Sprinkle with a little salt.

6 Repeat until all the vegetables are used up. If the oil starts to spit, carefully take the pan off the heat and let it cool down slightly before moving it back on the heat and continuing. Add more oil if it becomes too shallow.

7 Put all the vegetable crisps from the kitchen roll into a bowl and serve next to the dips.

Per serving: *Calories 634 (From Fat 225); Fat 25.0g (Saturated 5.0g); Cholesterol Trace; Sodium 199mg; Carbohydrate 92.6g; Dietary Fibre 23.2g; Protein 9.6g.*

Home-Made Pizza

Pizzas are fairly cheap to buy, but don't give you that extra edge of creativity. You can't buy a pizza modelled on your best friend's face, or that spells out Happy Birthday in pepperoni. But you can make one. . . .

This is a fairly basic recipe, but go ahead and freestyle on the ingredients to personalise it. As you undoubtedly know, pizza is delicious hot or cold.

Preparation time: *2 minutes*

Cooking time: *15 minutes*

Makes: *2 Home-Made Pizzas*

2 pizza bases

Tomato purée

2 tins of chopped tomatoes, with excess liquid drained

3 big handfuls of grated Cheddar cheese

2 handfuls of pepperoni or other spicy sausage slices

1 small green pepper, sliced

1 small red pepper, sliced

1 small red onion, sliced

1 Preheat the oven to 220°C and place the pizza bases on a baking tray.

2 Starting from the middle and working outwards, spread the pizza bases with tomato purée and then spoon over the drained chopped tomatoes.

3 Cover both pizzas with grated cheese and then top with the onion, peppers and pepperoni.

4 Place in the preheated oven for around 15 minutes or until the topping is bubbling.

5 Allow to cool slightly before slicing and serving.

Per serving: Calories 454 (From Fat 176); Fat 19.5g (Saturated 9.0g); Cholesterol Trace; Sodium 566mg; Carbohydrate 51.5g; Dietary Fibre 2.9g; Protein 18.1g.

Cheese and Ham Quiche

Face facts, a party isn't a party without a bit of quiche. They're surprisingly easy to make, but you need a 9-inch quiche tin to cook it in.

Preparation time: *5 minutes*

Cooking time: *40 minutes*

Makes: *1 Cheese and Ham Quiche*

300-gram packet of shortcrust pastry	*Salt and pepper*
3 eggs	*2 slices of ham, cut into strips*
240 millilitres of single cream	*80 grams of grated cheese (Emmental cheese is very nice)*

1 Preheat the oven to 200°C.

2 Roll out the pastry until it's about half a centimetre thick and line the tin with it.

3 Crack the eggs in a bowl and whisk until thoroughly mixed. When whisked, beat in the cream and add salt and pepper.

4 Place the ham and three-quarters of the cheese into the tin and pour the cream and egg mixture over the cheese and ham. Scatter the rest of the cheese over the top. Crimp (gently press) the edges of the pastry to make it look a little more quiche-like.

5 Pop in the oven for 40 minutes and allow to cool slightly before removing from the tin, slicing into portions and serving.

Variation: Cheese and ham is a pretty basic filling for quiches, so go ahead and try swapping the ham with spinach and tomato; cooked bacon and leek; fried mushrooms or smoked salmon.

Per serving: *Calories 358 (From Fat 245); Fat 27.2g (Saturated 10.6g); Cholesterol Trace; Sodium 216mg; Carbohydrate 17.6g; Dietary Fibre 0.6g; Protein 10.6g.*

ᗯPotato Salad

Potato salad is a nice refreshing snack for parties in the summer. People can eat as much or as little as they like, and it's suitable for vegetarians too.

Preparation time: *10 minutes*

Cooking time: *15 minutes*

Makes: *1 bowl of Potato Salad*

500 grams of new potatoes

3 spoonfuls of mayonnaise

½ lettuce (iceberg or little gem is good), sliced into pieces

¼ cucumber, sliced, then halved

2 spring onions, finely chopped

1 Bring a saucepan of water to the boil and cook the potatoes for 10 to 15 minutes.

2 Drain and allow to cool.

3 Mix the potatoes with the mayo in a bowl.

4 Place the lettuce, cucumber and spring onions in a separate bowl and then add the potatoes. Mix well and serve.

Per serving: *Calories 79 (From Fat 33); Fat 3.7g (Saturated 0.6g); Cholesterol Trace; Sodium 25mg; Carbohydrate 9.8g; Dietary Fibre 1.5g; Protein 1.6g.*

Chicken Dippers

I remember having chicken dippers as a kid, but they make a great comeback on the buffet table. They're delicious dipped in some creamy mayo or tomato sauce.

Preparation time: *10 minutes*

Cooking time: *20 to 25 minutes*

Makes: *Around 10 chicken dippers*

3 slices of toasted bread, crusts removed

Pinch of chilli powder

Salt

2 eggs

4 chicken breasts,
cut into bite-sized pieces

Olive oil

1 Preheat the oven to 220°C.

2 Grate the bread or blitz in a blender until it turns into breadcrumbs.

3 Add a few pinches of chilli powder and some salt to the breadcrumbs and mix well. Place in a small bowl.

4 Crack the eggs into a clean bowl and whisk until smooth.

5 Dip the chicken pieces into the eggs, then into the breadcrumbs, coating them completely. Then place on a plate. Repeat with the other chicken pieces.

6 Lightly oil a baking tray and place in the oven for 5 minutes to get hot.

7 After 5 minutes, take the tray out and place the chicken on it. Put back in the oven and bake for 20 to 25 minutes.

8 Check that the chicken is cooked by cutting open a dipper and seeing if the middle is white, with any juices running clear.

9 Serve on a plate next to some dips.

Per serving: *Calories 164 (From Fat 34); Fat 3.8g (Saturated 1.0g); Cholesterol Trace; Sodium 115mg; Carbohydrate 4.6g; Dietary Fibre 0.2g; Protein 27.9g.*

Vodka slush puppy

Every party needs a signature drink. Well, this won't last long, so make sure you have lots on standby.

Place 1 mug of vodka, 1 mug of cranberry juice, 1 mug of lemonade and 3 mugs of ice in a blender and blend until slushy.

Pour the drink into a bowl and place a ladle inside, allowing people to fill their own glasses. Put a pack of straws by the bowl to really recreate the Slush Puppy experience.

You can swap the cranberry juice for any other juice – pineapple, grapefruit, raspberry and tropical juice all work well.

Throwing a Party

Throwing a party is easy. Throwing a decent one that people will remember for years to come is a little more difficult and requires careful preparation and planning.

Plus, for your sake, you need to ensure that things don't get out of hand. If you're in private accommodation, you're responsible for whatever you wake up to the morning afterwards, and a few easy precautions will make sure that you get to see your bond again.

So follow these few nuggets of advice to help you make the most of your party:

Planning your party:

✔ **Get the word out about a week before the big day.**
This gives people a chance to put it in their diaries and make sure that they can come. Planning in advance gives everyone time to work out if they can make it, and plan around sport fixtures or important deadlines.

However, be careful where you publicise your party! Posting the party on a social networking site such as Facebook is a great idea, but *don't* give out your address! Your mates already know it, and putting the time and location of your party means *everyone,* including people you may not want at the party, will know what's happening.

✔ **Give your party a theme or hold it on the day of an event.** Theme parties are so much more fun than normal parties. People get more creative thinking about their costumes and what they can bring and look forward to seeing what everyone else will be going as. Having a theme makes you a bit more creative with the music, decoration and food. Event parties, such as Eurovision or Grand National parties make for unmissable parties as the event only happens once a year – when it's gone, it's gone!

✔ **Let your neighbours know.** If you're in private accommodation, let your neighbours know that you'll soon be having a party. Not only is it polite, but it also gives them a bit of prior warning that there'll be a bit more noise than usual. You're neighbours are less likely to come round and complain if they know about your party.

On the day:

- ✔ **Make sure that you buy enough food and drink.** Head to the market or a budget supermarket to buy food and drink in bulk. Get more than you think you'll need. It's better to have more than not enough, and you can eat anything leftover throughout the week.

- ✔ **Rearrange the furniture.** Make as much room as possible. Move any small tables and sofas into your bedroom (stopping people getting into your room). Move any laundry, expensive items like laptops, and anything that can be broken into a safe place.

- ✔ **Make room for coats.** Plan a room to put people's coats and bags in. Make sure that it's got a door (preferably lockable) for a bit of added security. Be wary – burglars could spot the house as being an easy target with the door unlocked and lots of drunk people around, making it very easy for someone to nip in and rummage through a bedroom or even worse, the room with everyone's coats and bags in. . . .

- ✔ **Get the music ready.** A good playlist is the pulse of the party. If you're like me, you'll be spending a good seven hours meticulously preparing and honing this important feature, subtly expressing your deep and eclectic taste in music.

On the evening:

- ✔ **Get the food and drink ready.** Make sure that everything's finished at least 30 minutes before anyone is due to arrive so that the food is fresh and at its best. Make sure that you have non-alcoholic drinks, and vegetarian and vegan options so you cater for everyone. Sounds silly, but labelling the dishes is a good idea in case people have allergies to certain foods. And it's not pleasant picking up what you think is a salt and vinegar crisp only to discover that it's your nemesis flavour – cheese and onion.

- ✔ **Be prepared to open windows.** Your house may get very hot and sweaty very quickly.

✔ **Clean as you go.** Okay, this tip sounds so boring, but you'll thank yourself in the morning. Pick up any discarded bottles or cans and chuck them into a bin liner throughout the night. This stops the rubbish piling up and people accidentally treading on bottles. Ouch.

✔ **Look out for everyone, but remember to enjoy yourself.** Without turning into a Butlins holiday rep, make sure that everyone has everything they want and are enjoying the night, but remember to kick back and relax as well.

Keeping an eye on the pennies

You can spend a lot of money on your party without even realising it. By the time you've bought decorations, cleaning stuff and enough food and drink to feed 30 students, you're easily looking at close to £100. But throwing a party doesn't have to be such an expense. Here are a few tips to save your cash and still have a great time:

✔ **Ask people to bring their own booze.** Most people will bring some alcohol without you having to ask; it's that unwritten party rule. But it doesn't hurt if you suggest it to people who are coming. You'll get a much more varied selection of beers and wines that way.

✔ **Buy less and make more food.** Anything home-made is generally cheaper than anything bought at the supermarket, so make as much home-made food as you can. The budget range of party food in supermarkets can be pretty shocking.

✔ **Improvise with what you have in your cupboards.** If you have loads of pasta knocking around, make a pasta salad. Eggs? Make the Cheese and Ham Quiche or the Mini Roast Beef and Yorkshire Puds in this chapter.

✔ **Consider buying paper cups and plates.** They'll work out cheaper than buying more glasses or plates that will break during the night. And you can recycle them and save on the washing up.

✔ **Ask friends to bring snack food.** If you're supplying most of the home-cooked grub, feel free to ask friends to bring along some crisps, nuts and other snacks. Or challenge them to bring something home-made that can beat your own creations!

Part V
The Part of Tens

In this part . . .

If your eyes are stinging from chopping too many onions or you have trouble turning pages as your fingers are covered in chocolate sauce, you'll love Part V. It's a big old juicy round up of the very best of the book and all the essential info you need to know about cooking at uni, all in jaw-droppingly good top ten lists. Enjoy.

Chapter 16

Ten Tips for Cooking at Uni

In This Chapter

▶ Saving time and money

▶ Getting savvy when you're shopping

▶ Knowing what to buy and where to buy it

▶ Kitting out your cupboard

*1*f you need to get up to speed on your culinary knowledge faster than the time it takes to burn your toast, you're going to love this top ten list. This chapter is a quick-fire run through of the essential info you need when you're cooking at uni.

Why can't lectures be as brief as this?

Stick to Your Shopping List

The *best* way to save money when you're cooking at uni is also the simplest. Making a shopping list forces you to buy only what you need, not what looks tempting. So how do you do it?

Start by flicking through the recipes in this book and planning which meal you're going to eat every day. This may sound like an incredibly geeky task that only that weird guy down the corridor would do, but trust me, you'll end up saving loads of money (which means more money to spend when you go out. Now who's geeky?).When you've worked out your week's meals, work out what ingredients you need by looking through your cupboards and seeing what you have already and what you need to buy.

Compile that magical list of the things that you need to buy, gallivant off to the nearest supermarket or market and start shopping, safe in the knowledge that you're spending your money efficiently, on only the things that you need.

Buy Frozen Veg

Now, I'm a big advocate of buying fresh vegetables when possible. Nothing beats seeing a cupboard or fridge full of fresh and colourful vegetables. Just looking at them makes you feel healthy. Fresh vegetables, bought in season, are bursting with flavour. But that's not to say that frozen vegetables are a poorer option.

Frozen vegetables are as healthy and nutritious for you as fresh veg; in fact, possibly better for you. Fresh vegetables lose nutrients as they age. However, vegetables are frozen very quickly after they leave the ground, so all the nutrients freeze as well. So even if that packet of frozen veg has been in your freezer for months, when you defrost it, it's as if it's fresh from the earth.

Frozen vegetables are often cheaper than fresh vegetables, and are a great option when you just need a selection of vegetables when you're cooking stir-fries or need some veg as an accompaniment to a meat dish.

All this applies to frozen fruit as well (perfect when you're making smoothies).

Wash Up While You're Cooking

Imagine the scene – you finish a delicious meal, feeling full (and slightly drunk from the wine) and then realise you have a small mountain of dirty pots, pans and plates to clean.

The very simple solution to this age-old problem is to clean as you cook. Before you start cooking, fill the sink with hot water (put your housemates' dirty dishes on the floor outside their rooms!) and just chuck into the sink any utensils you use as you cook.

As you cook, you naturally have gaps of time where you're simply waiting for something to finish cooking. These gaps are perfect opportunities to keep on top of the washing up and wash stuff as you go.

By the time you serve up, all that's left to clean is your plate and a couple of pans; the rest is all done.

Eat Locally and Seasonally

Eating seasonally doesn't mean gorging on food during the spring and summer months and hibernating during autumn and winter. It means buying only the food that's growing in Britain in the current season.

For example, pears are harvested in Britain from September to January. You can still buy pears outside of these months, but more often than not, they'll be of a poorer quality and may be imported from abroad, causing pollution to the atmosphere and adding to the price.

Buying locally ensures you buy the freshest and tastiest meat and vegetables, and most importantly means you support the local food industry. Buying meat that's come from a farm down the road or in the next town is much better than buying it from a farm hundreds of miles away or even in another country.

The only downside to buying locally and seasonally is that you have less choice, but part of the fun is seeing your meals and diet change with the seasons. Plus, you feel more connected to nature, man. . . .

Of course, you don't have to be so strict that the *only* food you eat is seasonal. Don't skip a good deal at the supermarket or miss taking advantage of a bumper bag of frozen veg if you know you're going to use them. Just make seasonal eating a habit, not a rule.

To find out more about buying and eating seasonally, refer to Chapter 2.

Don't Buy Expensive Kitchen Utensils

You won't need or use a fancy electric tin opener or hand-made bamboo steamer; your bog standard ones from your local hardware store or supermarket will do. You can kit out your kitchen from scratch for about £20. You can make your own steamer by placing a colander over a pan of boiling water and placing a clean tea towel over the top.

The only utensil you should spend a bit of money on is a good knife. A good knife lasts all through your time at uni, plus you can always sharpen it if it goes a little blunt.

Buy Meat in Bulk and Freeze the Extra

Buying in bulk is a great way to save money and works particularly well with meat. A local butcher is more likely to round down the price or throw in a few extra things if you buy a lot. If you see a buy one get one free offer (BOGOF) on meat at the supermarket, remember that you can take advantage of the offer and freeze whatever you don't use straight away.

Split up the meat into portion sizes and pop it into freezer bags. Wrap the bags in a carrier bag to avoid freezer burn, label it and whack it in the freezer.

Buying in bulk may sound slightly contradictory to sticking to your shopping list (earlier in this chapter), but just use your head when you're shopping. If you see a good deal and know that you'll use everything in that deal, go for it!

Make Sunday Lunch Last until Wednesday

Cooking a big Sunday lunch may seem like a lot of effort and result in a lot of leftover food, but it's actually a great way of saving money and feeding yourself for the next few days.

For example, if you've done a roast chicken on Sunday, set aside some meat that you can use on Monday night in a chicken curry. If you've done roast beef, chop up the leftovers and use them in a cottage pie.

As for roast vegetables, use them in a delicious roast vegetable soup or whack 'em in a home-made curry.

Using leftovers involves you learning a few recipes (all of which are in this book), but get it right and you'll be laughing.

Cook for Your Mates

This tip works on a few levels. Not only will you be admired by all your friends and peers and increase your pulling power (there's always something sexy about someone who knows how to cook), but it's also a great way of saving a bit of cash.

The deal goes like this. You invite your friends round to yours and say you'll cook for them. They each give you a fiver towards the meal. You'll have around £20 to £25 to throw on a great spread for four or five people, which you can do easily. You don't pay anything towards the meal, but instead you cook it. So essentially, you get a free meal and usually some leftover grub that you can use to magic up something for the next night.

Plus, you'll have some fantastic food, a few beverages and a great evening's banter with your mates. Try it and you'll have some very memorable evenings at uni.

Keep an Eye Open for Special Offers

Even though I include a tip about making and sticking to a shopping list, don't be afraid to veer off it if you spot a special offer or bargain that would be useful.

Only buy something if you'll actually *use* it.

The most useful offers are on meat or bread, or anything you can freeze and use at a later date. For example, a BOGOF on minced beef is handy because you know you can freeze one pack and get round to using it later.

However, special offers on fresh items such as fruit and veg aren't usually worth it, as they'll just sit in your cupboards, slowly going mouldy.

Buy Meat and Fish from Your Local Butcher or Fishmonger

Butchers and fishmongers, and any local independent shop or trader, soon become your best friends when you're at uni or cooking on a budget.

Buying meat and fish from your local butcher or fishmonger is important for many reasons. Firstly, they know more about meat and fish than anyone working in a supermarket. They'll know the farm the meat comes from, the abattoir used, and sometimes the farmer who's reared the animal. Fishmongers know everything there is to know about fish, from where it's been caught, to who caught it, and most importantly, how to cook it. All this means that butchers and fishmongers put their names and their reputations to a series of establishments and other businesses that they trust.

Also, butchers and fishmongers are skilled at their job. Fishmongers can help you choose a fish, prepare it for you and tell you how to cook it. Butchers do the same with meat, and both are likely to give you a student discount if you ask nicely. Plus, you can buy as little or as much meat or fish as you like. If you just want 100 grams of minced beef for a couple of home-made kebabs, you can get it for under £1 at your local butcher's. Supermarkets don't sell in such small quantities because doing so makes too little profit.

When you're a butcher or a fishmonger, the only thing that sets you apart from the competition is the quality of your produce. Unlike supermarkets, where people shop for many different items, you only go to a butcher for meat, so the meat has to be the best, otherwise the customer will go somewhere else. This quality, coupled with the knowledge they have of where their produce comes from, sets butchers and fishmongers miles apart from supermarkets.

Chapter 17

Ten Ways to Eat on the Cheap

In This Chapter

▶ Feeling full with empty pockets

▶ Saving money when cooking at uni

▶ Finding ways to eat on the cheap

*A*part from learning to cook healthy and low-budget meals, other, more ingenious tricks can help you save a few pounds and still end the day with a full stomach. In this chapter, I give you loads of little tips and tricks to get free food when you're at uni, and not all of them involve cooking!

Work in a Restaurant or Uni Catering Hall

Yep, it worked for me when I was at uni, and it'll work for you. Getting a part-time job at somewhere that serves food usually means you get some of that food on your break. Working at the uni catering hall is a perfect example. Even if you're just serving or washing up, you can eat the meals for free on your lunch or dinner break. Plus, your job is right on campus and you can see your friends a bit more.

Restaurants may not give you as much free food as working in a uni catering hall, but the food is often of a much higher quality. Working with chefs is usually a laugh, and you get free cooking tips from professionals.

Enjoy Early Bird Menus

If you and your friends want a bit of a mid-week treat and an evening eating out, lower the cost a little by looking for restaurants that do Early Bird Menus, which are designed to get customers in during a restaurant's quiet period, usually between 6 and 7.30 p.m. Prices on the Early Bird Menu are generally much cheaper than usual and often offer set meal combinations (starters and mains, or mains and dessert) for really great prices. Being a student, you should be fairly flexible for time and can make this a cheap way of eating out.

Pick Up Supermarket Magazines

Apart from the articles on how Elaine from Bolton lost 7 stone by eating celery for a week, supermarket magazines are full of interesting and useful advice on cooking. Not only do they have many cheap and easy to follow recipes, but also the magazines usually have coupons and vouchers that you can use to get money off useful ingredients. Oh, and the mags are usually free.

Cook in a Group

By cooking in a group, you end up saving quite a bit of money and having more of a laugh than cooking on your own. If everyone throws in a set amount of money every week towards food, you find that the cost per head of feeding everyone falls, as ingredients are cheaper to buy in large quantities.

For example, say four of you share a flat. If everyone gave £15 a week to pay for seven nights' meals, you end up with a £60-a-week food budget. Now think about how cheap it is to make a shepherd's pie for one: about £3. Making one big enough to feed four doesn't quadruple the price to £12, but only bumps it up to about £5 or £6. So you can see straight away how much money you can save if you cook in a group.

Charge Your Flatmates for Washing Up Duties

Bit of an odd one this, I'll give you that, but it may earn you a bit of cash. There's always one or two students in your house or corridor that never wash up after cooking and leave dirty pots and pans on the side, slowly cultivating a new species of mould. If you're clearing up after yourself, you can add their dirty pots and pans to your washing up duties and charge them a couple of quid per item. They end up never having to wash a dirty pot for a year, and you end up with slightly sore hands and a smile on your face from the few extra quid in your back pocket. Okay, it might not work for most people, but there'll be someone lazy and rich enough for you to do it, guaranteed.

Buy Supermarket-Own Brands

Supermarket-own brands are pretty good when you're on a budget. Don't worry about buying a branded pack of pasta or rice; the supermarket version is cheaper and tastes pretty much the same. It's only when you get to a higher level of cooking that you need more expensive ingredients, but when you're a student and on a budget, then supermarket-own brands are real bobby dazzlers.

Minimise Your Leftovers

Throwing food away that you can use again is like throwing away money. Us Westerners are lucky enough that no matter how poor we get, we can still afford *something* to eat. Only 8 per cent of the world are in this privileged position. So, learn to minimise or make the most of your leftovers. For example, you can refrigerate extra mashed potato and make it into fish cakes (see the Smoked Haddock Fish Cakes in Chapter 7 for a recipe); you can reheat leftover chilli con carne and pour it over a jacket potato, making another meal. Always think about how you can rescue your leftovers and try to throw as little away as possible.

Use Cheaper Cuts of Meat

Cheap meat and cheaper *cuts* of meat are two very different things. Although cheap meat can be good quality if it's well sourced from your local butcher, most cheap meat means meat that's been cheaply produced, with little money spent on the living conditions and rearing of the animals.

Cheap cuts, however, are parts of the animal that aren't as popular as other cuts, which means they're less expensive. Generally speaking, the front end of the animal produces the cheaper cuts, such as shoulder of lamb or pork, beef shin and lamb shank. These cuts tend to be a little tougher and more muscley than cuts like breast or leg, but can still be a delicious meal. Because they're tougher, you need to cook them for longer and on a reasonably low temperature so that they end up juicy and tender and just falling off the bone.

Try mutton (meat from an older sheep) instead of lamb. The meat is slightly tougher, but lovely if you cook it slowly or use it for mince.

Check out Chapter 13 for some great recipe ideas.

Visit the Market at the End of the Day

Market traders aim to finish each day with as little as possible so that they can start a new day with fresh produce and don't have to spend ages packing everything away. So, at the end of the day market stalls do some amazing deals just to get rid of their stock. This is the best time to go to the market. You'll find that you can get everything you buy rounded down to a ridiculously low price and get stuff thrown in for free if you ask nicely. See how much you can blag, and you'll come back with bags stuffed with food.

Make Friends with Catering Students

The benefits of being mates with catering students are pretty obvious really. You get good food cooked for you, free cooking tips and a chance to eat what they've learned to cook during the day. Take a catering student with you when you go food shopping, and he or she will know exactly what to buy too, as well as potentially being best buddies with some of the market traders. You're also guaranteed a wild night out with them!

Chapter 18

Ten Replacements for Expensive Ingredients

*I*f you read a recipe that asks for ingredients that you just don't have or can't afford, rather than ditching the recipe, you can always swap some of the ingredients for cheaper alternatives. The tricky bit, of course, is knowing what you can swap and use instead.

Well, help is at hand with the top ten expensive ingredients that you can swap for cheaper alternatives. I'm not saying that they'll be as good as their originals, but they're worthy replacements.

Dried Herbs

Fresh herbs are far, far better than dried, and don't cost a lot to buy, but the trouble is, you have to use them a lot to get your money's worth. A pot of basil may look attractive on the windowsill, but you have to cook a lot of Italian dishes to get full value. Plus, its survival rate in a student kitchen is very slim.

So instead, dried herbs are a good substitute. They cost about the same price as a pot of fresh herbs, but last a lot longer – up to a year if not more. Sure, they won't look or taste the same as a pot of fresh herbs, but they're a good student option.

If you're really short on money, opt for the single jar of mixed dried herbs. This is a really cheap way of cooking, and does the job.

Tinned Plum Tomatoes

Tins of plum tomatoes make a great substitute for tins of chopped toms. Some cheap cans of chopped tomatoes contain more liquid than tomato, whereas tins of plum tomatoes always contain a hefty amount of tomato goodness. Simply chop them up yourself when you get them out of the tin.

Chilli Powder

Fresh chillies are tastier than dried and are readily available in supermarkets all year round, but if you want an ever-ready, cheap chilli kick, chilli powder is the way to go. With chilli powder, you can always add more heat than you'd get from a single chilli, and like dried herbs, it lasts a lot longer than buying fresh. For a stronger taste, buy dried chillies.

Spaghetti

Making a stir-fry but run out of noodles? Reach for the spaghetti. It's sometimes difficult to tell the difference between the two, and spaghetti is cheaper than noodles!

Home-Made Herb Stock

If you've got halfway through a recipe and found that you're out of vegetable stock, try mixing a few pinches of a selection of dried herbs in 150 millilitres of water (depending on the recipe). Basil, oregano, thyme and rosemary are good ones to use because the last three are quite pungent. Home-made stock isn't the same as proper vegetable stock, but it is a cheap substitute.

Greek Yogurt

Some recipes ask for crème fraîche, which can be a little pricey. For a much cheaper alternative, use Greek yogurt or better still, supermarket-brand Greek yogurt. Greek yogurt tends to be slightly runnier than crème fraîche, so be prepared to use a spoonful or two more than the recipe suggests.

Fish

If you're making a fish pie, fish cakes, or basically anything where fish is mixed in with other ingredients, you can use cheaper species of fish to save on pennies and still get a great taste. A good idea is to bulk up most of the recipe with cheap species of fish and use a few pieces of a strong-tasting fish or smoked fish to carry most of the flavour. Fish is pretty cheap anyway, but cutting corners with tricks like this makes fish dishes even easier to have at uni.

Your fishmonger can advise you on exactly what to buy and will probably give you a discount too.

Red Wine

If you have a drop of leftover red wine, instead of downing it, turn it into a red wine stock cube. Pour the wine into an ice cube tray and pop in the freezer. Next time you need to add a dash of red wine to a recipe, don't buy a new bottle; whip out your tray of red wine stock cubes and throw a couple into the pot.

Home-Made Garlic Bread

Although garlic bread is pretty cheap to buy, an even cheaper version is to make your own. Check out Chapter 12 to find out how.

Use margarine rather than butter, which is more expensive, and look out for baguettes that have been reduced. They may be a little hard, but hey, it doesn't matter because you're going to grill them anyway!

Home-Made Sauces

Don't buy readymade sauces such as bolognaise or curry sauce. You can make them yourself for a fraction of the cost, using ingredients like chopped tomatoes, tomato purée, garlic and herbs for an Italian sauce, and onions, chillies, curry paste and stock for a curry sauce. All the info you need on making them is in this book!

Appendix

Cooking Terms (I've Got to Do What?!)

*B*lanch it, baste it, whisk it and then parboil it until it's al dente, bind it so it's slightly puréed, then try to remember what you were making in the first place. You don't have to speak another language to cook, but sometimes it helps; especially when there are so many fancy words to explain something so simple. Here's an A to Z of what the most popular cooking terms mean.

Al dente: When cooked pasta is firm and not too soft. It should still have a 'bite' to it. (*Al dente* is Italian for 'to the tooth'.)

Au gratin: When a dish is topped with breadcrumbs or grated cheese.

Baste: To brush something (usually meat) with an ingredient to give some moisture, extra flavour or both. A typical example is basting a roast chicken with butter or oil during cooking.

Bind: To make a liquid thicker by using an ingredient that acts as a thickening agent @@nd flour or butter for example.

Blanch: To dip vegetables briefly into boiling water. Blanching often helps to bring out the colour of vegetables.

Bone: To get rid of the bones from meat, fish or poultry.

Braise: To fry meat lightly and then finish off the cooking slowly by stewing the meat in liquid.

Bread: To cover an ingredient in breadcrumbs.

Brown: To cook food briefly over a high heat until it turns brown.

Chill: To put food in the fridge until its temperature reduces to below room temperature.

Cool: Allowing the temperature of food to reduce to about room temperature, or so that it's cool enough to touch.

Core: To remove the core of an ingredient, usually a fruit or vegetable.

Crumble: To break up food into smaller pieces using your hands.

Cube: To cut food into cubes (getting the hang of this?).

Deglaze: To cook something in a pan and then use a little liquid to lift any bits stuck on the inside of the pan.

Dice: To cut into small cubes.

Dilute: To reduce the strength of one liquid by adding another.

Drizzle: To pour a small amount of liquid (usually oil) over an ingredient.

Fillet: To remove the bones from a fish. As a noun, a cut of meat or fish.

Glaze: To coat an ingredient with a liquid (often melted butter) to give it a shine.

Grease: To rub butter or fat over an ingredient or cooking equipment to make food easier to remove when cooked.

Grill: To cook food under a grill.

Julienne: Pronounced *shzou-lee-en,* it means to cut vegetables into thin strips.

Marinate: To place a food in flavoured liquid (a marinade), allowing it to soak up some of the flavour from the liquid.

Mince: To cut food up into very small fine pieces, or to walk in a rather camp fashion.

Parboil: To place vegetables in boiling water for a short amount of time, to partially cook them.

Poach: To cook a food (often eggs and fish) in simmering water.

Preheat: To set the oven or grill to a required temperature before popping the food in.

Purée: To mash food to a pulp. As a noun, the pulp.

Reduce: To boil a liquid until it reduces in volume and concentrates in flavour.

Roast: To cook food in the oven.

Roux: A mix of flour and butter used to make a white sauce, for example, for lasagne.

Sauté: To cook food very quickly over a high heat.

Score: To make shallow incisions in an ingredient.

Sear: To brown meat very quickly in a frying pan.

Season: To sprinkle salt and pepper, or herbs, over an ingredient or meal.

Sift: To shake powder, such as flour or icing sugar, through a sieve to make it finer.

Simmer: To bring water or a liquid to just before boiling.

Skewer: To push meat, vegetables or other ingredients onto a metal or wooden skewer.

Steam: To cook an ingredient with steam. An easy way to steam something is to place the ingredient in a colander and cover with a clean tea towel. Then place the colander over a pan of boiling water, allowing the steam to rise into the colander.

Stew: The name of a dish and also the process of cooking meat very slowly in liquid in a covered pot.

Stir-fry: The clue is in the name. To fry and stir meat and vegetables over a high heat. The ingredients are usually in small pieces so that they cook quickly.

Stock: Proper stock is a liquid produced from cooking meat or fish with vegetables, herbs and spices. You can also buy stock cubes that you mix with hot water, which are an easy way of recreating the flavour from stock.

Strain: To pour liquid through a sieve to separate any solids from the liquid.

Stuff: To fill the inside of a piece of meat or vegetable (usually peppers) with another ingredient. You're most likely to stuff poultry, such as chickens and turkeys.

Stuffing: A mixture of herbs and breadcrumbs placed inside poultry to give flavour.

Tenderise: To pound meat (usually with a wooden hammer) to soften and weaken the muscle structure, making the meat more tender.

Toss: To lightly mix ingredients together; usually a salad.

Whisk: To blend ingredients together using . . . a whisk.

Zest: To finely grate the skin of citrus fruit, such as lemons and limes. As a noun, the zest is this fine peel.

Index

FOR

DUMMIES®

Making Everything Easier! ™

UK editions

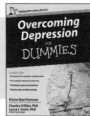

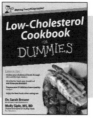

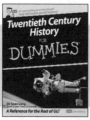
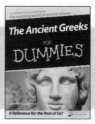

FOR DUMMIES®

The easy way to get more done and have more fun

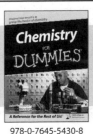

FOR DUMMIES

Helping you expand your horizons and achieve your potential

COMPUTER BASICS

978-0-470-27759-1

978-0-470-13728-4

978-0-471-75421-3

DIGITAL LIFESTYLE

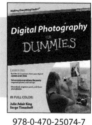

978-0-470-25074-7

978-0-470-39062-7

978-0-470-42342-4

WEB & DESIGN

978-0-470-39700-8

978-0-470-32725-8

978-0-470-34502-3

Access 2007 For Dummies
978-0-470-04612-8

Adobe Creative Suite 3 Design
Premium All-in-One Desk Reference
For Dummies
978-0-470-11724-8

AutoCAD 2009 For Dummies
978-0-470-22977-4

C++ For Dummies, 5th Edition
978-0-7645-6852-7

Computers For Seniors For Dummies
978-0-470-24055-7

Excel 2007 All-In-One Desk Reference
For Dummies
978-0-470-03738-6

Flash CS3 For Dummies
978-0-470-12100-9

Green IT For Dummies
978-0-470-38688-0

Mac OS X Leopard For Dummies
978-0-470-05433-8

Macs For Dummies, 10th Edition
978-0-470-27817-8

Networking All-in-One Desk Reference
For Dummies, 3rd Edition
978-0-470-17915-4

Office 2007 All-in-One Desk Reference
For Dummies
978-0-471-78279-7

Search Engine Optimization
For Dummies, 3rd Edition
978-0-470-26270-2

The Internet For Dummies,
11th Edition
978-0-470-12174-0

Visual Studio 2008 All-In-One Desk
Reference For Dummies
978-0-470-19108-8

Web Analytics For Dummies
978-0-470-09824-0

Windows XP For Dummies, 2nd Edition
978-0-7645-7326-2

06439_p4